The Ethics of Educational Leadership

Ronald W. Rebore
St. Louis University

Merrill
Prentice Hall

Upper Saddle River, New Jersey
Columbus, Ohio

Library of Congress Cataloging in Publication Data

Rebore, Ronald W.

     The ethics of educational leadership / Ronald W. Rebore.

        p.   cm.

     Includes bibliographical references and index.

     ISBN 0-13-787920-2

     1. School administrators—Professional ethics—United States. 2. Educational leadership—Moral and ethical aspects—United States   I. Title.

    LB1779.R42 2001

    174'9371—dc21

00-035133

Vice President and Publisher: Jeffery W. Johnston
Editor: Debra A. Stollenwerk
Editorial Assistant: Penny S. Burleson
Production Editor: Linda Hillis Bayma
Copy Editor: Jenifer Cooke
Design Coordinator: Diane C. Lorenzo
Cover Designer: Linda Fares
Text Designer: Mia Saunders
Cover art: © SuperStock
Production Manager: Laura Messerly
Electronic Text Management: Marilyn Wilson Phelps, Karen L. Bretz, Melanie N. Ortega
Director of Marketing: Kevin Flanagan
Marketing Manager: Amy June
Marketing Services Manager: Krista Groshong

This book was set in Baskerville by Prentice Hall. It was printed and bound by R.R. Donnelley & Sons Company. The cover was printed by Phoenix Color Corp.

10 9 8 7 6 5 4 3 2 1
ISBN: 0-13-787920-2

I dedicate this book to my mother,
Harriet M. Rebore

No issue has captured the interest and imagination of the American public more than the subject of ethics, particularly in relation to leadership in the public sector. Further, ethical issues in education now concern not only the conduct of administrators, teachers, and staff members in relation to how they fulfill their responsibilities in schools and school districts, but also the ethics of their private lives. The public makes little distinction between the arenas in which educational leaders deal with ethical situations. People are concerned with the ethical fiber of superintendents, principals, and other administrators regardless of the situations in which they perform an action. They are public figures and as such are expected to be role models for students, other educators, and the public in general.

In treating the subject of ethics as it relates to educational leadership, the material and argumentation in this text are organized so that they support Standard Five of the Interstate School Leaders Licensure Consortium (ISLLC) Standards for School Leaders. This standard is concerned with the ethics of school leadership. The works of important philosophers provide the basis for the development of the ethical principles presented in this book. Equally important is the methodology that these philosophers used in arriving at ethical insights. The lasting benefit to students of educational-leadership ethics is understanding their method of analysis. Two philosophers from the classical period are presented, along with six from the modern period and fifteen from the contemporary period. These philosophers were chosen because their ideas and concepts are relevant to the American ethos and to the practice of educational leadership.

The Ethics of Educational Leadership should be of interest to three groups of people: professors of educational leadership who have the instructional responsibility of teaching courses in ethics; practicing central-office and school-building administrators who want to become more familiar with the field of ethics; and members of the general public who have an interest in how ethics relates to educational leadership.

The book is organized into five parts. Part One, "The Ethical Administrator," comprises Chapters 1 through 3 and is concerned with establishing the fundamental principles endemic to being an ethical person who is also an educational leader. Part Two, "The Ethical Practice of Educational Leadership," includes Chapters 4 and 5, which concentrate on the ethical practice of central-office and school-building administration. Part Three, "Equity and Educational Leadership," contains Chapters 6 and 7. These chapters deal with gender equity and how other kinds of equity issues can be addressed in a pluralistic society. In addition, this section discusses equity from the perspective of social justice and considers how public discourse can contribute to the development of educational administration policies. The Epilogue constitutes the fourth part of this book, and sets forth some final thoughts about ethics. Last is the Appendix, which contains a self-assessment instrument that will help the reader ascertain his or her understanding of ethical principles in relation to educational leadership activities.

Several pedagogical features will help the reader understand the nuances of the material. Each chapter contains the following sections: "Other Philosophical Approaches to the Issues in This Chapter," "Crosswalk to ISLLC Standard Five" (except Chapter 1), "Ethical Considerations Presented in This Chapter," "Summary," "Discussion Questions and Statements," and "Selected Bibliography," as well as one or more case studies (except Chapter 1). Further, the text includes several excerpts from the writings of important philosophers and from documents that set forth principles that have an impact on ethical conduct.

ACKNOWLEDGMENTS

I am especially grateful for the support which I received from my wife, Sandy, my son, Ron, and daughter, Lisa, both of whom are teachers. I could not have completed this book without the encouragement and support of Debbie Stollenwerk, my editor at Merrill/Prentice Hall. Her insight helped me focus the book so that it better serves the needs of the academic community.

Finally, I wish to thank the reviewers for their comments and suggestions: Clinton Collins, University of Kentucky; David A Erlandson, Texas A&M University; Beverly Geltner, Eastern Michigan University; Robbe Lynn Henderson, California State University, Dominquez Hills; Larry W. Hughes, University of Houston; Stephen Jacobson, State University of New York at Buffalo; and Spencer Maxcy, Louisiana State University.

BRIEF CONTENTS

CONTENTS

Chapter 3
The Ethics of Power and Duty in Educational Leadership   55

PART ONE

The Ethical Administrator

1

The Purpose and Structure of the Book

THE FOCUS

The content of this book is rooted in Standard Five of the Interstate School Leaders Licensure Consortium (ISLLC) Standards for School Leaders. These standards are the product of the Council of Chief State School Officers. They were drafted by professionals from twenty-four state education agencies and representatives from professional associations. The standards are compatible with the new National Council for the Accreditation of Teacher Education (NCATE) curriculum guidelines for school administration. The model standards are being used by many states to assess candidates seeking licensure as school administrators.

ISLLC Standard Five states: "A school administrator is an educational leader who promotes the success of all students by acting with integrity, fairness, and in an ethical manner." This standard is operationalized through three dimensions: knowledge, dispositions, and performances. The following list[1] details various aspects of these dimensions and gives the chapters in this book in which they are addressed. Not all aspects are treated with the same depth, but they are all covered to some degree except for that part of the knowledge section that deals with the philosophy and history of education.

Knowledge

The administrator has knowledge and understanding of:

◆ the purpose of education and the role of leadership in modern society (Chapters 2, 3)

◆ various ethical frameworks and perspectives on ethics (Chapters 2–7)

◆ the values of the diverse school community (Chapters 6, 7)

- professional codes of ethics (Chapters 4, 5)
- the philosophy and history of education (not covered)

Dispositions

The administrator believes in, values, and is committed to:

- the ideal of the common good (Chapter 7)
- the principles in the Bill of Rights (Chapters 4–7)
- the right of every student to a free, quality education (Chapters 4, 5)
- bringing ethical principles to the decision-making process (Chapter 2)
- subordinating one's own interest to the good of the school community (Chapters 2, 3)
- accepting the consequences for upholding one's principles and actions (Chapter 2)
- using the influence of one's office constructively and productively in the service of all students and their families (Chapters 4, 5)
- development of a caring school community (Chapters 4, 5)

Performances

The administrator:

- examines personal and professional values (Chapters 2, 3)
- demonstrates a personal and professional code of ethics (Chapters 4, 5)
- demonstrates values, beliefs, and attitudes that inspire others to higher levels of performance (Chapters 2, 3)
- serves as a role model (Chapters 4, 5)
- accepts responsibility for school operations (Chapters 3–5)
- considers the impact of one's administrative practices on others (Chapter 2)
- uses the influence of the office to enhance the educational program rather than for personal gain (Chapters 2–5)
- treats people fairly, equitably, and with dignity and respect (Chapters 2–7)
- protects the rights and confidentiality of students and staff (Chapters 4, 5)
- demonstrates appreciation for and sensitivity to the diversity in the school community (Chapters 6, 7)
- recognizes and respects the legitimate authority of others (Chapter 3)
- examines and considers the prevailing values of the diverse school community (Chapters 6, 7)
- expects that others in the school community will demonstrate integrity and exercise ethical behavior (Chapters 3–5)
- opens the school to public scrutiny (Chapters 4, 5, 7)

   ◆ fulfills legal and contractual obligations (Chapter 2)
   ◆ applies laws and procedures fairly, wisely, and considerately (Chapters 3–7)

THE CONTEXT OF ETHICS

Although Standard Five deals with the ethics of educational leadership, in itself it presents neither a theoretical foundation nor the nuance of implementation. Those issues are left to endeavors such as this book.

Ethics has a long and varied history. There is no way of knowing how humans wrestled with ethical issues before the advent of writing, but they must have confronted difficult situations that required reflection about what was the right way to act. The classical beginnings of ethical consideration are found in Plato's account of Socrates' trial. Socrates was accused of disturbing the social order because he went about Athens asking citizens their opinions concerning the ultimate meaning of human existence. At his trial he accepted the death penalty and drank hemlock rather than give up his search for truth.

The study of ethics is an extremely complex enterprise because the subject matter is human conduct. In humans, conduct does not merely occur, but emanates from the totality of the person. Children, adolescents, and some adults tend to react to situations rather than act according to certain principles. Everyone is prone at times to the reactive type of behavior. However, mature adults are expected to put thought and reflection behind their actions. Only in this way can human beings maintain a stable and equitable society.

Endemic to reflection on the most desirable course of action are three fundamental questions that all philosophizing in some way attempts to tackle:

   ◆ What does it mean to be a human being?
   ◆ How should human beings treat one another?
   ◆ How should the institutions of society be organized?

It is true that these questions are not explicitly set forth in every deliberation, and they are often debated separately. However, what it means to be a human being is fundamental to human conduct. For example, when ethnic cleansing becomes a national policy, those supporting such a policy cannot possibly consider those to be eliminated as fully human as they consider themselves. Implicit within such a policy is a distortion of what it means to be human. Other examples are found in U.S. society, such as racial segregation and poor treatment of women, people with disabilities, and older adults in general and discrimination in the workplace in particular.

How human beings should treat one another is thus predicated on certain notions about humanity. Those notions are significantly influenced by the culture and traditions of each society. History has verified that societies are ever changing either for the better or the worse. Governmental and legal structures, economics, and scientific advances also have influenced notions about humanity.

Concepts about humanity and human conduct affect the way people organize and deliver education, health care, and governmental and social services. When certain people are not valued in society, individual responsibility is lessened and institutional care is abrogated. Ethics as a discipline is much more complex than merely making decisions about the right or wrong way to act in a given situation.

As a philosophical enterprise, ethics is about rational inquiry for the purpose of acquiring knowledge that can be used in making decisions about present and future actions. As such, the study of ethics is a search for truth. The ultimate goal of ethics is normative, the establishment of standards of conduct.

Ethics is concerned with human conduct, as distinguished from mere human behavior. *Conduct* implies that there is a choice; people can choose one course of action or an alternative course of action. *Behavior* is a descriptive term referring to all human activities. People can behave in a rational or irrational manner. The underlying assumption is that conduct is rational because it is intentional.[2]

There are two traditional approaches to the study of ethics: the deontological approach and the teleological approach. The former approach is concerned with the rightness or wrongness of a given action. It is usually understood within the context of duty. What is the right thing to do? That is the million-dollar question, of course, and there is no scarcity of opinions in almost every situation as to what that right thing is. That there are many interpretations of what is the right thing to do will be clear from the philosophical selections included in this book. Some opinions are rooted in utilitarianism, which holds that the consequences of an action should be the standard for what makes something right. Others indicate that a person's motivation or the nuances of the situation itself are the determinants that make an action right or wrong.

The teleological approach considers the goals of action in terms of goodness and badness. The major concern of this approach is what is meant by goodness. The seeking of pleasure is set forth by some philosophers as the ultimate goodness, whereas others value intrinsic qualities. A number of interpretations to this fundamental question are presented in the philosophical works quoted in this book.

As suggested by the three fundamental questions posed earlier, this book takes an approach that is both deontological and teleological. It is difficult in practice to utilize just one approach and to neglect the other. Rather, both considerations are presented in this book and thus a nexus is created in which both approaches are intermingled.

Another distinction usually made in the study of ethics is that between normative ethics and meta-ethics. Normative ethics is the study of human conduct, whereas meta-ethics is the study of conditions that affect normative ethics. Such controversies as the relationship between free will and determinism, between authority and intuition, between deductive and inductive reasoning, and between skepticism and cognitivism are the subject matter of meta-ethics. This presentation treats both normative and meta-ethical issues.[3]

Ethics is part of a much larger tradition. It is an academic discipline taught in colleges and universities along with other philosophical disciplines. It is difficult to categorize an academic discipline, but it will be helpful to situate the study of ethics in relation to the common understanding of many people. Figure 1.1, although not the definitive explanation of how ethics fits into the philosophical enterprise, should be of some help in understanding the differences between ethics and other philosophical disciplines. It should be kept in mind that the distinctions made in this figure are approximations and that different elements in the various disciplines overlap. Finally, the titles and designations for the various disciplines are not universal.

The Relevance of Ethics to Educational Leadership

It is important for educational leaders to incorporate ethical analysis as an ongoing way of thinking for three reasons. First, the issues that ethics explores are important not only because they provide a framework for decision making, but also because they require reflection upon values that are at the core of a given

---

Philosophical Disciplines

Aesthetics: Study of the meaning of beauty and aesthetic judgments

Cosmology: Study of nature, the universe, and such issues as time and motion

Epistemology: Study of the meaning of truth and knowledge

Ethics: Study of human conduct

History of philosophy: Study of the context in which the various trends in philosophical thought have developed

Human nature: Study of the human phenomenon

Logic: Study of the processes of human understanding

Metaphysics: Study of reality in its ultimate principles

Theodacy: Study of what can be known about a supreme being from reason

Philosophy of Academic Subjects

Mathematics: Study of how and why reality is quantified

Science: Study of the nature of scientific theory and the scientific method

Social science: Study of the principles involved in human engagement and in the creation of human institutions

---

FIGURE 1.1
Traditional Categories of Philosophical Disciplines

human enterprise. It is possible to be a thoughtful and reflective administrator without an understanding of, for example, genetics, but it is not possible to be so without an understanding of ethics. The use of student assessment as an indication of how effectively a school is meeting its instructional objectives raises significant questions about the purpose of education itself and the validity of using student assessment to evaluate a program. Equally important is the issue that is raised in relation to teacher performance if student test scores fall below a given standard.

Second, an ethical approach addresses issues through a disciplined way of thinking. The success factor that seems to be so important in contemporary public education, exemplified by mandates in many states for the publication of student test scores, also raises significant questions about students who are not achieving. For example, many nonachieving students are nonconformists in their behavior, which can lead to bullying by their classmates. Making the connection between one set of circumstances and others is a common thread that runs through all ethical analysis.

Finally, ethical analysis offers educational administrators a unique kind of response to leadership issues—different from the response that might be expected from one who takes a management or even an instructional point of view. This is not to imply that it is unimportant to analyze issues from a management or instructional perspective; rather, an ethical analysis can enhance the strategies developed through these other approaches. These other approaches might answer the questions of *how* and *what*, but the ethical approach answers the question of *why*. Why are certain students disenfranchised?

The Framework and Methodology

Because educational leaders practice within the larger community, selections from the writings of philosophers who have exerted a significant influence on this larger community are included in this book, and what these philosophers have developed as philosophical principles are applied to the practice of educational leadership. More important, however, is the method they employed to arrive at their ethical insights. Each philosopher's method of analysis provides long-term benefit to the student of educational leadership ethics. The nuance of situations will change, but the analytical argumentation endures. The methodology employed by the various philosophers can be difficult to discern, as they usually have not set forth their methodology in pedagogical terminology. Uncovering this methodology, then, is part of the task at hand.

The ethical positions set forth in this book come from two philosophers of the classical period, six of the modern period, and fifteen of the contemporary period, as follows:

Classical Period

Marcus Aurelius Antoninus
Aristotle

Modern Period

Jeremy Bentham
Georg Wilhelm Friedrich Hegel
Thomas Hobbes
Immanuel Kant
John Stuart Mill
Jean-Jacques Rousseau

Contemporary Period

Susan Bordo
Simone de Beauvoir
. Teilhard de Chardin (philosopher/paleontologist)
John Dewey
Erik Erikson (philosopher/psychologist)
Michel Foucault
Viktor Frankl (philosopher/psychologist)
Jürgen Habermas
Sandra Harding
Carl Jung (philosopher/psychologist)
Lawrence Kohlberg (philosopher/psychologist)
Jean-François Lyotard
John Rawls
Jean-Paul Sartre
Edith Stein

Human thought not only draws on the contributions of past generations, but also is conditioned by the problems, issues, and trends of the milieu within which it is developed. Philosophers from past generations have provided current philosophers with maps, which contemporary philosophers use to develop their own analysis about the times in which they live. The insights of philosophers from past and present generations have been applied in this book to the problems and issues of educational leadership.

In addition, this book includes several documents: codes of ethics and other documents of professional organizations and selections from the Declaration of Independence, the Bill of Rights, and the Constitution of the United States of America. These documents embody much of what is contained in the writings of many philosophers, but they are also stand-alone philosophical treatises that can be of significant help in arriving at ethical decisions.

Interpreting the Philosophical Works and Other Documents

Throughout this book the works of certain philosophers are set forth, interpreted, and applied to the practice of educational leadership. The word *interpreted*, rather than, for example, *explained*, is used here deliberately and in a philosophical sense.

To understand the point, it is beneficial to begin with Aristotle's dictum, "All men by nature desire to know."[4] This knowing is quite different from explaining. When people read a book, document, essay, or any literary work, they seek to understand the words, sentences, paragraphs, and meaning conveyed by the writer. When people seek the assistance of others, conveyed either orally or in writing, they usually are seeking an explanation of the author's work so that they can understand the meaning of the text. What they get, however, is an interpretation of the work; and indeed, what people get in subsequent explanations, predicated on a secondary source, are interpretations of an interpretation. Even the primary-source author, in explaining concepts or ideas or describing a sequence of events, has filtered the facts or information through his or her repertoire of experience and thus has engaged in interpretation.

The word *hermeneutics* is derived from the Greek word, *hermeios*, which referred to the priests at the Delphic Oracle. The wing-footed messenger-god Hermes probably derived his name from the same Greek source. It is interesting to note that Hermes' function was to communicate what was beyond human understanding in a form that humans could grasp. For this reason, the early Greeks attributed Hermes with the discovery of language and writing as the vehicle for conveying meaning.[5]

Of course, language itself is a symbolic expression of thought, and written language is the most important sign system ever invented. Many linguists hold the position that human beings are born with the ability to speak, evidenced by the fact that the inhabitants of every known society have used speech to communicate and organize their lives.[6] In contrast, many societies have not had a written language. Writing is a cultural achievement, and it has become the linchpin in modern societies. "This is not to say that writing causes civilization, but the reverse is not the whole truth either. Rather, writing has to be seen as a result as well as a condition of civilization, as a product shaped by civilization and a tool shaping it."[7]

Through the influence of writing, revolutions have occurred that have changed the world. The documents supporting the founding of the United States, such as the Declaration of Independence and the Constitution, are excellent examples of such influence. The writings of the philosophers presented in this book, of course, have also shaped the culture of Western societies. Florian Coulmas has extensively researched written language and its significance to the development of culture.

> It has often been said that writing is a very recent achievement which emerged late in culture and societal history. This is undoubtedly true although *recent* is, of course, a relative notion. It is recent if compared with speech or the upright gait; recent in terms of the emergence of its earliest predecessors some 10,000 or maybe 12,000 years ago (Schmandt-Besserat 1978); and more recent still in terms of its almost universal spread in some societies (Oxenham 1980). Yet, despite its comparatively late advent, the invention of writing has had such pervasive effects on the development of civilization that for all of us who have grown up in a literate culture it is extremely difficult to imagine a world without

writing. Almost none of the familiar features of modern society would survive this test; there would be no books, no newspapers, no letters, no tax reports, no pay checks, no identity cards, no lecture notes, no street signs, no labels on commercial products, no advertisements, no medical prescriptions, no systematic education, no dictionaries or encyclopedias, no instructions manuals for radio, cars or computers, a very different kind of religion, a very different kind of law and no science in the proper sense of the word; there would be no linguistics either. A non-literate modern society is a contradiction in terms. Even though the dawn of the post-literate era has been proclaimed by scholars, such as McLuhan (1962) and Ong (1977), writing is, and will be for some time to come, one of the corner-stones of modern life. The entire civilization of the West as well as the East is unthinkable without it.

. . . The step from simple mnemonic devices such as tally sticks to the first conventional system of writing capable of recording information on clay tablets was immeasurably greater than all subsequent steps combined leading up to the modern technology of recording information on microchips. Basically, microchips are merely a technical improvement over clay tablets. The invention of writing, however, was the invention of an entirely new technology. . . .

. . . the most obvious function of writing is memory supportive. . . . A related function is that of expanding the communicative range. . . . Communicating in speech requires the presence together of speaker and listener. Writing, by contrast, enables communication over any distance in space or time. . . . [8]

When the written text is dislocated from the originating person and becomes available to other people or to the originator at a later date, the text assumes the quality of an object, in contrast to oral communication, which disappears as soon as it materializes. Further, since written artifacts have the quality of permanence, they also have the potential for regulating social behavior. Therefore, as Florian Coulmas affirms, "The notions of law and right, of standard and correctness, are closely linked with writing. It is, after all, *the letter of the law.* Notice, incidentally, that the words author and authority have the same etymology." [9]

Finally, written artifacts can create novel types of coordinated action. Legal documents, instruction manuals, recipes, and style sheets will influence the behavior of others. [10] This is the rationale from which the writing of the philosophers presented in this book and the insights of others who have produced relevant or ancillary written material will be interpreted in the context of contemporary educational leadership.

This view of writing raises several questions. "Does interpretation lead or extend beyond itself? Does it refer to an external world, a specific field of objects that stand outside the linkage of interpretation?" [11] These questions give rise to one that is even more pervasive: Can human desire for absolute knowledge ever be satisfied, or must people be content with a chain of interpretations? In a sense, the interpretation enigma frees humanity from the desire for absolute knowledge. Interpretation does not include predetermined meanings; it mediates and is mediated by this desire. Interpretation creates connections, which bring about unity and harmony and can result in an understanding of totality. [12]

Interpretation becomes the methodology by which the ideas and concepts of different philosophers are renewed and utilized in subsequent generations. Thus, the works of Aristotle, Immanuel Kant, Jürgen Habermas, and others are pursued and consulted by commentators in reflecting on the problems, issues, and trends of their contemporary milieus.

It is important to address three questions in a more systematic way: What does each person bring to the interpretation of philosophical works? What is the meaning of the text? What is the relevance of the philosophical work for the practice of educational leadership?

What does each person bring to the interpretation of philosophical works?   Several philosophers have devoted some portion of their energies to researching, discoursing, and writing about hermeneutics. Wilhelm Dilthey (1833–1911) made a significant contribution to the process of interpretation. He was concerned with the effect of a given person's psyche on his or her interpretation of the written word. Specifically, Dilthey highlighted the role a person's interests play in his or her understanding of writings.[13]

Of course, the major concern of a person who is interpreting a given work or text is objectivity, although he or she should also be concerned with clarity, precision of expression, and logical consistency. Reflecting on one's personal history will help bring about objectivity. The reader of a philosophical work may be a female high school principal who was educated in public schools and who received her Ph.D. from a large research university on the East Coast of the United States. She may have been a special education teacher before becoming an administrator. She may be married with one child and her husband may be an assistant principal in a middle school. She may be the youngest of three children whose parents were very religious. And so on. We bring who we are as individual people to every interpretation, and the task at hand is to be aware of these factors in order to guard against their inappropriate intrusion into our interpretation of a certain text.

What is the meaning of the text?   First and foremost it is important to understand what the text meant to its original audience and in its original setting. This approach is commonly referred to as the historical-critical method of interpretation. Because of the quality of formal education in the United States, it will be rather easy for educators to understand the historical documents, position statements of professional organizations, and philosophical excerpts presented in this book. For the most recent documents and texts, thought patterns and cultural nuances are shared by both reader and writer. Translations of foreign-language documents are more than adequate. However, for writings that are somewhat removed from the contemporary setting, some historical-critical information is provided, which will enhance the understanding of the ethical positions developed in this book. For the person who wishes to become more adept at interpretation, Figure 1.2 provides a series of questions that can serve as a guide in such an endeavor.

What is the relevance of the philosophical work or document to the practice of educational leadership?   Perhaps the best way to answer this question is to consider the

Declaration of Independence. The founders of the United States proclaimed, "We hold these truths to be self-evident, that all men are created equal, that they are endowed by their Creator with certain unalienable Rights, that among these are Life, Liberty, and the pursuit of Happiness." At the time this document was written, extending these rights to women was not a consideration. It took subsequent generations to recognize that the rights set forth in this document were also applicable to women and that such rights had to be safeguarded through decisions of the United States Supreme Court. Further, how the rights set forth in this document were to be implemented had to be clarified through the enactment of federal legislation and even through amendments to the Constitution. Thus, what the Declaration of Independence stated had significance not only for the time in which it was written, but also for subsequent generations, which extended its principles to a larger number of people and applied these principles in specific ways. This potential lives in all philosophical works. What has changed? The people who read the documents.

The scope of exploration into the milieu within which educational leadership functions is infinitely expanded through the principles of interpretation. Daring creativity becomes the norm against which solutions can be sought to the problems facing educational administrators. Liberation replaces the insecurity that results from attempts by educational leaders to force a rigid ethical viewpoint on dilemmas that call for a much more pervasive resolution. Thus, the educational leader becomes a person who melds together the personal and professional dimensions of his or her life. The educational leader recognizes that ethics springs from his or her personal perspective of what is contained in authoritative documents.

OTHER PHILOSOPHICAL APPROACHES
TO THE ISSUES IN THIS CHAPTER

The study of ethics is predicated on the use of reason as the vehicle for developing norms of conduct. Rational analysis is assisted by knowledge and information derived from anthropology, the fine arts, biology, drama, genetics, management science, psychology, technology, sociology, and all other human endeavors.

However, norms of conduct may be derived from another source, which, although beyond the scope of this presentation, must nonetheless be acknowledged—religious faith. The Commandments found in the Jewish scripture, the Beatitudes of the Christian faith, the sayings of Muhammad, and the Noble Eightfold Path of Buddhism are only a few of the many religious sources used by the faithful in guiding their conduct.

Often the norms of religious faith are referred to as moral norms, in contrast to ethical norms established through reason. However, these two terms are used interchangeably by philosophers and in common language usage.

Literary Criticism Questions

1. What literary forms are used in the text?
2. What is unique about the images evoked in the text?
3. What is the thought pattern set forth in the text?
4. What is unique about the words used by the author?
5. What is unique about the symbols and/or dialogue used by the author?
6. What unique images are evoked by the literary style?
7. How does the literary form contribute to the content?
8. What sources did the author use?
9. How did the author use these sources?

Hermeneutical Criticism Questions

1. If the text is a translation, what philosophy of translation was used?
2. How is the meaning of the text influenced by literary criticism?
3. How did the author's life situation influence the text?
4. What was the historical context within which the document was written?
5. What personal influences does the reader bring to his or her interpretation of the text?
6. What did the text mean to the people for whom it was written?
7. What is the relevance of the text for today's reader?
8. What is the literal meaning of the text?

FIGURE 1.2
Critical Interpretation Questions

ETHICAL CONSIDERATIONS PRESENTED IN THIS CHAPTER

◆ All ethical considerations are ultimately affected by the educational leader's understanding of what it means to be a human being and his or her understanding of how human beings should treat one another.

◆ This understanding will have a significant influence on the way in which the educational leader will administer his or her school or school district.

◆ It is extremely difficult for a principal or superintendent to administer a school or school district effectively without confronting his or her ethical values.

◆ Ethical analysis will enhance management and instructional analyses of educational issues.

◆ Studying the ethical works of philosophers, the ethical documents of professional organizations, and the founding documents of the United States will provide the educational leader with authoritative bases for making ethical decisions.

SUMMARY

The content of this book is rooted in Standard Five of the Interstate School Leaders Licensure Consortium (ISLLC) Standards for School Leaders.

Standard Five states: "A school administrator is an educational leader who promotes the success of all students by acting with integrity, fairness, and in an ethical manner." This standard is operationalized through three dimensions: knowledge, dispositions, and performances.

The classical beginnings of ethical consideration can be found in Plato's account of Socrates' trial. Socrates' claim that the unexamined life is not worth living sets the stage for the approach to ethical consideration taken by this book. Endemic to all ethical decision making are three fundamental questions: What does it mean to be a human being? How should human beings treat one another? How should the institution of society be organized?

The ultimate goal of ethics is to establish standards of conduct. Conduct implies that humans can choose one course of action or an alternative.

There are two traditional approaches to the study of normative ethics. The deontological approach is concerned with the rightness or wrongness of a given action. The teleological approach is concerned with the goals of action in terms of goodness and badness. In this book both approaches are intermingled through an explication of ISLLC Standard Five. In like manner, meta-ethics, which is the study of those conditions that affect normative ethics, is also melded into this presentation.

There are three important reasons for educational leaders to incorporate ethical analysis as an ongoing way of thinking: ethics explores important issues that act as a framework for decision making based on core values; ethics utilizes a disciplined way of thinking; and ethics provides a unique kind of response to leadership issues.

The writings of certain philosophers, the ethical statements of professional associations, and significant public-policy documents have been selected as foundational to an appropriate interpretation of this ISLLC Standard Five and its various dimensions. From this interpretation philosophical principles have been developed and are applied through this book to the practice of educational leadership.

This presentation draws on the works of philosophers from different periods. Thus, the insights from past and present generations have been applied to the ethical problems and issues facing educational leaders.

The aspect under which this interpretation takes place is hermeneutical. Hermeneutical interpretation tries to answer three questions in a systematic way: What does each person bring to the interpretation of a given work? What is the meaning of the text? What is the relevance of the work to the practice of educational leadership?

DISCUSSION QUESTIONS AND STATEMENTS

1. What is the importance of the ISLLC Standards in relation to the practice of educational leadership?
2. What are the three major questions concerning the human phenomenon that are endemic to ethical considerations?
3. How are these questions related to the practice of educational leadership?
4. Explain what is meant by the deontological and teleological approaches to the study of ethics.
5. Define meta-ethics.
6. How is the study of ethics situated in relation to the other philosophical disciplines?
7. How do philosophers of the past influence contemporary ethical opinion?
8. What is hermeneutics?
9. What is the difference between interpreting and explaining ethical treatises?
10. What is the significance of language to ethical understanding?
11. What is the significance of the three major questions concerning interpretation to the practice of educational leadership?

SELECTED BIBLIOGRAPHY

Barrett, William. *Irrational Man: A Study in Existential Philosophy*. Garden City, N.Y.: Doubleday Anchor Books, 1962.

Cahoone, Lawrence, ed. *From Modernism to Postmodernism: An Anthology*. Cambridge, Mass.: Blackwell Publishers, Inc., 1996.

Copleston, Frederick. *A History of Philosophy*. 9 vols. Garden City, N.Y.: Image Books, 1994.

Cottingham, John, ed. *Western Philosophy: An Anthology.* Cambridge, Mass.: Black-well Publishers Inc., 1996.

Coulmas, Florian. *The Writing Systems of the World.* Cambridge, Mass.: Basil Black-well, Inc., 1990.

Ingram, David, and Julia Simon-Ingram. *Critical Theory: The Essential Readings.* New York: Paragon House, 1992.

Ong, Walter J. *Orality and Literacy: The Technologizing of the Word.* New York: Routledge, 1995.

Ormiston, Gayle L., and Alan D. Schrift, eds. *The Hermeneutic Tradition: From Ast to Ricoeur.* Albany: State University of New York Press, 1990.

Palmer, Richard E. *Hermeneutics: Interpretation Theory in Schleiemacher, Dilthey, Hei-degger, and Gadamer.* Evanston, Ill.: Northwestern University Press, 1985.

Thonnard, F. J. *A Short History of Philosophy.* New York: Desclee Company, 1956.

Wallace, William A. *The Elements of Philosophy: A Compendium for Philosophers and Theologians.* New York: Alba House, 1979.

CHAPTER 2

Developing a Personal Approach to Ethics

This chapter is divided into two main sections. The first section, The Dynamics of Ethics, explicates various concepts and ideas that will be helpful to educational leaders and those planning a career in educational leadership as they seek out and develop their own personal ethical system. The second section, The Search for Meaning in Life, attempts to establish a framework within which educational leaders and those preparing to become educational leaders can reflect on the search for meaning given the ideas and concepts presented in section one.

THE DYNAMICS OF ETHICS

Pose the following question to any educational leader: Are you conscious? He or she probably would respond *yes*, with great reservation concerning the motive of the questioner. Most people would react this way or would suspect that a punch line was sure to follow. Yet this is the seminal question that must be addressed in any discussion about personal ethics. Of course, the context within which the term *consciousness* is being used here refers to the process of reflection that is absolutely necessary if an individual is to develop a personal ethical approach to being an educational leader.

This section begins by setting forth a foundational approach to ethical norms. The first part incorporates the insights of Teilhard de Chardin on evolution and delineates the context of ethical norms as emerging from a revised worldview that radically alters the concept of natural law. This section proceeds with a discussion of social ethics, which is pertinent because of the social dimension of educational leadership. Next is a treatment of consequences, which situates the remnants of unethical actions and leads to an explication of the four moral virtues. This section ends with an explanation of various methods for making ethical decisions.

Ethical Norms

Educational leadership must be situated within the context of all other human activities because it is impossible to isolate the responsibilities of leadership from other human responsibilities. It is the total person who administers educational programs. From this perspective the insights of contemporary astronomy and the new physics are of particular interest. These insights have renewed attention to the evolutionary process, which has much to say about the antecedents and future experiences of every person. Of course, the touchstone for the presentation here is educational leadership.

Teilhard de Chardin. An understanding of human evolution is the key to understanding the ethical issues that have been and will continue to be unleashed with great magnitude on the unsuspecting educational leader. Scientists recognize that evolution proceeds from the simple to the more complex: electron to atom, atom to molecule, molecule to cell, cell to organism, inferior organism to humans. This is the *law of continuity.* Further, evolution is governed by the *law of design:* the growth in complexity does not mean merely an accumulation of elements; rather, when a certain degree of complexity has been reached, evolution must proceed to a new plane in order for the process to continue. Thus, a real metamorphosis occurs—a necessary discontinuity within the necessary continuity of evolution.[1]

Teilhard de Chardin, the noted paleontologist and philosopher, postulated a concept, which he termed *spirit-matter,* that was a stumbling block for many scholars during his lifetime but that has gained many supporters since his death in 1955. Spirit-matter is the stuff from which everything in the entire universe is formed. Matter and spirit are not two separate concepts, but are inseparable and present at the most elementary physical level. As an example, humanity possesses the spiritual potential to exercise freedom; thus, according to Chardin's reasoning, since humanity evolved from other, nonhuman forms, and because of the continuity of the evolutionary process, these forms must have possessed elements of freedom.[2]

The greatest discontinuity, then, occurred with the appearance of humanity, which ushered in the spirit endowed with thought, reflection, and liberty. Thus, human consciousness emerged and began a new evolutionary process toward ever greater complexity and consciousness. Once this process began, it became irreversible and subject to the laws of continuity and design. Thus, the evolution of humanity will eventually reach a critical point of complexity, which will necessitate ascendance to a higher plane.[3]

Evolution always succeeds in safeguarding previous stages of development, the synthesis that evolution produces. Therefore, the spirit not only will remain, but also will move forward to a new plane. Only speculation is possible as the future is contemplated, but it is certain that the social aspect of humanity will also be affected by future evolution. Consciousness necessitates a greater awareness of the interrelatedness of social experience and the need for better communication among human beings; thus the emergence of communicative technology. In fact, all technology has an effect, direct or indirect, on communication, which accounts for the recognition that there is a communication component to most human problems.[4]

The question of human freedom arises in any discussion of evolution because of the inherent issue of the biological determinants of evolution. Teilhard de Chardin pointed out in the *Phenomenon of Man* that humanity became a new form of biological life that had certain characteristics: the emergence of internal arrangements above the factors of external arrangements in individual life; the appearance of true forces of attraction and repulsion (sympathy and antipathy); the awareness of an aptitude to foresee the future and thus the consciousness of a state of absolute irreversibility.[5]

The Context of Ethical Norms.   From the wellspring of evolved human consciousness flows the context within which ethical norms are identified. *Thought, reflection,* and *liberty* constitute the essence of consciousness, which is operationalized through human experience, understanding, and judgement; hence, the emergence of ethical norms.

The evolutionary perspective revealed through research and scholarship has ushered in a new vision that compels humanity to reevaluate previous ethical norms. For the sake of clarification, the previous perspective will be designated the *classical worldview* and the current perspective will be designated the *modern worldview*.[6]

The classical worldview sees the world as a finished product and holds that the experiences of people will allow them to grasp a clear understanding of immutable essences. Therefore, people can have a high degree of certitude that ethical principles will remain valid forever. The true path to right conduct can be formulated using universal principles and a deductive method that will yield secure and complete conclusions. Individuals with this viewpoint emphasize preestablished norms and conformity to authority, as well as duty and obligation.

The modern worldview sees the world as dynamic and evolving, hallmarked by progressive growth and change; the experiences of people allow them to identify individual traits within concrete and historical particulars. The path to right conduct is primarily through induction from specific experiences. Some conclusions may change with an increase in knowledge. Thus incompleteness and error are possible and could lead to a revision of principles. This viewpoint emphasizes responsibility and adaptation to changing times.[7]

These two perspectives are presented here in their purest form. However, most people would agree that the prudent approach to developing ethical norms lies somewhere in the middle. Plagiarism by a student, the faking of an injury by a school staff member in order to receive workers' compensation benefits, sexual harassment of a teacher by a principal, and refusal of a teacher to help a student who is failing are examples of unethical conduct that will always be unethical. However, psychology, sociology, and philosophy admonish educational leaders to use understanding and kindness when dealing with people who have committed these wrongs. Circumstances may diminish their culpability. Certainly some form of disciplinary action must follow from such conduct, but a one-fits-all disciplinary approach also can be unethical.

The modern worldview is most compelling when educational leaders face policy issues, such as what constitutes a just wage for teachers or what is the right of students to the use of computers for instruction.

Natural Law.   Perhaps the most misunderstood concept in ethical discourse is the concept of natural law. The confusion lies in thinking that *natural law* is synonymous with *law of nature*. The notion of natural law does not refer to a codified body of precepts; rather, used in its widest sense, natural law refers to the parameters that define the milieu of *being*, what follows from the essential nature of humanity. Further, natural law should not be identified with physical, chemical, or biological laws, which explain how the natural world works.[8]

When some people observe the conception, growth, and development of nonhuman life, they project on human life the laws governing these phenomena—a practice usually referred to as physicalism. Yet the presentation of human evolution has underscored the uniqueness of humanity in relation to nature. If we observe the behavior of primates, such as gorillas and chimpanzees, from a law-of-nature perspective, the projection to humans would be that when males and females reach the age of puberty, they pass into the realm of adulthood and therefore they are expected to procreate. Given the cultural, economic, educational, legal, and social milieus of contemporary Western society, such a practice would be disastrous. The jargon for this situation is "children raising children." Further, with most animals the female is the primary caregiver for newborns, whereas with humans caregiving is often shared by both parents, other family members, and even family friends. Shared caregiving allows women to continue with their careers. When a woman is a single parent, shared caregiving allows her to keep a job in order to make a living. The economic and quality-of-life benefits to society from the employment of women as professionals, researchers, and in the general workforce also cannot be overestimated. Thus, humanity does not and should not adhere to the law of nature, but must help mold and adhere to the natural law.

Although it is extremely difficult to define natural law, it is possible to set forth certain ideas to help clarify the role that natural law plays in our ethical decision making.

- ◆ Natural law is discovered through discourse, research, and reflection on humanity. Thus, rationality is the foundation of the natural law inherent to human beings. Humanity is always mysterious, not only because it is evolving, but also because it is affected by history and culture.[9]

♦ There are levels within natural law. The most general tenet of natural law is Do good and avoid evil, which for most people is self-evident and requires only common sense. However, more complex issues require more deliberation, often involving dialogue and study. For example, the issue concerning the educational rights of children with disabilities and how their rights affect the rights of nondisabled peers requires a great deal of involvement by many people, including students, parents, teachers, and administrators. Further, researchers and scholars in other disciplines, such as law, medicine, political science, psychology, and sociology, also should be consulted.[10]

♦ Deliberation concerning natural law must take into account the social dimension of humanity. Everything humans do probably has some effect on others, if not immediately, then at some time in the future. The enactment of a zero-tolerance policy calling for the expulsion of students who possess, use, or sell drugs in school would probably keep drugs out of the hands of some students but would deprive the expelled students of an education if an alternative school program was not available.

♦ Using the tenets of natural law allows all people to enter into rational debate concerning our collective humanity, which is critical in a pluralistic society. Thus, school-attendance policies, student-achievement goals, and teachers' rights and responsibilities can be publicly debated without offending particular groups.[11]

Natural law thus extends beyond physical, chemical, and biological precepts to include the social, spiritual, and psychological aspects of human existence. Nature provides the material people use to promote the well-being of humanity; through the use of reason, people reflect on what natural law requires. The correct approach, however, must take into account certain givens of human existence that contribute to the well-being of humans, such as living in harmony with members of the community and, as educational leaders, working in harmony with colleagues. It is equally important not to attribute the givens of human nature as beyond the control of human creativity.

The use of reason as the vehicle for knowing the natural law must be understood as the capability within the person to understand reality in relation to human experience. People must make use of observations, human testimony, research, analysis, logic, intuition, common sense, art, film, music, poetry, theater, and so on to understand reality. Two caveats should be considered as individuals exercise their right to discover the natural law and to apply it to particular ethical issues: reason's grasp of reality is always partial and limited; and reason is limited by a person's capability, emotions, and cultural conditioning.

In conclusion, there are four aspects to the development of ethical norms.

1. It is the responsibility not only of each person, but also of the community in the aggregate, to search for what is ethically good.

2. Norms should emerge from our experience of what it means to be truly human.

3. Norms should recognize the unfinished evolutionary character of humanity and the world.

4. The principle of proportionality, which testifies that people are doing what is ethical when they achieve the greatest possible proportion of good, should be observed.[12]

Social Ethics

The roots of social ethics are embedded in the realization that good and sincere people may be implicated in structures, institutions, or systems that inflict harm and injustices on other people. *Structures* are patterns of relationships that have become routine and involve policies and institutions. Economic, political, and cultural structures are the most common. *Institutions* are complexes of actions that control human conduct through predefined patterns, such as organized religion, marriage, and education. *Systems* are complexes of structures and institutions, such as civil authority.

Unethical actions by individuals can have a power that transcends the individual and can induce others to be unethical. Unethical attitudes can be transmitted to children and other people and become situated in their thoughts and actions, facilitating their mistreatment of others. In a sense, we inherit the unethical actions of past generations. Members of various groups, such as women, people belonging to ethnic minorities, people with disabilities, and elderly people, have had firsthand experiences that exemplify the symbolic, mythic, and linguistic structures that perpetuate injustice. The suffering caused by bigotry is far different from the suffering caused by disease or natural disaster. Bigotry is passed on from one generation to another; it is a learned condition. Individual actions that demean the humanity of others can eventually become embodied in institutions, structures, and systems. The segregation of African Americans in public schools is an obvious example of how the individual attitudes and actions of bigoted people eventually transcended those individuals and became institutionalized in public education.[13]

The free decision of one person sometimes places another person in a situation that requires that other person to make a decision. The decision is the link with the first person's reaction; the second person must decide to act or not to act. Hence, an unethical act invites another person to act unethically. History becomes a series of decisions and situations.[14]

It is easy to affirm what people know from experience; even though humanity is uniquely individual, people can develop and grow to their fullest potential only within the context of community. Principals and superintendents are usually aware of this reality and can take advantage of every opportunity to instill this notion in the curriculum and in other aspects of student life.

A discouraging realization about unethical institutions is that complexity plays a major role in efforts to change them; political and socioeconomic relationships and structures take on a life of their own, which would be threatened by efforts to eradicate the unethical component of the institutions. Patterns of behavior and relationships are difficult to break down once the embodiment occurs.

For example, court orders to desegregate schools sometimes failed to eradicate racial prejudice because the remedy did not solve the problem. Most school-desegregation programs simply bused African American students into predominantly European American schools and at the end of the school day bused them back into predominantly African American neighborhoods. This practice did not solve the underlying problem of segregated communities.

Personal and social unethicality are truly dimensions of the same phenomenon and can be understood only in relation to one another. From a social perspective, unethicality is experienced as external, inherited, overbearing, and seductive; from a personal perspective unethicality is experienced as freely chosen and incurring blame. Unethicality is powerful and fascinating, often addictive and alluring. Some ethicists speak of unethicality as a knowing ignorance, which requires the active collaboration of individuals. There is a reciprocal relationship between humanity and society; as humanity is creating social institutions, structures, and systems, society is transforming humanity in an ethical or unethical manner. Unethicality unfolds as a universal condition of humanity, encountered through social relationships and manifested by a person's active participation. Humanity creates society and society creates humanity.[15]

Consequences of Human Actions

When a person does something that he or she considers unethical, the consequence of that unethicality does not vanish, but remains in its core. That core is the decision the person made that oriented him or her in that direction. From the moment in each person's life when he or she begins the exercise of reason, and therefore of freedom, the circumstances of the person's life become the milieu in which he or she exercises freedom. With each subsequent decision, the person further restricts himself or herself; therefore, a person is always situated because of prior decisions. From this perspective, each person is the ultimate cause of the kind of person he or she becomes.

After an unethical action is carried out, the externalization fades away, but the person's attitude or disposition remains. A superintendent who falsely prejudices individual school-board members against an assistant superintendent whom he sees as a rival for his job could eventually harden his attitude to the point of total selfishness, which, in turn, would affect his relationship with other colleagues and even with people outside the professional milieu. When certain actions are repeated over a period of time, eventually the person becomes more inclined in the direction of those actions.

A person's self-centeredness and selfishness engender a unique response to others: the other people do not change, but the view the unethical person holds of them changes. Others are seen more as objects to be dealt with than as people to be encountered. It becomes easier to abuse others because they are not perceived as people with dignity and freedom; instead, they are viewed as a means or an obstacle to the person's self-interest. As a consequence of objectifying others, the self-centered person may experience a profound sense of loneliness and, because of this self-imposed isolation, a sense of anxiety.

Emerging from the analysis of unethical behavior and its consequences is the focused realization that people act from the totality of their beings. A person's attitudes, dispositions, and powers are expressed in every action. Thus, a person's actions tell others something about who that person is in the core of his or her being, and that something can act as a stimulus or invitation to other people to emulate. Positions in educational leadership impose a responsibility on the leader to demonstrate appropriate ethical behavior. When an educational leader does not demonstrate this quality, but acts in an unethical manner and either implicitly or explicitly tries to involve another staff member, the fear of losing professional opportunities and amenities controlled by the leader adds a dimension of pressure that can affect the staff member's ethical balance. The educational leader thus not only abrogates a responsibility, but also inflicts an ethical injury. Further, as staff members internalize the content of an educational leader's conduct, values and ethical norms become somewhat obscured, and once again, a stimulus or invitation is issued to emulate the unethicality.[16]

The ultimate goal of the ethical person is the integration of all his or her attitudes and dispositions (passions, powers, and tendencies) in order to become oriented toward ethical relationships with other people in his or her personal and professional lives. The conversion of an unethical person into an ethical human being is a very difficult process because it requires him or her to reinvest others with human dignity. In popular language, this process is called unhardening the heart.[17]

As a final note, Western civilization has a long history of glorifying rugged individualism that neglects the social aspects of individual actions and omissions. Thus, ethics has become a private affair.[18] This understanding is the antithesis of a social ethical perspective on educational leadership.

The Virtues

Educational leaders desirous of leading an ethical life must eventually come to grips with the virtues: prudence, justice, fortitude, and temperance. However, in contrast to past dialectics, the contemporary understanding of virtue must be viewed in the context of human development in general; also, human development must be viewed as a process, which begins in early childhood, extends into adulthood, and terminates only with death. Further, as a species, humans are still in a state of evolution.

The insights of two noteworthy scholars of human growth and development, Erik Erikson and Lawrence Kohlberg, will be presented in this chapter. Erikson began his research from a psychoanalytic perspective, but eventually pulled away from this approach to develop his own. He was concerned with aspects of human life manifested in the somatic, societal, and ego processes. Erikson viewed these processes as interrelated and emphasized that all three must be taken into consideration when analyzing a particular human situation.

Necessary to understanding Erikson's stages of development is the principle of *epigenesis*, which is part of the somatic process. Basically, this principle states that as a person develops in intervals, certain significant potentialities come to pass only during later intervals in life; therefore, although the beginnings of development are important, development that occurs later in life is important also.

Erikson's societal process strongly asserts the influence of the community on the development of the individual and the influence of the individual on the development of the community. For this reason, Erikson's theory is often termed *psychosocial*. Erikson's belief that a person's encounter with others plays a major role in the person's development goes beyond the inherent determinants characteristic of the psychoanalytic school of psychology.

The ego process constitutes the organizing and balancing principle for the person; it keeps everything in perspective. The ego process is critical to a person's individuality, and it is also an integrating agent. The ego keeps the person's instincts in check and maintains the person's vision of wholeness.

Erikson's *stages of moral development* present phenomena, called crises of development, that are critical points during times of transition from one stage to the next. Each person must resolve these crises during a given life period in order to be prepared for the next stage. To go to the next stage without a positive resolution of the crisis from the current period will cause problems in the person's further development. It is not necessary, however, for the resolution to be totally positive; indeed, some negativity can be helpful as a person progresses through the life cycles. For example, a principal or superintendent may need to exercise caution in considering communications from people concerning the actions and intentions of others. Thus, a certain amount of mistrust is advantageous. The goal for a person should be achieving a favorable ratio of positive to negative.

The stages of moral development should be considered as a continuum rather than as discrete periods. People may experience the stages in varying degrees of intensity and may even oscillate between them. Table 2.1 presents Erikson's eight stages of development and their corresponding crises. Also listed are the strengths that will emerge from the successful resolution of the crisis in each stage (Erikson used the term *strength* rather than *virtue*).

Lawrence Kohlberg was greatly influenced by Jean Piaget. He modified and extended Piaget's approach in setting forth his own theory of ethical develop-

TABLE 2.1
Erikson's Eight Stages of Moral Development

Stages	Crises	Strengths
Stage One: Infancy	Basic trust vs. basic mistrust	Hope
Stage Two: Early Childhood	Autonomy vs. shame, doubt	Will
State Three: Play Age	Initiative vs. guilt	Purpose
Stage Four: School Age	Industry vs. inferiority	Competence
Stage Five: Adolescence	Identity vs. identity confusion	Fidelity
Stage Six: Young Adult	Intimacy vs. isolation	Love
Stage Seven: Adulthood	Generativity vs. stagnation	Care
Stage Eight: Old Age	Integrity vs. despair	Wisdom

Source: From John W. Crossin, *What Are They Saying about Virtue?* (New York: Paulist Press, 1985), pp. 58–64.

ment. Kohlberg's approach is commonly referred to as a *structural-developmental approach.*

In his research Kohlberg asked participants to respond to a story that set forth an ethical dilemma. He then probed and analyzed the reasoning behind their responses. His research resulted in his identifying six stages of moral development, described in Figure 2.1. These stages are universal to all people and, according to Kohlberg's theory, once a person has passed through a given stage, that person will not regress. Further, the development of ethical principles is not related to specific religious beliefs; rather, ethical principles develop through interaction with the environment and with other people that results in the person's restructuring of his or her experiences to achieve ethical growth.

The key virtue for ethical growth at each stage of development is justice. Kohlberg considers his research and conclusions related to the philosophies of both Immanuel Kant and John Rawls, who contributed significantly to the body of knowledge about justice. Justice is concerned with equality and reciprocity in the sense that each person has a responsibility to treat others as equals.

Educational administrators who promote the dignity of all employees and recognize the contribution made to the education of children not only by teachers and other professionals, but also by cooks, custodians, school-bus drivers, and secretaries, exemplify the virtue of justice.

From the developmental and structural perspectives of human growth, it is now possible to proceed with a contemporary understanding of the ethical virtues. A functional definition of *virtues* should include the following:

◆ Virtues are qualities that shape the very core of who a person is.

◆ Virtues are flexible and adaptable to the milieu within which a person must act.

◆ Virtues shape human inclinations and dispositions to act in a certain way.

Level A: Preconventional Level

Stage One.   Punishment and Obedience
Right is literal obedience to rules and authority, avoiding punishment, and not doing physical harm. This stage takes an egocentric point of view.

Stage Two.   Individual Instrumental Purpose and Exchange
Right is serving one's own or others' needs and making fair deals in terms of concrete exchange. This stage takes a concrete individualistic perspective.

Level B: Conventual Level

Stage Three.   Mutual Interpersonal Expectations, Relationships, and Conformity
Right is playing a good (nice) role, being concerned about other people and their feelings, keeping loyalty and trust with partners, and being motivated to follow rules and expectations. This stage takes the perspective of the individual in relationship to other individuals and stages of development.

Stage Four.   Social System and Conscience Maintenance
Right is doing one's duty in society, upholding the social order, and maintaining the welfare of society or the group. This stage differentiates societal point of view from interpersonal agreement or motives.

Level C: Postconventional and Principled Level

Stage Five.   Prior Rights and Social Contract or Utility
Right is upholding the basic rights, values, and legal contracts of a society, even when they conflict with the concrete rules and laws of the group. This stage takes a prior-to-society perspective, that of a rational individual aware of values and rights prior to social attachments and contracts.

Stage Six.   Universal Ethical Principles
This stage assumes guidance by universal ethical principles that all humanity should follow. This stage takes the perspective of a moral point of view from which social arrangements derive or on which they are grounded. The perspective is that of any rational individual recognizing the nature of morality or the basic premise of respect for other persons as ends, not means.

FIGURE 2.1
Kohlberg's Philosophy of Moral Development

From Lawrence Kohlberg, *Essays on Moral Development: The Philosophy of Moral Development,* vol. 1 (New York: HarperCollins Publishers, Inc., 1981), pp. 409-412. Excerpts, as submitted, from *Essays on Moral Development: The Philosophy of Moral Development* (volume 1) by Lawrence Kohlberg. Copyright © 1981 by Lawrence Kohlberg. Reprinted by permission of HarperCollins Publishers, Inc.

◆ Virtues integrate a person's emotional and intellectual life in such a way as to facilitate arriving at ethical judgments with ease.

◆ Virtues must be cultivated over time in order to facilitate a certain way of acting.

This last point suggests that virtues are analogous to the abilities acquired by athletes or musicians who must practice certain skills over a prolonged period of time. In like manner, virtues can be strengthened through practice or weakened if neglected.

Prudence.   The bedrock of the virtues is prudence, because it permeates all decision making and thus operates in concrete situations. The practice of prudence entails memory, foresight, imagination, and docility. The prudent person attempts to recall past experiences and similar experiences when he or she faces an issue or problem that requires a decision; he or she also tries to predict the possible consequences associated with various options. Developing alternative solutions to issues and problems requires creative and, at times, daring decision making. Docility does not mean passivity, but means the openness to learn from others that is a key aspect of this virtue.

Prudence is called for when the threat of a teacher strike over wages occurs after at-the-table negotiating has failed. The superintendent of schools will be required to evaluate the situation and make difficult decisions about the teachers' demands. Acquiescing to the demands will probably require a change in the priorities embedded in the school-district budget; standing firm could result in a strike, which would have a significant affect on students.

Justice.   Justice is concerned with the individual's relationship to others in the various communities in which he or she lives. There are three kinds of justice: *distributive justice* is concerned with the obligations of society to individuals; *legal justice* is the justice required of individuals to the society in which they live; and *commutative justice* regulates the relationships among individuals. These three types of justice bestow rights and responsibilities on each individual and the societies to which they belong. There is a corresponding responsibility for each right. The major question that sets the stage for public discourse is, On whom does a given right place a claim? There are two distinct kinds of rights: the first is a claim to something, such as the right to an education; the second is a claim against interference, such as the right to privacy.

The issue of inclusion of students with disabilities in the regular classroom requires administrators to respect the rights of both students with disabilities and nondisabled students in the allocation of human, financial, and material resources.

Fortitude.   Principalships and superintendencies in contemporary society are fraught with pressures that emerge from the psyche of educational leaders in the form of anxiety and fearfulness. Once found only in large, urban school districts, this phenomenon is now fostered in suburban and country districts as well. Fortitude not only helps people moderate their fear and anxiety, but also helps individuals overcome their weaknesses in the pursuit of doing good in their private and public lives. A weakness manifested in a fear of making commitments can paralyze an educational administrator. Fears of criticism, failure, disappointment, and humiliation on the part of a principal or superintendent can be devastating to a school or school district. Always taking the safe way is more than likely the wrong way to lead. Fortitude helps individuals overcome obstacles and strengthens them to look beyond their fears in pursuit of what they believe is the right course of action.

Temperance.   There are educational administrators who make a fetish out of their responsibilities, sometimes even putting work ahead of the well-being of themselves and their families. The human desires for pleasures and comforts are truly at the heart of an ethical life. Without such desires the individual will eventually blunt his or her sensibilities for anything except knowing that the tasks related to his or her responsibilities have been completed. On the other extreme are those administrators who indulge so much in pleasures that they neglect their responsibilities or perform them at a minimal level. Temperance is a flexible virtue and as such requires the individual to learn his or her limits in order to recognize when gratification begins to obscure other values.[19]

Making Ethical Decisions

Conscience is that essential human dimension that prompts everyone to make correct ethical decisions. It may be described in one of two ways: as an inclination or instinct that helps a person decide how to act in relation to a particular ethical dilemma, or as a skill, acquired through experience, that a person uses to make an informed judgment. The initial sign of conscience usually appears in children when they realize that a given action, thought, or omission is either right or wrong. The former is more complex because in most situations, a person must choose among many different *goods* in order to establish a balance.[20] A building principal may be caught between recommending the termination of employment of an incompetent teacher or letting the teacher remain for one more year so that he or she can qualify for retirement. It is necessary for all educational leaders to develop a process that will provide them with a foundation for probing the ethical depths of each situation that calls for a judgment.

Of the many approaches to making ethical decisions, three appear to have the greatest application to educational leadership: *strict consequentialism, mixed consequentialism,* and *deontologism.*

Joseph Fletcher is perhaps the best-known strict consequentialist because of his much celebrated book, *Situation Ethics: The New Morality.* Strict consequentialists use the following approach in making ethical decisions:

- Identify the problem
- List alternative courses of action
- Predict the consequences for each alternative
- Assign a value to the good produced by each alternative
- Select the alternative that produces the greatest good

The major objection to this approach is the subjectivism that is involved in determining both what is meant by *good* and how the good is to be *produced*.

Peter Knauer, Bruno Schüller, Josef Fuchs, and Louis Janssen are the most well-known mixed-consequentialists. Their approach can be summarized as follows:

- Identify the problem
- Analyze the problem (who, what, context)
- Analyze the values involved that are influenced by a person's beliefs and convictions
- Identify norms that should guide the action that protects the person's values
- Explore the consequences of the action
- Compare the consequences with the values
- If the consequences and the values are inconsistent, explore other alternatives and test them to gain feedback about the norms that protect the person's values
- If the consequences and the values are consistent, perform the action

The *principle of universalizability* can act as a quality check on the decision. Basically, this principle asks the question, Would everyone who has the same characteristic and values as the person performing the action act in a similar fashion?

The third approach is usually identified with Germain Grisez, William E. May, and Paul Ramsey. The process of the deontologist position is as follows:

- Identify the problem
- Match up alternative courses of action with corresponding norms (comparing the alternatives with the norms should yield one of the following conclusions: one alternative is consistent with the norms; several alternatives are consistent with the norms; one alternative is consistent with one or more norms but is in conflict with one or more other norms)
- The higher norm is the one that should be acted on

This approach appears to be the more defensible because it tempers the subjective element of consequences but recognizes the importance of striving toward the good.[21]

One final note on forming moral judgments: sometimes people defer to the law as the norm they must follow. A director of personnel for a school district may follow all the provisions of civil-rights legislation in terms of procedure, but violate the spirit of the law. There is a certain amount of subjectivity in almost all hiring decisions, and it is possible for a bigoted administrator to manipulate the interpretation of an individual's qualifications for a position when that person is a certain gender or a person of color. People who have hardened and focused their attitudes in unethical directions may eventually become so self-deceiving that they do not fully realize what they are doing.

THE SEARCH FOR MEANING IN LIFE

The coming of the third millennium has prompted a great deal of analysis about the current century. People are *event* driven in the sense that they take stock of who they are at key anniversaries. Birth dates, death dates, employment or termination dates, graduation reunions, religious and national holidays, and wedding anniversaries all evoke memories and feelings. Obviously, some of these memories and feelings are pleasant and others are painful. One aspect of this rather complicated phenomenon is the meaningfulness factor. People engage in event analysis, hoping to find that their lives have purpose and meaning.

This section attempts to set a framework within which educational leaders and those preparing to become educational leaders can reflect on the meaning of their professional lives. Thus the discussion is organized around three topics: the search for meaning, human suffering, and liberation from suffering.

The Search

In a significant way, the writings of Viktor Frankl[22] address a core question facing contemporary educational administrators: Has my professional career made a difference? The monumental demands on administrators range from bureaucratic red tape to keeping schools safe and secure. The level of violence has escalated so much that some schools make use of metal detectors to prevent students from bringing weapons into the buildings. Most people enter the education profession with an expectation and desire to make a difference in the lives of students; it can be devastating to realize that making a difference often has nothing to do with learning in the traditional sense and everything to do with trying to motivate students simply to come to school.

The noted psychiatrist and author Viktor Frankl epitomized in his own life a struggle to find meaning. His parents, brother, and wife were victims of the Holocaust. He and his sister were the only concentration-camp survivors in his entire family. He lost everything in the camps, from possessions to human dignity.

Frankl asserted that the search for meaning is the primary motivator in life for everyone and that meaning is unique to each person. Because of this uniqueness, meaning can be found only through individual efforts. The dimensions of meaning are exemplified in ideals and values. The terminology used by Frankl, *the will to meaning,* gives priority to the personal freedom of each person to effect and sustain a direction in life that continually seeks out meaning not only in major life events but also in everyday living.

The search for meaning is fundamentally related to each person's profession or occupation. Although people engage in work to make a living, it is clear that for many (if not for most) people their profession or occupation is either a hindrance or help as they search for meaning. Like others, some educational administrators have lost a sense of meaning in their lives such that they cannot detect the difference they make in the lives of faculty members, staff members, students, and parents with whom they interact.

Active imagination is the tool that can help administrators understand their contributions to the profession and give overall meaning to life. The unique abilities, skills, and talents of each educational leader cannot be duplicated by other people, simply because they are unique. Frankl, however, was concerned with the existential moment. He believed that the search for meaning must be grounded in the reality of the here and now. As a point of departure from more classical approaches, he insisted on the position that the world, and not a person's psyche, is the milieu within which the person will find the meaning of life.

Frankl also had a profound understanding of how interpersonal relationships shape a person's search for meaning. Ultimately, the meaning of life is always about human relations. Educational administrators are fortunate in the fact that their entire professional careers are devoted to actualizing human potential. In fostering the instructional and learning processes through administrative practices, educational leaders can experience firsthand how faculty, staff, students, and parents have changed their lives for the better.

In a unique way human potentiality can easily slip away without being actualized. Frankl lamented that the opportunity to actualize this potential is the only transitory aspect of life. However, once actualized, potentiality becomes part of a past that is irrevocably stored and thus is retrievable. This concept accounts for the progress individuals make and how that progress affects others. It also smacks of Carl Jung's theory of the collective unconscious and the evolutionary propositions of Teilhard de Chardin. Principals, superintendents, and other administrators can be assured of a legacy through the potentiality that they actualize both in themselves and in others. Administrators, along with teachers, are the benefactors of the accomplishments produced by students in school and throughout their lives.

Educational administrators, teachers, and staff sometimes forget that students are constrained by biological, psychological, and sociological conditions. Frankl believed that human beings are capable of growing beyond these constraints and can change not only themselves but also their environment and even the world. Human existence is fraught with pain, guilt, and death. Yet Frankl called this condition a tragic optimism because it offers individuals the opportunity to change themselves for the better.

Selected Reading 2.1 contains an excerpt from *Man's Search for Meaning* in which Viktor Frankl set forth the philosophical tenets of his approach to therapy.

Human Suffering

Suffering is the most universal experience of humanity. Because no one escapes this existential reality, it provides a shared experience that can be a vehicle for human empathy and understanding. It is also a private phenomenon in the sense that no one can truly alleviate the suffering of another person. Pain can be alleviated through medication and other therapies, but suffering cannot.

Defining suffering is problematic; however, for ease of understanding, suffering can be considered as arising from personal experience or from symbiotic experience. Personal suffering is always the stimulus of fundamental questioning: Why me? Thus, personal suffering is expressed as victimization, and the anguish of suffering is its meaninglessness. Symbiotic suffering arises from a felt kinship with other people who are suffering.

A principal, teachers, and staff members from a particular school experience symbiotic suffering when a child attending their school dies. The superintendent of schools will also suffer from such an incident, but to a lesser degree than those who had personal contact with the child.

All people suffered from the horrendous tragedy that took place in Littleton, Colorado, at Columbine High School. People suffer from the occurrence of spousal and child abuse and large-scale natural disasters such as floods and tornadoes. Although to a much lesser degree, people share the anguish of those who have personally experienced a tragedy and its seeming meaninglessness. It is easy to conclude that people live on a continuum with meaning and happiness on one end and meaninglessness and sorrow on the other end. Viktor Frankl would hold that the primary motivational force in human life is the quest for meaning, which is continually being frustrated by suffering.[23]

Self-Agency.   The response people make to their own suffering and to the suffering of others is of particular concern to educational leadership because of the effect of suffering on the character formation of children and young adults. The suffering of educational administrators, teachers, and staff can become a force in the school community when these people model responses that children and others should make to suffering.

The self-agency approach places emphasis on each person's beliefs, intentions, and actions as a response to suffering. People are viewed as self-determining through their own personal life history. The person who suffers is changed

ᔌ Selected Reading 2.1

Man's Search for Meaning
Viktor E. Frankl (1905–1997)

Man's search for meaning is the primary motivation in his life and not a "secondary rationalization" of instinctual drives. This meaning is unique and specific in that it must and can be fulfilled by him alone; only then does it achieve a significance which will satisfy his own *will* to meaning. There are some authors who contend that meanings and values are "nothing but defense mechanisms, reaction formations and sublimations." But as for myself, I would not be willing to live merely for the sake of my "defense mechanisms," nor would I be ready to die merely for the sake of my "reaction formations." Man, however, is able to live and even to die for the sake of his ideals and values!

Noogenic neuroses does not emerge from conflicts between drives and instincts but rather from existential problems. Among such problems, the frustration of the will to meaning plays a large role. . . .

. . . After a few interviews, it was clear that his will to mean was frustrated by his vocation, and he actually longed to be engaged in some other kind of work. As there was no reason for not giving up his profession and embarking on a different one, he did so, with most gratifying results. . . .

. . . some amount of conflict is normal and healthy. In a similar sense suffering is not always a psychological phenomenon; rather than being a symptom of neurosis, suffering may well be a human achievement, especially if the suffering grows out of existential frustration. I would strictly deny that one's search for a meaning to his existence, or even his doubt of it, in every case is derived from, or results in, any disease. Existential frustration is in itself neither pathological nor pathogenic. A man's concern, even his despair, over the worthwhileness of life is an *existential distress* but by no means a *mental disease*. . . .

To be sure, man's search for meaning may arouse inner tension rather than inner equilibrium. However, precisely such tension is an indispensable prerequisite of mental health. There is nothing in the world, I venture to say, that would so effectively help one to survive even the worst conditions as the knowledge that there is a meaning in one's life. There is much wisdom in the words of Nietzsche: "He who has a *why* to live for can bear almost any *how*." . . .

The existential vacuum is a widespread phenomenon of the twentieth century. This is understandable; it may be due to a twofold loss which man has had to undergo since he became a truly human being. At the beginning of human history, man lost some of the basic animal instincts in which an animal's behavior is imbedded and by which it is secured. Such security, like Paradise, is closed to man forever; man has to make choices. In addition to this, however, man has suffered another loss in his more recent development inasmuch as the traditions which buttressed his behavior are now rapidly diminishing. No instinct tells him what he has to do, and no tradition tells him what he ought to do; sometimes he does not even know what he wishes to do. Instead, he either wishes to do what other people do (conformism) or he does what other people wish him to do (totalitarianism). . . . The existential vacuum manifests itself mainly in a state of boredom. Now we can understand Schopenhauer when he said that mankind was apparently doomed to vacillate eternally between the two extremes of distress and boredom. . . .

. . . For the meaning of life differs from man to man, from day to day and from hour to hour. What matters, therefore, is not the meaning of life in general but rather the specific meaning of a person's life at a given moment. . . . One should not search for an abstract meaning of life. Everyone has his own specific vocation or mission in life to carry out a concrete assignment which demands fulfillment. Therein he cannot be replaced, nor can his life be repeated. Thus, everyone's task is as unique as is his specific opportunity to implement it. . . .

By declaring that man is responsible and must actualize the potential meaning of his life. I wish to stress that the true meaning of life is to be discovered in the world rather than within man or his own psyche, as though it were a closed system. I have termed this constitutive characteristic "the self-transcendence of human existence." . . .

Love is the only way to grasp another human being in the innermost core of his personality. No one can become fully aware of the very essence of another human being unless he loves him. . . .

Those things which seem to take meaning away from human life include not only suffering but dying as well. I never tire of saying that the only really transitory aspect of life are the potentialities; but as soon as they are actualized, they are rendered realities at that very moment; they are saved and delivered into the past, wherein they are rescued and preserved from transitoriness. For, in the past, nothing is irretrievably lost but everything irrevocably stored. . . .

By the same token, every human being has the freedom to change at any instant. Therefore, we can predict his future only within the large framework of a statistical survey referring to a whole group; the individual personality, however, remains essentially unpredictable. The basis for any predictions would be represented by biological, psychological or sociological conditions. Yet one of the many features of human existence is the capacity to rise above such conditions, to grow beyond them. Man is capable of changing the world for the better if possible, and of changing himself for the better if necessary. . . .

Let us first ask ourselves what should be understood by "a tragic optimism." In brief it means that one is, and remains, optimistic in spite of the "tragic triad," as it is called in Logotherapy, a triad which consists of those aspects of human existence which may be circumscribed by: 1. pain; 2. guilt; and 3. death. . . . And this in turn presupposes the human capacity to creatively turn life's negative aspects into something positive or constructive. In other words, what matters is to make the best of any given situation. "The best," however, is that which in Latin is called *optimum*—hence the reason I speak of a tragic optimism, that is, an optimism in the face of tragedy and in view of the human potential which at its best always allows for: 1. turning suffering into a human achievement and accomplishment; 2. deriving from guilt the opportunity to change oneself for the better; and 3. deriving from life's transitoriness an incentive to take responsible action.

Source: Excerpts from pages 105–109, 111, 113, 115, 116, 123–124, 133, 139–140 of *Man's Search for Meaning* by Viktor E. Frankl. © 1959, 1962, 1984, 1992 by Viktor E. Frankl. Reprinted by permission of Beacon Press, Boston.

by the experience; and the change can be enhancing or destructive depending on how the individual perceives the event that caused the suffering.[24]

Life narrative becomes a type of ongoing historical account of a person's successes, failures, happiness, and suffering. Suffering does not occur as an unexpected event, with the person hoping that the disconcerting effects will dissipate over time. Rather, suffering is seen as a condition of life that transforms the person, that becomes a part of the person's life narrative.

The following criteria can help in determining the effectiveness of a person's response to suffering.

◆ The narrative must have power to release the person from destructive alternatives.

◆ The narrative must help the person see through current distortions.

♦ The narrative must have the power to keep the person from resorting to violence.

♦ The narrative must help the person transform the suffering into meaning.[25]

People falsely assume that life is good only when they are free from suffering. Yet often people are able to achieve meaning in life only when they are willing to accept their own suffering and the suffering of others.[26]

In the face of tragedy, people rise to greater heights than they thought possible of themselves. It is almost an involuntary response for the principal, teachers, and staff members of a school to raise money and offer support to a child and his or her parents when their house is destroyed by fire. School administrators are always eager to open the doors of their schools to the victims of floods and other natural disasters. A television camera captured a principal who was waiting for the school bus to arrive so that he could take the hand of a child and lead him into school through a crowd of protesting parents because the child had been diagnosed with AIDS.

Taking Responsibility.   When people think about their responsibilities they may not immediately think of freedom. Yet freedom is the foundation of responsibility. No one can be responsible for anything either as a duty or as a consequence without freedom of choice. Guilt and innocence have no meaning without freedom.

One of the most solemn and yet poignant treatises on freedom and responsibility was written by Jean-Paul Sartre. The concept of self-agency is enhanced by Sartre's work, even though he tended to be negative about the exercise of freedom. Selected Reading 2.2 contains an excerpt from Sartre's treatise, which begins by stating that human beings are the initiators of everything in the world and thus they should not attempt to disguise the fact that they are also responsible for everything in the world. As an existentialist, Sartre was concerned with combating a worldview that placed blame for the human condition on extraneous forces. According to Sartre, people are capable of almost anything, including waging war and torturing other people; thus it is blatantly incorrect to term some types of behavior *nonhuman*.

Using the situation of war as an example of his position, Sartre stated that participation in war is a conscious choice because people could have done something even as tragic as suicide or as difficult as desertion in order to get out of the situation. Although these two alternatives are possible, they are not probable, because most people do not see them as alternatives. Sartre's point, however, is that people must take on themselves their share of the responsibility. It becomes the individual's war through participation; it is not someone else's war in which people are participating; it is their war.

The most important aspect of Sartre's discourse is the recognition that everyone is ultimately alone in making his or her decisions. Further, the person making a decision is at the same time *creating* himself or herself because of the impact every decision has on the person who makes it.

Selected Reading 2.2

Freedom and Responsibility
Jean-Paul Sartre (1905–1980)

Man being condemned to be free carries the weight of the whole world on his shoulders; he is responsible for the world and for himself as a way of being. We are taking the word "responsibility" in its ordinary sense as "consciousness (of) being the incontestable author of an event or of an object." In this sense the responsibility of the for-itself is overwhelming since he is the one by whom it happens that *there* is a world; since he is also the one who makes himself be, then whatever may be the situation in which he finds himself, the for-itself must wholly assume this situation with its peculiar coefficient of adversity, even though it be insupportably. He must assume the situation with the proud consciousness of being the author of it, for the very worst disadvantages or the worst threats which can endanger my person have meaning only in and through my project; and it is on the ground of the engagement which I am that they appear. It is therefore senseless to think of complaining since nothing alien has decided what we feel, what we live, or what we are.

Furthermore this absolute responsibility is not resignation; it is simply the logical requirement of the consequences of our freedom. What happens to me happens through me, and I can neither affect myself with it nor revolt against it nor resign myself to it. Moreover everything which happens to me is *mine*. By what happens to me *qua* man, for what happens to a man through other men and through himself can be only human. The most terrible situations of war, the worst tortures do not create a non-human state of things; there is no non-human situation. It is only through fear, flight, and recourse to magical types of behavior that I shall decide on the non-human, but this decision is human, and I shall carry the entire responsibility for it. But in addition the situation is *mine* because it is the image of my free choice of myself, and everything which it presents to me is *mine* in that this represents me and symbolizes me. Is it not I who decide the coefficient of adversity in things and even their unpredictability by deciding for myself?

Thus there are no *accidents* in a life; a community event which suddenly bursts forth and involves me in it does not come from the outside. If I am mobilized in a war, this war is *my* war; it is in my image and I deserve it. I deserve it first because I could always get out of it by suicide or by desertion;

these ultimate possibilities are those which must always be presented for us when there is a question of envisaging a situation. For lack of getting out of it, I have *chosen* it. This can be due to inertia, to cowardice in the face of public opinion, or because I prefer certain other values to the value of the refusal to join in the war (the good opinion of my relatives, the honor of my family, etc.). Any way you look at it, it is a matter of a choice. This choice will be repeated later on again and again without a break until the end of the war. Therefore we must agree with the statement by J. Romains, "In war there are no innocent victims." If therefore I have preferred war to death or to dishonor, everything takes place as if I bore the entire responsibility for this war. Of course others have declared it, and one might be tempted perhaps to consider me as a simple accomplice. But his notion of complicity has only a juridical sense, and it does not hold here. For it depended on me that for me and by me this war should not exist, and I have decided that it does exist. There was no compulsion here, for the compulsion could have got no hold on a freedom. I did not have any excuse; for as we have said repeatedly in this book, the peculiar character of human-reality is that it is without excuse. Therefore it remains for me only to lay claim to this war.

But in addition the war is *mine* because, by the sole fact that it arises in a situation which I make be and that I can discover it there only by engaging myself for or against it, I can no longer distinguish at present the choice which I make of myself from the choice which I make of the war. To live this war is to choose myself through it and to choose it through my choice of myself. There can be no question of considering it as "four years of vacation" or as a "reprieve," as a "recess," the essential part of my responsibilities being elsewhere in my married, family, or professional life. In this war which I have chosen I choose myself from day to day, and I make it mine by making myself. If it is going to be four empty years, then it is I who bear the responsibility for this.

Finally, as we pointed out earlier, each person is an absolute choice of self from the standpoint of a world of knowledge and of techniques which this choice both assumes and illumines; each person is an absolute emergence at an absolute date and is perfectly unthinkable at another date. It is therefore a waste of time to ask what I should have been if this war had not broken out, for I have chosen myself as one of the possible meanings of the epoch which imperceptibly led to war. I am not distinct from this same epoch; I could not be transported to another epoch without contradiction. Thus *I am* this war which restricts and limits and makes comprehensible the period which preceded it. In this sense we may define more precisely the responsibility of the for-itself if to the earlier quoted statement, "There are no innocent victims," we add the words, "We have the war we deserve." Thus, totally free, indistinguishable from the period for which I have chosen to be the meaning, as profoundly responsible for the war as if I had myself declared it, unable to live without integrating it in *my* situation, engaging myself in it wholly and stamping it with my seal, I must be without remorse or regrets as I am without excuse; for from the instant of my emergence in being, I carry the weight of the world by myself alone without anything or anyone being able to lighten it.

Yet this responsibility is of a very particular type. Someone will say, "I did not ask to be born." This is a naive way of throwing greater emphasis on our facticity. I am responsible for everything, in fact, except for my very responsibility, for I am not the foundation of my being. Therefore everything takes place as if I were compelled to be responsible. I am *abandoned* in the world, not in the sense that I might remain abandoned and passive in a hostile universe like a board floating on the water, but rather in the sense that I find myself suddenly alone and without help, involved in a world for which I bear the whole responsibility without being able, whatever I do, to tear myself away from this responsibility for an instant. For I am responsible for my very desire of fleeing responsibility. To make myself passive in the world, to refuse to act upon things and upon others of being-in-the-world. Yet I find an absolute responsibility for the fact that my facticity (here the fact of my birth) is directly inapprehensible and even inconceivable, for this fact of my birth never appears as a brute fact but always across a projective reconstruction of my for-itself. I am ashamed of being born or I am astonished at it or I rejoice over it, or in attempting to get rid of my life I affirm that I live and I assume this life as bad. Thus in a certain sense I *choose* being born. This choice itself is integrally affected with facticity since I am able not to choose, but this facticity in turn will appear only insofar as I transcend it toward my ends. Thus facticity is everywhere but inapprehensible; I never encounter anything except my responsibility. That is why I cannot ask, "*Why*

In this view, the decisions principals make are free choices, even though they flow from the policies of the board of education or from the administrative procedures of the superintendent. They are free choices because the principal is not extraneous to the principalship of a given building. It is his or her principalship. A disciplinary decision made by a principal based on the board of education's policy pertaining to student rights and responsibilities carries a personal consequence for that principal. He or she personally changes with every decision. The only way a principal can extricate himself or herself from a professional decision is through resignation, which, of course, is also a decision that the principal must make alone and that will irrevocably change him or her.

was I born?" or curse the day of my birth or declare that I did not ask to be born, for these various attitudes toward my birth—i.e., toward the fact that I realize a presence in the world—are absolutely nothing else but ways of assuming this birth in full responsibility and of making it *mine*. Here again I encounter only myself and my projects so that finally my abandonment—i.e., my facticity—consists simply in the fact that I am condemned to be wholly responsible for myself. I am the being which *is* in such a way that in its being its being is in question. And this "is" of my being *is* as present and inapprehensible.

Under these conditions since every event in the world can be revealed to me only as an *occasion* (an occasion made use of, missed, neglected, etc.), or rather since everything which happens to us can be considered as an *opportunity* (i.e., can appear to us only as a way of realizing this being which is in question in our being) and since others as transcendence-transcended are themselves only *occasions* and *opportunities*, the responsibility of the for-itself extends to the entire world as a peopled world. It is precisely thus that the for-itself apprehends itself in anguish; that is, as a being which is neither the foundation of its own being nor of the Other's being nor of the in-itself which form the world, but a being which is compelled to decide the meaning of being—within it and everywhere outside of it. The one who realizes in anguish his condition as *being* thrown into a responsibility which extends to his very abandonment has no longer either remorse or regret or excuse; he is no longer anything but a freedom which perfectly reveals itself and whose being resides in this very revelation. But as we pointed out earlier, most of the time we flee anguish in bad faith.

Source: Jean-Paul Sartre, *Being and Nothingness,* trans. Hazel Barnes (New York: Philosophical Library, Inc., 1956), pp. 553–556. Reprinted with permission.

OTHER PHILOSOPHICAL APPROACHES TO THE ISSUES IN THIS CHAPTER

The approach taken in this chapter to the development of ethical norms is predicated on an inductive approach that begins with human experience. The mandate derived from this approach is an ongoing analysis of the human phenomenon. Thus this approach is concerned with continually asking the three ethical questions presented in Chapter 1: What does it mean to be a human being? How should human beings treat one another? How should the institutions of society be organized? Some may take the position that this approach is relativistic in nature.

Another approach to the development of ethical norms, often referred to as ethical objectivism, takes the position that some ethical principles are universal to all people at all times. The strictest adherents of objectivism would state that there is always one right answer to every question, that the one right answer is valid regardless of the circumstances, and that one ethical principle cannot be overridden by another ethical principle. The minimalist taking the objective approach would probably state that circumstances exist in which a universal principle cannot be applied and that a certain principle may override another principle in certain situations.

Perhaps the most relevant proponent of the objectivist approach was Thomas Aquinas. His notion of the natural law was the keystone for his ethical objectivism. According to Aquinas, the natural law is based on the divine law, which means it is eternal. The natural law is imprinted on universal human nature and therefore is applicable to all people regardless of historical circumstances. It is discoverable through human reason. Further, it is the basis for all civil law. The influence of ethical objectivism cannot be overstated; it is perhaps the most widely held position, even though many people who take this position are not familiar with the writings of the various philosophers who have advocated it. Of the many other philosophers who could be classified as objectivists, two of the most prominent are Jacques Maritain and Louis Pojman.

CROSSWALK TO ISLLC STANDARD FIVE

The contents of this chapter support the following dimensions of ISLLC Standard Five.

Knowledge
The administrator has knowledge and understanding of:
- the purpose of education and the role of leadership in modern society
- various ethical frameworks and perspectives on ethics

Dispositions
The administrator believes in, values, and is committed to:
- bringing ethical principles to the decision-making process
- subordinating one's own interest to the good of the school community
- accepting the consequences for upholding one's principles and actions

Performances
The administrator:
- examines personal and professional values

♦ demonstrates values, beliefs, and attitudes that inspire others to higher levels of performance

♦ considers the impact of one's administrative practices on others

♦ uses the influence of the office to enhance the educational program rather than for personal gain

♦ treats people fairly, equitably, and with dignity and respect

♦ fulfills legal and contractual obligations

ETHICAL CONSIDERATIONS PRESENTED IN THIS CHAPTER

♦ Research in the social and physical sciences has revealed that the universe and humanity are much older and more dependent on each other than was once believed.

♦ Humanity gradually evolved onto higher planes of thought, reflection, and liberty.

♦ Human consciousness comprises thought, reflection, and liberty, which are the necessary components of human experience, understanding, and judgment.

♦ The conscious exercise of human reason in making judgments is the context within which educational leaders can develop ethical norms.

♦ Because human experience is dynamic and continually evolving, educational leaders can derive ethical norms primarily through inductive reasoning.

♦ It is the responsibility of each educational leader and the education community in the aggregate continually to search for what is ethically good in providing services for students and in supporting the activities of school-district employees.

♦ Because schools and school districts are human institutions, it is incumbent on educational leaders to change the structure of these institutions when they cease to promote the common good.

♦ Cultivating the virtues of prudence, justice, fortitude, and temperance can aid educational leaders in the ethical exercise of their responsibilities.

♦ Developing a systematic approach to ethical decision making can help educational leaders confront the complex issues facing contemporary education.

♦ Educational leaders can sustain an ethical direction in their professional lives only through continual striving to find meaning in their daily activities.

◆ When educational leaders are faced with human tragedy and suffering, they are presented with a choice of how they will reaction to the experience, which will lead either to optimism or to despair.

∽ SUMMARY

Recent research not only in the social sciences but also in the physical sciences testifies that the universe and humanity are much older, more dependent on each other, and more complex than once believed. Because of this research, the question of evolution has been raised again.

The two laws of evolution most relevant to an understanding of humanity are the law of continuity and the law of design. The law of continuity states that evolution proceeds from the simpler to the more complex. The law of design holds that growth in complexity does not mean merely an accumulation of elements; rather, when a certain degree of complexity is reached, evolution must proceed to a new plane in order for the process to continue.

Teilhard de Chardin created the concept of spirit-matter—the stuff from which everything in the universe is formed. With relation to the evolution of humanity, he postulated that since people possess the spiritual potential to exercise freedom and since humanity evolved from nonhuman forms, those forms must have possessed elements of freedom.

Humanity is endowed with thought, reflection, and liberty. Humanity will eventually reach a critical point of complexity that will necessitate ascendance to a higher plane.

Consciousness brings with it a greater awareness of the interrelatedness of social experiences and the need for better communication among human beings and thus has led to communicative technology.

From evolved human consciousness develops the context within which ethical norms are identified. Thought, reflection, and liberty constitute the essence of consciousness, which is operationalized through human experience, understanding, and judgment. In relation to the study of ethics, these ideas underscore the need to reevaluate previous ethical norms. The classical worldview sees the world as a finished product and holds that the experiences of people allow them to obtain a clear understanding of immutable essences. Thus, people can have a high degree of certitude about ethical principles, which remain valid forever. Right conduct can be formulated using universal principles in a deductive method that will yield secure and complete conclusions.

In contrast, a more modern worldview sees the world as dynamic and evolving. The experiences of people allow them to identify individual traits within concrete and historical particulars. The path to right conduct is formulated primarily through inductive reasoning from particular experiences.

The distinction between the law of nature and natural law emerges as a consequence of this modern worldview. Natural law is not a codified body of precepts, but refers to the parameters that define the milieu of being, that which follows from the essential nature of humanity. Natural law should not be identified with physical, chemical, or biological laws that explain how the natural world works.

Natural law is discovered through discourse, research, and reflection on humanity; the more complex the issue, the more deliberation, dialogue, and study will be required. Rationality is thus the foundation of natural law. Deliberations concerning natural law must take into account the social dimension of humanity. Finally, using natural law as a foundation allows all people to enter into rational debate concerning our collective humanity, which is critical in a pluralistic society.

The development of ethical norms has four aspects: (1) it is the responsibility of each person and of the community in the aggregate to search for what is ethically good; (2) norms must emerge from our experience of what it means to be truly human; (3) norms should be in concert with the unfinished evolutionary character of humanity and the world; and (4) the principle of proportionality should be observed.

The institutions, structures, and systems created by humanity are situated either for or against the common good or for the good of some segment of society. Structures are patterns of relationships that have become routine and involve policies and institutions; institutions are complexes of actions that control human conduct through predefined patterns; systems are complexes of structures and institutions. This is the realm of social ethics.

The free decisions of a person can place others in situations that require them to make decisions whether to act or not to act for good. History becomes a series of decisions and situations. Personal and social unethicality are dimensions of the same phenomenon and can be understood only in relation to one another. From a social perspective unethicality is experienced as external, inherited, overbearing, and seductive; from a personal perspective unethicality is experienced as freely chosen and incurring blame.

The decision to act unethically becomes a core orientation, which, in turn, becomes the milieu in which future freedom is exercised. A person is restricted in making decisions because of prior decisions. People act from the totality of their being, and each person is the ultimate cause of the kind of person he or she becomes. The ultimate goal of the socially ethical person is the integration of all his or her attitudes or dispositions in order to orient himself or herself toward ethical relationships with other people.

Erik Erikson viewed the somatic, societal, and ego processes as interrelated and emphasized that all three must be taken into consideration when analyzing a particular human event. Lawrence Kohlberg extended Piaget's approach in developing his own structural-developmental approach. Kohlberg posited six stages of moral development that are universal to all people. The key virtue for ethical growth and development at each stage is justice. Once a person has passed through a given stage, he or she will not regress.

Cultivating the virtues of prudence, justice, fortitude, and temperance can strengthen an individual and even rectify the wrongs committed by people against others and against the community. Contemporary thought views these virtues in the context of the process of human development, seeing them as qualities that shape the very core of a person; are flexible and adaptable to the milieu within which the person must act; shape human inclinations and dispositions to act in a certain way; must be cultivated over time; and facilitate arriving at good moral judgments.

The bedrock of the virtues, prudence, permeates all decision making and operates in concrete situations. Exercising prudence involves attempting to recall past similar experiences and trying to predict consequences associated with various options. Justice is concerned with the individual's relationship to others in the community. There are three kinds of justice: distributive, legal, and commutative. There is a corresponding responsibility for each right. The virtue of fortitude helps people moderate their fears and anxieties and overcome their weaknesses in the pursuit of doing good in their private and public lives. Temperance is a flexible virtue that requires a person to learn his or her limits in order to recognize when gratification begins to obscure other values.

Conscience is the essential human dimension that prompts everyone to make appropriate ethical decisions. It refers both to the sensitive inclination or instinct that helps a person decide how to act in relation to a particular ethical dilemma and to a skill, acquired through experience, that a person uses to make an informed judgment. There are three approaches to making ethical decisions: strict consequentialism, mixed consequentialism, and deontologism.

The contemporary milieu within which educational administration is practiced sometimes makes it difficult for administrators to realize the value and meaningfulness of their professional and personal lives. Viktor Frankl asserts that the search for meaning is the primary motivator in life for everyone and that meaning is unique to each person. The dimensions of meaning are exemplified in ideals and values. Frankl's concept of the *will to meaning* gives priority to the freedom of each person to effect and sustain a direction in life that continually seeks out meaning both in major life events and in everyday living. The search for meaning is fundamentally related to each person's profession or occupation.

Frankl's concept of *tragic optimism* is a perspective for people who have experienced great tragedy in their lives. Optimism cannot be commanded or thrust on a person; it can only be reached through personal striving and suffering. The opposite of tragic optimism is despair.

The self-agency approach to suffering places emphasis on each person's beliefs, intentions, and actions as a response to suffering. The person who suffers is changed by the experience, and the change can be enhancing or destructive depending on how the individual perceives the event that caused the suffering. People have a choice in how they will react to suffering. Sartre pointed out that everyone is alone in his or her decision making. The person making a decision is creating himself or herself because every decision has an impact on the person who makes it.

DISCUSSION QUESTIONS AND STATEMENTS

1. Explain the relationship between the *law of continuity* and the *law of design*.
2. What is Teilhard de Chardin's position concerning human freedom as it relates to the nonhuman matter from which humanity has been formed?
3. How is it that human consciousness is the context within which ethical norms can be identified and developed?
4. Compare and contrast the classical worldview with the modern worldview.
5. Explain the difference between the *law of nature* and the *natural law*.
6. How does a person discover the natural law?
7. What are the four aspects endemic to the development of ethical norms?
8. Explain what is meant by institutions, structures, and systems from a social ethics perspective.
9. Define social ethics.
10. How are the consequences of unethical conduct inherited by future generations?
11. Explain how practicing the virtues of prudence, justice, fortitude, and temperance can enable an educational leader to fulfill his or her professional responsibilities.
12. Explain the difference between Erik Erikson's *eight stages of moral development* and Lawrence Kohlberg's *philosophy of moral development*.
13. Compare and contrast the strict consequentialist, mixed consequentialist, and deontologistic approaches to decision making.
14. Under what two aspects can human conscience be considered?
15. Explain Viktor Frankl's concept of the *will to meaning*.
16. How is Frankl's idea of *tragic optimism* linked to his concept of the will to meaning?
17. What is the difference between personal suffering and symbiotic suffering?
18. Explain Jean-Paul Sartre's notion about human freedom and responsibility.

The Gay Teacher

The principal of the high school has been very successful and attributes this to the fact that he has an experiential understanding of the community and the students because he was born and raised in the same region. He has been the principal for nineteen years.

The school has an enrollment of about 1,600 students. The students are excellent not only academically, but also in the manner in which they conduct themselves at school and in the community. The athletic program is very good, and interscholastic athletic events are attended by students, parents, and others in the community as well. Such events unify the community, which is very supportive of the entire school district. The tax levy is $5.72, which is high for that area of the state.

The students are respectful of adults and caring for each other. Parents see to it that their children come to school ready to learn. Although there are the usual problems associated with adolescence, as well as problems with some parents, there is generally nothing that cannot be handled. There is a relatively low incidence of alcohol and drug abuse among the students, and the local police department cooperates fully with the school when there is an incident.

There is little turnover in the faculty because the district provides a competitive salary schedule and benefits package. However, the strong student and parental support is the compelling reason that most faculty members like to teach in the district and live in the community.

The faculty like the principal very much because he is reasonable and supportive. Similarly, the principal likes the faculty as a whole because they are generally competent and cooperative. There are two assistant principals. One of the assistants is a woman who has been in her position for eleven years; the other is a first-year assistant who was chosen from the faculty after he completed a master of arts degree in educational administration. All three administrators complement each other and have no difficulty working as a team.

One of the physical education teachers also coaches basketball and has led the team to three conference championships in five years. He is extremely popular not only with the students and their parents, but also with the faculty and administrators at both the building and district levels.

During spring break, the physical education teacher was seen in a restaurant in another city with another man by one of the basketball players and his parents. Before the student and his parents could make their way over to the teacher's table to say hello, the other man leaned forward, clasped the physical education teacher's hand, and kissed him on the cheek. At that moment, the physical education teacher looked up and saw the student and his parents standing less than five feet from the table. He could tell from the expressions on their faces that they were shocked. Everyone simply stared silently at one another. The student and his parents turned around and left the restaurant.

The principal received a telephone call from the superintendent of schools on Sunday evening, the day before classes reconvened after spring break. The superintendent said that he had a delicate issue to discuss. He had received telephone calls from the parents of every student who played on the basketball team and from every member of the board of education. The issue was the physical education teacher's lifestyle. The parents claimed that the physical education teacher was gay. The superintendent described the incident that took place in the restaurant and told the principal to investigate the accusation and, if it was true, to convince the physical education teacher to resign.

Immediately on arriving at school, the principal met with the two assistant principals and explained the situation to them. Both of them agreed with the superintendent that the teacher had to resign.

The physical education teacher had already heard the rumors when the principal confronted him with the accusation. The teacher stated that his personal life was private, and he refused to discuss the issue. He further stated that he did not see the connection between his private life and the fact that he was a good teacher and coach and that he had no intention of resigning. The principal informed the superintendent about the conference. The superintendent was direct and emphatic, stating that the teacher had to resign or his employment would be terminated.

The principal considered the teacher a good coach and teacher. He agreed with the teacher that his private life should not nullify his excellent teaching and coaching record. The principal knew as well that the teacher's conduct at school and in the community was exemplary. Thus, the principal decided that he would try to resolve the issue in favor of the teacher, even though he thought that anything less than the teacher's resignation could jeopardize his own position as principal.

Discussion Questions and Statements

1. What virtues are being exhibited by the principal's decision to try resolution of the issue rather than forcing the teacher to resign or terminating his employment?

2. Explain how this case exemplifies the tension between the classical and modern worldviews.

3. What dimensions of the natural law are being exemplified in the principal's behavior?

4. Can the principal's decision to attempt resolution of the issue be characterized as fundamental to who he is as a person?

5. How has contemporary society been situated by the attitudes of past generations toward people who are gay?

6. Apply the three approaches to decision making to this situation.

CASE STUDY 2.2

Student Violence

The new middle school was built to alleviate the crowded conditions at another middle school in the district. It is a state-of-the-art school: its classrooms are arranged in a pod formation that supports team teaching, and it uses a core-curriculum approach that was resurrected after having been abandoned for five years. A huge gymnasium and swimming pool are in an adjacent wing of the building. Student physical fitness is the goal of the superintendent of schools, who convinced the board of education that future middle schools and high schools should have excellent physical-fitness facilities.

The school district is experiencing tremendous growth. The economy in the area has been booming because of the concentration of corporations specializing in technology development and production. As these corporations have increased their workforces, so have the businesses providing services and products to these workers.

Most of the people in the middle-school attendance area are in their thirties; there are approximately two children per family. The parents are well educated and demand the same for their children. It was relatively easy for the school district to pass a bond referendum to build three new schools, including the middle school. The superintendent predicts that the enrollment will increase approximately 12 percent per year for the next five years. With this increase, the school district will become the second largest in the suburban area.

The principal of the middle school was hired specifically for the new school. She was the assistant principal at another school in the district. Her appointment as principal was made two years before the school opened its doors. She was allowed to participate in the facility planning process with the architect. She was also able to be a key person in the faculty and staff hiring processes as well as in the curriculum-development process for the new school. This was one of those rare opportunities for an administrator to plan and staff the school he or she will lead.

Most people working in the school and the parents of the children are delighted with the principal because they recognize that she is a very competent administrator. Further, the students like her because she is a caring person who treats them with respect.

A fifth-grade teacher is having a difficult time motivating a student to participate in classroom activities. Furthermore, his attendance at school is sporadic. The teacher referred the student to the school counselor, who talked with him and his parents. The boy's parents are separated and will probably get divorced but appear to be very concerned and supportive of their son. However, the student showed no improvement and resented the teacher and the guidance counselor for having talked with his parents. He told the teacher and the counselor that he was old enough to handle his own problems. The teacher and the counselor both talked to the principal and suggested that she talk with the student, and the three professionals planned to meet to develop a strategy to help him.

The principal talked with the student while walking in the halls of the school. She thought that this informal approach would be more comfortable for him. He was very resistant to her involvement and did not say much. She told him that she wanted to talk with his parents to get their help.

During lunchtime the student managed to leave school without being seen by the teachers who were monitoring the cafeteria. He returned within a half hour, walked directly to principal's office, took a gun from his jacket, and shot the principal. The secretary ran out of the outer office and called the police from the nurse's office. The police arrived within ten minutes and found the student sitting on the floor next to the principal. He gave no resistance.

The principal was in critical condition for two weeks. The bullet damaged her spinal cord; the prognosis calls for months and maybe years of therapy. Most probably, she will remain partially paralyzed.

Discussion Questions and Statements

1. What personal characteristics and resources will the principal need in order to face her permanent disability?
2. Can a person find meaning in this type of tragedy? If so, how?
3. Can there be emancipation in the principal's suffering?
4. Describe the response that students, parents, and faculty might have to this tragedy.
5. Explain the ethical issues that surround student violence.
6. What are some ethically inappropriate responses to student violence?

SELECTED BIBLIOGRAPHY

Allen, Diogenes. *Philosophy for Understanding Theology*. Atlanta: John Knox Press, 1985.

Allen, Diogenes, and Eric O. Springsted, eds. *Primary Readings in Philosophy for Understanding Theology*. Louisville, Ky.: Westminster/John Knox Press, 1992.

Berman, Marshall. *All That Is Solid Melts into the Air*. New York: Simon & Schuster, 1982.

Douglas, Mary, and Steven M. Tipton, eds. *Religion and America*. Boston: Beacon Press, 1983.

Frankl, Viktor E. *Man's Search for Meaning: An Introduction to Logotherapy.* New York: A Touchstone Book, Simon & Schuster, Inc., 1984.

Garfield, Jay L. *Foundations of Cognitive Science: The Essential Readings.* New York: Paragon House, 1990.

Gutierrez, Gustavo. *A Theology of Liberation.* New York: Orbis, 1973.

Hauerwas, Stanley. *Naming the Silences: God, Medicine and the Problem of Suffering.* Grand Rapids, Mich.: William B. Eerdmans Publishing Co., 1990.

Lonergan, Bernard J. F. *Insight: A Study of Human Understanding.* San Francisco: Harper & Row, Publishers, 1978.

Sartre, Jean-Paul. *Being and Nothingness.* Trans. Hazel Barnes. New York: Philosophical Library, Inc., 1956.

Teilhard de Chardin, Pierre. *The Phenomenon of Man.* New York: Harper Torchbooks, Harper & Row, Publishers, 1961.

Towers, Bernard. *Teilhard de Chardin.* Atlanta: John Knox Press, 1975.

Toynbee, Arnold. *Mankind and Mother Earth.* New York: Oxford University Press, 1976.

CHAPTER 3

The Ethics of Power and Duty in Educational Leadership

This chapter treats the practice of educational administration in relation to two variables that have a profound effect on the quality of leadership. The first is the use of power within schools and school districts. All professional relationships with a supervisor-employee dimension involve power. When a person has the authority to employ, encourage, foster, censure, discipline, and terminate the employment of others, he or she is a powerful person. The responsibility of the supervisor is to exercise this power for the welfare of those who are affected by the performance of the employee. The most effective way to fulfill this responsibility is to promote the growth and development of employees, which will enable them to improve their performance and thus will enrich the quality of the service they provide. The dimensions and exercise of power are complex; this treatment intends to explicate the intricacies of this phenomenon.

Power in educational administration is obviously exercised only within schools and school districts. These educational agencies, however, have a cultural dimension that affects the use of power in the supervisor-employee relationship. This chapter identifies ten characteristics of organizations that can serve as criteria to assess the quality of the cultural climate within schools and school districts. The cultural climate is the milieu within which power is exercised, and it affects the purpose of and method used in exercising that power. Clearly, exercising power and fostering a positive culture within a school or school district fall within the domain of educational leadership.

The second variable presented in this chapter is duty. Duty influences leadership at the individual rather than the organizational level. Thus, there is a balance between the organizational and the personal dimensions of educational leadership. Both perspectives are necessary. The effective educational leader will recognize that these perspectives are complementary and not mutually exclusive. The section on duty begins with a treatment of the charisma of leadership. The charisma of educational leadership is viewed in relation to the current milieu within which it is exercised. The insights of Carl Gustav Jung are used to help explicate this treatment of charisma.

Leadership is exercised through the performance of duties. Understanding the nuances of duty is not always easy, however, and there are different opinions as to how duty is operationalized.

THE USE OF POWER IN SCHOOLS AND SCHOOL DISTRICTS

The phenomenon of educational leadership is about power, and ethics is about the proper use or misuse of power. The growth or disintegration of the ethical fiber of each person is the center from which he or she exercises this power. The neophyte administrator learns quickly about the intricacies of power, usually when someone manipulates him or her to use the power of his or her office to accomplish what that person desires. For a superintendent of schools it might be simply intervening on a person's behalf with another administrator. For instance, after the building principal has denied a teacher's request to attend a whole-language workshop, the teacher might convince the superintendent to allow him or her to attend by pointing out that the district is considering such a program. Similarly, a first-year building principal could be vulnerable to such maneuvering on behalf of parents who complain that their child's underachievement rests with the incompetency of the teacher. The "I'll take care of it" response of the principal will echo for a long time in the teachers' lounge.

In the first case, the superintendent should have consulted the principal about the reason for refusing to send the teacher to the workshop before making a commitment. In the second case, the principal should have known that the correct response to the parents would have been that he or she would review the allegation with the teacher and perhaps schedule an appointment with the teacher and the parents to address the allegation at a later date.

On a more malevolent level, a superintendent may reassign a principal whom he or she suspects is not supporting a project that the superintendent is promoting even without compelling proof of the suspicion. A principal eager to comply with a goal established by the board of education for improved parent-principal relations may support a group of vocal parents who are not happy with the discipline strategies of a tough but fair teacher in order to gain recognition as a parents' advocate.

The power of office is wielded not only by administrators and teachers, but also by support staff, such as secretaries, cooks, custodians, bus drivers, and maintenance personnel. Consider that superintendents, principals, curriculum coordinators, directors of transportation, and so on usually have secretaries who control access to them. The heating-ventilating-air conditioning system in schools is controlled by maintenance personnel; the cleanliness of lunchrooms and bathrooms, and thus health risks from infection arising from unsanitary conditions, are under the control of the custodial staff.

In large, urban school districts, the assistant superintendent for human resources or director of personnel is responsible for recommending who should be hired and whose employment should be terminated by the superintendent and, ultimately, by the board of education. The director of facilities recommends which companies should receive lucrative construction and remodeling contracts.

The following aspects of the power of office are refinements people have developed to enhance that power:[1]

Inspirational power: Influence of a person based on other people's admiration and desire to model themselves after him or her

Charismatic power: Influence attributed to one's personal characteristics

Expert power: Influence based on special skills or knowledge

Persuasive power: Power derived from a person's ability to allocate and manipulate rewards

Knowledge power: Power derived from a person's ability to control unique and valuable information

Coercive power: Power based on fear

Inspirational power is enjoyed by very few people. Some administrators mistakenly believe that adulation of another administrator could hinder their ability to exercise power. However, almost everyone at some time has recognized greatness in a colleague, which has led him or her to emulate that person's leadership style and to accept that person's opinions and decisions without question. The danger in such power rests not with the person who has the power, but with the person who emulates him or her. Every administrator must develop a leadership style that is comfortable and, to a great degree, tailor-made.

All administrators must adapt their leadership styles to meet the ongoing changes and challenges endemic to their situations. Thus, the only effective way to emulate another person is to study that person over an extended period of time. This can be an effective way for novice administrators to learn the nuances of leadership. As the new administrator gains confidence in his or her ability, he or she will begin to develop a separate leadership style.

Inspirational power presupposes that the possessor is having a positive effect on the school or school district. The person's power base comprises those personal qualities that are recognized as being inspirational.

The superintendent of schools, building principal, or other administrator who places the responsibilities of office above his or her own professional welfare is worthy of emulation, especially when he or she must confront the board of education, parents, or colleagues over an issue or problem that could have an undesirable effect on his or her employment or compensation. Consider the superintendent who refuses to recommend the hiring of a person who is not the best candidate for a position but who is a friend of the board president and two other board members, all of whom have suggested that he or she would be an excellent teacher; or the principal who refuses to let the star quarterback of the football team play in the league championship because he has a grade point average below the norm for eligibility to play.

Charismatic power hinges on the personal characteristics of an individual. Being articulate, physically imposing, or competent is generally attractive to others and allows the charismatic person to follow successfully both professional and personal agendas. Many people have difficulty saying no to a charismatic individual.

Psychology teaches us that personality is a dynamic force that organizes a person's unique response and adjustment to his or her environment. Charismatic power is embedded in the dynamic organization of a person's personality. A major flaw in some administrators who wield charismatic power is disappointment when their charisma does not produce the results they expect. A superintendent who commands attention by his or her presence will represent the school district in a most effective manner, particularly at public events, such as board-of-education meetings. This superintendent also can represent the superintendency as a profession when called upon to lobby for legislation to improve the quality of education for all children and not just those in his or her school district. This awesome power creates an additional responsibility for the person who possesses it. It is possible to use such power in a manipulative manner to achieve personal objectives that are not conducive to the welfare of others.

Expert power sets apart people who have talents, experiences, or skills that are useful or necessary to other people. When a superintendent engages in the selection process for a director of accounting or business manager, he or she knows that this person will play a key role in the school district's organizational structure. Of course, every employee brings to his or her job specific talents, experiences, and skills. However, when a staff member's qualifications are very specialized and when serious and pervasive consequences could occur if that person made an error in carrying out his or her responsibilities, that person is said to possess expert power. Experts are listened to and consulted by others in the school district.

Business managers in many school districts prepare budgetary documents and keep the board of education, superintendent, and other administrators informed about progress in receiving revenues and making expenditures. The fiscal health of the district is dependent on the business manager's expertise in performing his or her responsibilities. The same can be said about the director of accounting, who provides much of the information needed by the business manager. Mistakes in projecting revenues could eventuate in a decrease in educational services to students.

Expert power is usually designated as influence because the power is not directly exercised, but instead impinges on the exercise of power by other administrators in a school district.

A person is said to have *persuasive power* when he or she can manipulate rewards. The superintendent of schools has the power to recommend the promotion of a faculty member to a principalship; principals receive higher salaries than teachers (assistant superintendents receive higher salaries than principals; custodial supervisors receive higher salaries than custodians; and so on). Thus, the superintendent controls the reward of promotion. This power is usually well understood by teachers and staff members.

Persuasive power is also exercised when the superintendent asks a teacher to serve on a curriculum committee charged with developing a new mathematics program in the secondary schools. If the teacher has aspirations of becoming a high school principal, he or she would welcome the opportunity to comply with the wishes of the superintendent. In essence, this is a symbolic reward, which could become a tangible reward if accommodating the wishes of the superintendent in this way were eventually to lead to the teacher's acquiring a principalship. The teacher in this situation would most likely have several motives for serving on the curriculum committee, among them the opportunity to fulfill a professional responsibility.

In school districts *knowledge power* is usually exercised by experts. The business manager who controls spending is a good example because he or she has access to budgetary information. In a well-managed school district, the superintendent will require the business manager to provide on-line data concerning their budgets, such as the amount of each line item in the budget along with current expenditures, encumbrances, and remaining balances, to the principals and other administrators.

Knowledge power is always exercised by the chief executive administrators of the respective departments and schools in a school district. All lines of communication impinging on the operations of these departments and schools usually converge in the offices of these top administrators. This is easily seen in relation to the superintendent of schools, who should have access to more information than any other administrator in the school district. Indeed, if the superintendent does not have this access, he or she will not be successful. The superintendent should have continual access to the members of the board of education, to all members of the administration, to colleagues in other school districts, to the presidents of the teachers' union and other employee unions, to parents, to citizens who do not have children in school, to private and parochial school administrators and teachers, to religious leaders in the community, to the business community, to public-services officials, to elected officials, and to members of the news media. Information about their concerns and interests, about their opinions and suggestions provides the superintendent with valuable knowledge, which certainly converts into a power base.

Similarly, a principal should have continual access to the teachers and staff members in his or her school, to colleagues, to parents, to citizens living in the attendance boundaries of the school, and so forth.

During the last few decades, a new phenomenon has come to the attention of the public through the news media: experts with knowledge power in some businesses and school districts have become whistle-blowers, some for good reasons and others for unjustifiable reasons.

The power that should be used least by an educational administrator is *coercive power,* power based on fear. Perhaps the most obvious example of coercive power is the threat to terminate someone's employment. At times, however, coercive power can be used to provide a wake-up call for someone whose behavior needs to change. A teacher who is using outdated instructional techniques and refuses to attend seminars or workshops to update his or her skills even when the school district offers to pay the costs should have his or her employment terminated by the board of education.

The use of coercive power should be the last resort in attempting to correct the behavior of staff members because it is demeaning to the humanity of people. People who wield coercive power without justification demean themselves also and project an image that is less than professional.

Power, then, is the capacity of a person to affect the behavior of another person. In school districts and schools, a person who holds power may use different aspects of the power of office, depending on his or her desire and purpose. Of the aspects of the power of office described herein, the first three, inspirational, charismatic, and expert, utilize influence rather than control. The last three, persuasive, knowledge, and coercive, utilize control rather than influence. Consequently, it is appropriate to consider these aspects as a continuum along which a shrewd power holder may move, depending on circumstances.

Few administrators have the capacity to utilize all aspects of the power of office with equal skill. Some administrators may possess only one or two of these aspects, which could be a detriment to fulfilling their leadership responsibilities. The building principal who is very controlling and lacking inspirational and charismatic powers must resort to strategies that will not endear him or her to faculty and staff members. Such strategies might include insisting on making the final decision on most issues that arise in the school, such as selecting instructional materials, ordering and purchasing supplies and materials, and scheduling extra duties. On the other hand, when a principal is trusting and empowers teachers to perform these tasks, the teachers are likely to take more ownership of the educational process, which could result in improved morale in the building.

The principal or superintendent also can be viewed as a strategist who augments the various power aspects of his or her office to produce the desired consequence. Reason can be employed by using data to support the logical presentation of ideas; friendliness refers to the creation of goodwill through flattery, humility, or by being personable prior to making a request. Coalition building is a strategy that involves securing the support of other people before making a request; bargaining occurs through the exchange of benefits or favors. The strategy of appealing to a higher authority is predicated on getting support for a request from the superintendent, in the case of a principal, or from the board of education, in the case of a superintendent. The two most severe strategies are assertiveness and sanctions. When an administrator uses assertiveness he or she employs a direct and forceful approach, such as demanding compliance, frequently repeating reminders to comply, or ordering the person to comply; an administrator uses sanctions when he or she rewards or punishes, for example, promising a salary increase, issuing an unsatisfactory evaluation, or possibly terminating the employment of the person to whom a request was made.[2]

The use of assertiveness or sanctions elicits the worst in people who are dependent on the educational leader for their job, salary, benefits, possible promotions, and rewards. When this approach is taken in a school or school district, dependent employees often employ techniques to try to make a favorable impression in order to counterbalance these power strategies:[3]

Conformity: Agreeing with someone else's opinion in order to gain his or her approval

Excuses: Explaining a predicament-creating event so as to minimize the apparent severity of the predicament

Apologies: Admitting responsibility for an undesirable even and simultaneously seeking to get a pardon for the action

Acclaiming: Explaining favorable events so as to maximize the desirable implications for oneself

Flattery: Complimenting others about their virtues in an effort to make oneself appear perceptive and likable

Favors: Doing something nice for someone to gain that person's approval

A rationale for the use of favorable-impression techniques can be found in the philosophy of Michel Foucault. One of the most influential postmodern philosophers, Foucault proposed that all life's activities are about power and truth, which cannot be separated into two different entities. Further, truth cannot be understood apart from social and political power. This notion about the circular relation of truth to systems of power situates each person's understanding about the reality of his or her life only as it relates to power. Life's struggles are encounters with power; thus, the unfolding of a person's life, his or her personal truth, takes places within these struggles.

The words of Michel Foucault are powerful. He viewed power only in its existential form as it is put into action, which then modifies other actions. Power does not require consent, but it is exercised only over free subjects; without freedom there would be no power. Because all life's activity is about power, power cannot be denied.

Foucault observed that a struggle occurs only when both participants have freedom. This observation certainly mirrors what takes place in schools and school districts. People who hold power can become locked in opposition to each other and as a consequence, can affect the morale of the other staff members who must witness the confrontation. By reason of his or her office an educational leader exercises power over others; therefore, he or she must recognize the far-reaching consequences of every action, because in essence, the educational leader is creating the milieu within which significant life decisions are made. Hence, influence is preferred over hegemony.

Being an ethical educational administrator is not only about conforming to a code of ethics; it is much more pervasive and encompasses every aspect of a person's life. According to Foucault, it is about how someone exercises power and how he or she reacts to the encroachment of power exercised by other people.[4]

The Culture of Schools and School Districts

When people come together for the purpose of collectively initiating some action, activity, or service, they create an *organization*. In its simplest form an organization may be a club that operates within a limited location; in its most complex form it may be a government that operates over vast territories with international interests and alliances. Along this continuum are corporations, schools, and school districts of varying sizes operating in diverse locations with adequate or inadequate resources.

Societies are groups of people with a similar language, heritage, customs, and traditions that form organizations; some societies join together with other societies because of a common purpose and thereby form organizations.

"When an organization becomes institutionalized, it takes on a life of its own, apart from any of its members."[5] However, organizations are constantly changing because they are composed of people who are constantly changing by reason of their knowledge, opinions, beliefs, and values. Because of the ongoing change in people and the change of people, a given school and school district will likely experience a change in culture either in a relatively short time or more gradually over a period of time. *Culture* is a quality inherent within an organization that creates an atmosphere setting it apart from other organizations with similar purposes.

The motives and behavior of individuals within a school or school district can affect the culture of the organization in a positive or a negative manner. This influence is most clearly seen in relation to the principal and superintendent of schools. The principal can have the most extensive impact on a school's culture and the superintendent can have the most extensive impact on a school district's culture, by virtue of the power of their offices.

The extent to which a principal or superintendent affects the culture of a school or school district is better understood when culture is viewed from a set of key characteristics of schools and school districts.[6] On a scale from 1 to 5, with 5 being the highest, the degree to which each of the following ten characteristics applies to a school or school district serves as an indication of that school's or school district's cultural quality:

> *Member identity*: the degree to which an administrator, teacher, or other staff member identifies with the school or school district as a whole rather than with his or her job or profession. If individuals closely identify with the

school or school district, then there is a positive culture operating within that school or school district.

Group emphasis: the degree to which administrators, teachers, and other staff members organize their work activities around groups rather than individuals. If the teachers in a school collaborate in developing aspects of the instructional program rather than relying upon the principal to organize this responsibility, the school exemplifies this characteristic. The obvious advantage of fostering group emphasis is the empowerment experienced by the teachers; the success of the instructional program then is not dependent on one person, the principal, who might retire or accept a position in another school district at some time in the future. Further, continuity remains even if certain teachers leave the school.

People focus: the degree to which administrators, teachers, and other staff members take into consideration the effects of their decisions on people. This consideration applies not only to decisions affecting staff members, but also to decisions affecting students, parents, and members of the community. A high degree of concern is a hallmark of the humanity of the decision makers.

Unit integration: the degree to which units in the school or school district are encouraged to operate in a coordinated or interdependent manner. A high degree of coordination and interdependence supports and strengthens the goal attainment of a school or school district.

Control: the degree to which rules, regulations, and direct supervision are used to control the behavior of administrators, teachers, staff members, and students. Less control and increased levels of trust and empowerment lead to greater commitment and success.

Risk tolerance: the degree to which administrators, teachers, and other staff members are encouraged to be aggressive, innovative, and risk seeking. A high degree of encouragement could lead to higher job satisfaction, high morale, and cutting-edge programming.

Reward criteria: the degree to which rewards and promotions are allocated according to performance rather than seniority, favoritism, or other nonperformance factors. Education has a long history at the low end of this characteristic. Thus, educational leaders will need a considerable amount of courage and resourcefulness to effect a change in how the system operates.

Conflict tolerance: the degree to which administrators, teachers, and other staff members are encouraged to express their criticisms openly. The educational leaders of some schools and school districts mistakenly believe that they can squelch criticism. Heavy-handed techniques used against staff members who publicly criticize will eventuate in deep-seated resentment and, in many cases, outright revolt. The mark of an effective school or school district is an atmosphere of openness within which everyone, including students, can be heard without reprisals. This kind of openness sends a signal to all members of the school community that people and their opinions and criticisms are valued and can make a difference in how the school or school district is administered. It is important for educational leaders to understand that criticism is not a sign of failure, but is an indication that something needs to change in order for the school or school district to progress and grow. The proper and effective handling of criticism is an important leadership skill, which not every leader has developed; it can enhance or detract from the culture of a school or school district.

Means-end orientation: the degree to which administrators, teachers, and other staff members focus on outcomes rather than on the strategies and processes used to achieve outcomes. Particularly in education, outcomes are not a good measure of progress or success. There are too many variables to control when dealing with people to measure outcomes accurately. Thus, a school or school district with a positive culture will be constantly engaged in developing, implementing, evaluating, and modifying strategies and processes.

Open-system focus: the degree to which a school or school district monitors and responds to changes in the external environment. Technology, corporate downsizing, shifts in population, violence, health issues, and all the other phenomena that constantly bombard our institutions require a response from educational leaders in relation to what needs to change in their school and school-district cultures.

THE DUTY OF EDUCATIONAL LEADERS

The Charisma of Leadership

Perhaps a significant transference of the hero archetype as expounded by the noted Swiss psychiatrist Carl Jung is the educational leader who fosters solidarity with people who are marginalized in society and advocates for universal education to create a just society. However, the discontent of people within our contemporary society with the strategies of educational leaders as they attempt to bring about educational reform is discouraging to those leaders.

There is no lack of expertise in the managerial operations of schools and school districts; accountants, budget analysts, transportation personnel, food-service personnel, human-services specialists, and the like are available in the job market. Pay the best wages and the most qualified people will probably be there waiting to be hired. Likewise, the academic expertise necessary for quality education in schools and school districts is available; administrators, classroom teachers, curriculum specialists, pupil-personnel specialists, special-education teachers, and educational therapists are available for hire.

There is also no shortage of applicants to graduate-degree programs in educational leadership. However, many administrators and professors of educational leadership are concerned that too many of their colleagues seem unprepared for the complex milieu within which they must practice. What may be lacking is a strategy that will connect the academic aspects of leadership with personal formation. The basis of this formation is presented here as the charisma of leadership.

Charisma in this context means a way of life dedicated to leadership within and on behalf of the academic community and profession, in contrast to merely a job as an administrator. The job mentality hinders effective leadership in the sense that the administrator becomes so concerned with performing tasks that little time is made for reflection on the purpose and goals of educational leadership. Further, the job mentality usually focuses the administrator on the requirements of a position in a specific school or district, resulting in the person's neglecting his or her responsibility to the academic community and profession at large.

Milieu.   The charisma of leadership becomes a lifelong process of discerning how a person can be of service to the academic community and profession while carrying out the tasks and responsibilities of his or her leadership position. A sense of service can be significantly sustained if a person recognizes the transcendental dimension of being human. Although repressed in Western society since the Enlightenment, this transcendental dimension is being rediscovered as an integral aspect of every facet of life. Its reemergence is easily seen in the large number of books, centers of study, and popular publications that flood our everyday life. Technology also has ushered in a system of worldwide communications that places before our attention events occurring in the most remote areas of the world. As a consequence, people can see the interrelatedness of every aspect of existence; diseases, environmental threats, hunger, ignorance, injustice, violence, and poverty are recognized as concerns that affect every person and nation on earth, wherever they are.

Because educational leaders as a group are concerned with human growth and development, they tend to be more open to diverse cultures and to view themselves as interrelated with other people throughout the world. Educational leaders recognize that there are no more ghettos of thought and that the values and philosophies of other people can have a profound effect on them and the people they serve.[7]

The last two decades have witnessed an ever-increasing immigration of people into the United States from all over the world. This situation heightens the expectation that educational leaders will be able to interact effectively with people from diverse cultures. The United States is experiencing a new georeligious reality; within its borders are significant numbers of second-generation Buddhists, Hindus, Jains, Muslims, and Sikhs. It is no longer possible to classify Americans as Catholic, Jewish, or Protestant. The number of ethnic groups has increased as well, and includes Cambodian, Chinese, Filipino, Hispanic, Japanese, Korean, Thai, and Vietnamese Americans in addition to African and European Americans.

Diversity and pluralism require that people engage in dialogue to seek understanding. Understanding does not require compromising beliefs and commitments, but it means holding values in relationship with the values of other people and not in isolation from them. [8]

The Transcendental.   Certain people from every generation and age have understood the deeply rooted human quest for a relationship with something beyond our own personal life existence. Yet many people have only a vague notion of this phenomenon, and it sometimes takes an event or an encounter to wake up a person from the sleep of everyday existence. Sometimes a life crisis, such as the death of a loved one, a serious illness, the loss of a job, or a divorce, produces the clarion call. When a catastrophic event, or even an event of lesser impact, occurs, the individual is free to respond or not to respond to its occurrence. Humans are free to make their decisions, even though they are not absolutely free because events can limit their freedom. Nevertheless, people are free, and freedom is the fundamental imperative when considering the ethics of human behavior.

The choice to question life's ambiguities instead of escaping into inactivity leads people down many paths and in seemingly diverse directions in search of meaning. Those who are animated on this journey seek a deeper consciousness, which brings with it a sense of the interconnectedness with other people.

Carl Gustav Jung.   Selected insights of Carl Jung properly finalize this discussion because of the profound effect he has had on the discipline of depth psychology. Perhaps the most important lesson taught by Jung was the primacy of the inner life that animates our external existence. The initial and yet obvious concept that must be understood is that human consciousness is capable of perceiving only a limited part of the world.

In the Jungian motif, consciousness is not a static phenomenon; it is a dynamic unfolding analogous to the process of waking up. With every new awareness and with every increase in the psyche's content, human consciousness is expanded by degrees. There is no end point. This process involves striking a balance between emotions and intellect, which leads to self-knowledge, which, if truly incorporated into a person's life, will eventually create an ethical confrontation with the person's deeper inner center, the self.

Within this motif the beginning of mature consciousness occurs when a person becomes conscious of the unconscious. In fact, Jung believed that no meaningful change can occur in personality and consciousness until a person develops an appropriate attitude not only toward the unconscious, but also toward the activities of the unconscious. Within the inner depths of the psyche can be found ethical conflicts, the resolution of which leads to higher levels of consciousness. Thus, there is reciprocity between consciousness and ethics; a change in one precipitates a change in the other. This phenomenon implies the necessity for each person to nurture a reflecting consciousness.

Jung also held the position that opposites could be mixed together without distinction in the unconscious.[9] A person can be tolerant and understanding and have great compassion for his or her children but be unforgiving of mistakes and failings in the teachers he or she supervises. Both attitudes can co-exist in the unconscious and bubble up to the surface of consciousness on specific occasions. This is the stuff of conflict. Resolving conflict is the path to heightened consciousness; conflict resolution also becomes the liberator of our personal striving for self-integration.

Knowledge obtained from depth psychology concerning the existence and functioning of the unconscious has certainly altered human understanding of ethics. Everyone experiences events that he or she has not taken note of but that have been absorbed into the unconscious. These events can emerge later in life, through intuition or during times of crises when the emotional and vital impact of the repressed events wells up from the unconscious.

Verification that the unconscious has a profound effect on consciousness occurs when someone overestimates his or her willpower, believing that nothing can affect his or her mind unless he or she intentionally causes it to by an act of the will.[10] Human experience testifies continually that attitudes, images, instincts, intuitions, thoughts, and urges seem to make themselves known to consciousness not only in times of crises, but also when nothing appears to prompt their appearance. This spontaneity is itself a result of other unconscious phenomena. Principals and superintendents sometimes place themselves in untenable positions, particularly with regard to their reactions to other people, because they neglect to recognize the effects of the unconscious.

The Nuances of Duty

Understanding and knowing one's duty can be difficult and at times ambiguous, whether the duty is one toward self, family, friends, colleagues, neighbors, or acquaintances, or one toward community, state, or nation. Further, there is often ambiguity in relation to the duty of an individual toward his or her profession, employer, and employees.

This section explores the concept of duty under five rubrics: the categorical imperative of Immanuel Kant, Georg Hegel's philosophy of right, Aristotle's duty of citizens, the meditations of Marcus Aurelius Antoninus, and the discourse ethics of Jürgen Habermas. Each addresses duty from a perspective that is certainly relevant to the practice of educational administration. The outcome of this treatment should be an understanding of duty both as a concept and in relation to the daily decision making of educational leaders.

The Categorical Imperative of Immanuel Kant.   For a person who had such a significant effect on the entire field of philosophy, Kant lived a rather uneventful life. He was born in 1724 in the city of Königsberg, where he attended grammar school and the university. Later he lectured at the university, and eventually he became a professor. He was an unmarried scholar who devoted himself to his studies. Kant was well versed in ancient and contemporary literature, but had little interest in the fine arts. Throughout his entire life, though, he had a keen interest in mathematics and physics, which acted as a diversion from his intense study of philosophy. Kant also was fascinated by the political events of his time and was a strong supporter of both the American and French revolutions.[11]

Kant was a sociable person known for his kindness and benevolence. He offered financial assistance to a number of poor people. He treated others with courtesy and respect and was a loyal friend. Kant did not observe a formal religion and was not inclined toward mysticism; however, he did possess a sincere belief in God. From Kant's perspective, morality is not derived from theology, either revealed or natural; rather, morality is derived through reason as manifested in consciousness of moral obligation. Kant's character is best understood in relation to his devotion to the idea of duty.[12]

The moral philosophy of Kant is found in three of his works: *Grounding for the Metaphysics of Morals* (1785), *Critique of Practical Reason* (1788), and *Metaphysics of Morals* (1797). In the preface to the *Grounding,* Kant states that the purpose of the treatise is to establish the supreme principle of morality, which is his categorical imperative: Always act in such a way that you can will that the maxim of your action should become a universal law. Kant believed that this principle was supreme in the field of morality, from the morality of politics to the moral requirements of duty to oneself and to others.[13]

Both the *Grounding* and the *Critique* establish the foundation and method of Kant's moral doctrine, which is set forth in the *Metaphysics.* As previously stated, in the *Grounding* Kant proposes that morality is derived from the supreme principle of pure reason; in the *Critique* he justifies this *a priori* principle as the fundamental principle of the autonomy of reason in action. In the *Metaphysics* Kant treats moral judgments in concrete situations.[14]

Kant's thought was influenced by two streams of philosophy, rationalism, especially that of Gottfried Leibniz, and empiricism, especially the empiricism of David Hume. The *Critique* sets forth a synthesis of rationalism and empiricism. Kant held the position that rationalism and empiricism considered separately present a distorted view of human knowledge.[15]

Selected Reading 3.1 is from the *Grounding.* Kant's logic is noteworthy. After enunciating the supreme principle of morality, the categorical imperative, he attempts to identify his idea of universal law with a willed idea of the natural order of life. Kant sets forth four examples, which explain his idea of duty based on the categorical imperative as a universal law of nature. In the first example, dealing with the internal conflict of a person contemplating suicide, he demonstrates that self-love that would eventuate in the self-destruction of a person's life contradicts a willed universal law of nature because the purpose of nature is to further the cause of life.

The second example, concerning a person's borrowing money knowing that paying it back will be impossible, is another illustration of an action that could not become a universal law of nature; in this case, because it would lead people into distrusting the promises of others.

The third example, concerning a person who has many talents that could be useful, adds a new dimension to Kant's argument. This person has a positive duty to others who could benefit from his or her talents. Willing that it should become a law of nature that people could neglect their talents and live a life of enjoyment contradicts the natural instinct of a person to develop all his or her faculties. Further, talents are meant to be developed for many different purposes; they are not merely for narcissistic pleasure.

The fourth example begins with the idea that everyone should be left alone to deal with his or her own problems or good fortune. Kant admits that such an approach would prevent people from taking advantage of others. However, willing this approach to become a law of nature would deprive a person of the assistance that he or she might need if troubles and problems should befall him or her.

It is clear from these examples how Kant intends people to reflect on the categorical imperative and how he viewed this as the universal principle of morality applicable in all situations. The major flaw with Kant's argument is that it relies on the ability of people to extrapolate how their possible actions would play out as a universal law of nature. The logic needed to analyze the potential consequences of an action in the context of a universal law of nature calls into question the practicality of such an approach, especially in times of great stress. However, for those with analytical ability and the restraint to think through the consequences of willing a potential action to become a universal law, Kant's approach is most appropriate.

Educational administrators have the ability and reflective time to utilize this methodology. Furthermore, Kant's examples are relevant to the practice of educational leadership. Today the demands and stress endemic to the life of educational administrators have a tremendous effect on their personal lives. Statistics on the numbers of administrators who suffer depression because of their profession are not readily available. However, experience suggests that educational administrators are as vulnerable as are people in the general population. Administrators who continually keep before themselves the idea that they are responsible to themselves and to their families for maintaining a balance between their personal and professional lives may be able to stay the temptation to become absorbed with their work to an unhealthy degree.

Trust is also a key element in the effectiveness of educational administration. Faculty, staff, parents, students, and members of the board of education must be able to trust administrators to keep their word and to fulfill their responsibilities. Anything less breaks down the entire structure of a school or school district. Those who tend to lie, exaggerate, or tell half-truths quickly lose the respect of others and place themselves in situations that could eventually result in the termination of their employment.

⌒ Selected Reading 3.1

Grounding for the Metaphysics of Morals
Immanuel Kant (1774–1804)

Hence there is only one categorical imperative and it is this: Act only according to that maxim whereby you can at the same time will that it should become a universal law.

Now if all imperatives of duty can be derived from this one imperative as their principle, then there can at least be shown what is understood by the concept of duty and what it means, even though there is left undecided whether what is called duty may not be an empty concept.

The universality of law according to which effects are produced constitutes what is properly called nature in the most general sense (as to form), i.e., the existence of things as far as determined by universal laws. Accordingly, the universal imperative of duty may be expressed thus: Act as if the maxim of your action were to become through your will a universal law of nature.

We shall now enumerate some duties, following the usual division of them into duties to ourselves and to others and into perfect and imperfect duties.

1. A man reduced to despair by a series of misfortunes feels sick of life but is still so far in possession of his reason that he can ask himself whether taking his own life would not be contrary to his duty to himself. Now he asks whether the maxim of his action could become a universal law of nature. But his maxim is this: From self-love I make as my principle to shorten my life when its continued duration threatens more evil than it promises satisfaction. There only remains the question as to whether this principle of self-love can become a universal law of nature. One sees at once a contradiction in a system of nature whose law would destroy life by means of the very same feeling that acts so as to stimulate the furtherance of life, and hence there could be no existence as a system of nature. Therefore, such a maxim cannot possibly hold as a universal law of nature and is, consequently, wholly opposed to the supreme principle of all duty.

2. Another man in need finds himself forced to borrow money. He knows well that he won't be able to repay it, but he sees also that he will not get any loan unless he firmly promises to repay it within a fixed time. He

wants to make such a promise, but he still has conscience enough to ask himself whether it is not permissible and is contrary to duty to get out of difficulty in this way. Suppose, however, that he decides to do so. The maxim of his action would then be expressed as follows: when I believe myself to be in need of money, I will borrow money and promise to pay it back, although I know that I can never do so. Now this principle of self-love or personal advantage may perhaps be quite compatible with one's entire future welfare, but the question is now whether it is right. I then transform the requirement of self-love into a universal law and put the question thus: how would things stand if my maxim were to become a universal law? He then sees at once that such a maxim could never hold as a universal law of nature and be consistent with itself, but must necessarily be self-contradictory. For the universality of a law which says that anyone believing himself to be in difficulty could promise whatever he pleases with the intention of not keeping it would make promising itself and the end to be attained thereby quite impossible, inasmuch as no one would believe what was promised him but would merely laugh at all such utterances as being vain pretenses.

3. A third finds in himself a talent whose cultivation could make him a man useful in many respects. But he finds himself in comfortable circumstances and prefers to indulge in pleasure rather than to bother himself about broadening and improving his fortunate natural aptitudes. But he asks himself further whether his maxim of neglecting his natural gifts, besides agreeing of itself with his propensity to indulgence, might agree also with what is called duty. He then sees that a system of nature could indeed always subsist according to such a universal law, even though every man . . . should let his talents rust and resolve to devote his life entirely to idleness, indulgence, propagation, and, in a word, to enjoyment. But he cannot possibly will that this should become a universal law of nature or be implanted in us as such a law by a natural instinct. For as a rational being he necessarily wills that all his faculties should be developed, inasmuch as they are given him for all sorts of possible purposes.

4. A fourth man finds things going well for himself but sees others (whom he could help) struggling with great hardships; and he thinks: what does it matter to me? Let everybody be as happy as Heaven wills or as he can make himself; I shall take nothing from him nor even envy him; but I have no desire to contribute anything to his well-being or to his assistance when in need. If such a way of thinking were to become a universal law of nature, the human race admittedly could very well subsist and doubtless could subsist even better than when everyone prates

about sympathy and benevolence and even on occasion exerts himself to practice them but, on the other hand, also cheats when he can, betrays the rights of man, or otherwise violates them. But even though it is possible that a universal law of nature could subsist in accordance with that maxim, still it is impossible to will that such a principle should hold everywhere as a law of nature. For a will which resolved in this way would contradict itself, inasmuch as cases might often arise in which one would have need of the love and sympathy of others and in which he would deprive himself, by such a law of nature springing from his own will, of all hope of the aid he wants for himself.

There are some of the many actual duties, or at least what are taken to be such, whose derivation from the single principle cited above is clear. We must be able to will that a maxim of our action become a universal law; this is the canon for morally estimating any of our actions. Some actions are so constituted that their maxims cannot without contradiction even be thought as a universal law of nature, much less be willed as what should become one. In the case of others this internal impossibility is indeed not found, but there is still no possibility of willing that their maxim should be raised to the universality of a law of nature, because such a will would contradict itself. There is no difficulty in seeing that the former kind of action conflicts with strict or narrow [perfect] (irremissible) duty, while the second kind conflicts only with broad [imperfect] (meritorious) duty. By means of these examples there has thus been fully set forth how all duties depend as regards the kind of obligation (not the object of their action) upon the one principle.

Source: From Immanuel Kant, *Grounding for the Metaphysics of Morals* with *On a Supposed Right to Lie because of Philanthropic Concerns*, 3d ed., ed. and trans. James W. Ellington (Indianapolis: Hackett Publishing Company, Inc., 1993), pp. 30–32. Third edition with new material copyright © 1993 by Hackett Publishing Co., Inc. All rights reserved.

An unfortunate situation arises when very talented administrators neglect to grow and develop in their profession. Becoming comfortable in life's routine is common in all professions, and the desire to improve skills and to develop abilities and talents is sometimes eclipsed by the demands of a position. The challenge is to recognize and accommodate growth activities into personal and professional schedules. Ultimately, becoming a better principal, superintendent, or other administrator benefits students, staff, and all others connected with a school or school district even if the benefits are not immediately apparent.

Perhaps the most tragic situation occurs when an administrator sees a situation in which he or she could be of assistance but doesn't provide that assistance, for one of a variety of reasons. When parents become unreasonably demanding, a principal may conclude that their problems must be resolved without his or her assistance. Some principals may resort to positive actions that exacerbate the problems in order to teach difficult parents a lesson. This same approach may be utilized with teachers or staff members who are uncooperative or troublesome. This type of vindictive neglect is clearly unethical. The profession of educational administration is a helping profession, and anything less on the part of an administrator is unacceptable.

The actions of an administrator may also be influenced by the potential dismissal of a teacher or staff member whose performance is not meeting the standards of the school district. In such situations the principal and the superintendent of schools are obligated to provide whatever assistance they can to give that person the opportunity to change his or her behavior. Of course, if the person persists in substandard performance, he or she must be considered for dismissal. The point that Kant made is most poignant: someday it may be the administrator who is in need of assistance.

Georg Wilhelm Friedrich Hegel's Philosophy of Right.   The German idealist Hegel was born in Stuttgart, Germany, on August 27, 1770. Although he did not distinguish himself as a student in grammar school, Hegel was greatly influenced by the plays of Sophocles, particularly *Antigone*. He entered the University of Tübingen in 1788 and enrolled in the Protestant Theological Foundation. It was then that he formed a friendship with Friedrich Schelling, who also was destined to become famous as an idealist philosopher. Both men studied the philosophy of Rousseau and had great enthusiasm for the spirit of the French Revolution.

At the university Hegel exhibited the same lackluster performance he showed in grammar school. However, his future claim to fame began to take shape with his interest in the relationship between philosophy and theology. After leaving the university, Hegel supported himself as a tutor. Relatively soon, though, his writings led to his being offered a variety of university positions, including the chair of philosophy at the University of Berlin. Hegel died in 1831 with a reputation that situates him as one of the most influential Western philosophers.[16]

Hegel published the *Philosophy of Right* in 1821. His view of duty as abstract and universal in character liberates people from performing their duties in order to obtain a particular end; instead, a person is to carry out his or her duty for duty's sake. From this perspective, the question concerning the performance of duty rests with the principles: Do what is right and Strive after welfare. (In this context, *welfare* pertains not only to the individual's own welfare but also to the welfare of others.)

According to Hegel, duty is a transcendental reality even though it emanates from these restricted principles (Do what is right and Strive after welfare). Duty is the essence of moral self-consciousness. The idea of what is good is also an abstract characterization and, as such, is subjective. Subjectivity is the inward certainty of a person that gives rise to the particular; thus, subjectivity is the determining dimension of a person's conscience.

A person's true conscience leads him or her to will what is absolutely good. This leads to the notion that in his or her conscience, a person is aware of certain principles that explicitly determine his or her duty. Conscience is only the formal side of the will, with no specific content. It is only in living out the ethical life that a person becomes aware of the objectivity of his or her duties. However, it is this subjectivity that allows a person to make judgments. It is in the existential moment that a person becomes aware that he or she could make a judgment that is potentially evil.

The exercise of duty allows a person to understand his or her freedom and in this sense liberates the person from the pull of natural impulses and from the threat of self-absorption, which leads to indeterminacy of action. Through the performance of duty people become self-actualized and thus acquire their substantive freedom.

Hegel believed that the private rights and welfare of people are subordinate to the rights and welfare of the state. Thus, a person's duty to family is subordinate to that person's duty to the state. However, Hegel recognized that the rights of the state are directed toward and are in complete unity with the welfare of individuals. Further, he asserted that people have a duty to the state in proportion to their rights granted by the state.

Hegel's position was that the state should enact laws to provide for the well-being and happiness of individuals and to provide services for them. There should be laws that deal with private rights and laws that deal with the rights of communities, corporations, and organizations. Hegel made an interesting observation about services. He stated that services must be considered in terms of money in order for them to be justly distributed; further, only when a person performs a service for money is he or she capable of exercising free will.[17]

On first reading it may appear that there are contradictions in Hegel's approach to the exercise of duty. His approach is theoretical as well as practical and has significant implications for the practice of educational administration. The approach is theoretical in the sense that Hegel conceived of duty as emanating from within a person as directed by his or her will and believed that duty should be performed for its own sake. It is practical in the sense that carrying out one's duty is a liberating experience because it forces a person to leave the comfort of his or her own self-absorption through the self-actualization of decision making.

The significance for educational administration lies in the juncture between the theoretical and the practical. Principals and superintendents are public figures who exert a significant amount of influence by their very actions. If the decisions of administrators are not prompted by their core values, their decision making will be dislocated from their genuine selves and certainly will be manipulated by circumstances and whims. Further, because the duties of people to the state have a priority over personal duties, educational administrators must attempt to keep their personal lives from affecting their professional decision making—a task that is often very difficult. Hegel's notion that the happiness and welfare of the individual is the proper object of legislation prompts educational administrators to formulate the rules and regulations of the school and school district so that they will be of service to students, parents, and the community at large.

Hegel's idea about money as the measure in the just appropriation of services carries an insight that is easily proven from human experience. Justice is made tangible through such a device. His understanding of the human dynamic at work in relation to financial compensation for rendering services makes sense in educational administration. People can make a decision based on their personal needs and values when they either accept or reject an offer to perform a service for a certain amount of money.

Aristotle and the Duty of Citizens.   The son of a physician, Aristotle was born in 384 B.C.E. in Stagira, which is in northern Greece. He spent twenty years as a student of Plato at the Academy. When Plato died, Aristotle left Athens; he was eventually invited by King Philip of Macedonia to become the teacher of his son, Alexander. After a few years, Aristotle returned to Athens and founded a school, called the Lyceum.

Aristotle's development of his own philosophy precluded his return to the Academy and was the main reason he founded the Lyceum. This new school had the character of a union or society in which mature thinkers could engage in scholarship and research. It also had some of the elements of a modern university, including a library and teachers who regularly gave lectures. The name of the school was derived from its location in the northeast section of the city, the precinct of Apollo Lyceus. However, the school was also known as the *Peripatos,* the Greek word for "walk," because the teachers carried on discussions with their pupils while walking up and down the covered ambulatory. After the death of Alexander, Aristotle had to leave Athens because of political reasons. He retired to Chalcis in Euboea, where he died in 322 B.C.E.[18]

Selected Reading 3.2 contains an excerpt from the *Politics* of Aristotle in which he presents his political philosophy. The purpose of the state, according to Aristotle, is to foster the supreme good: the moral and intellectual development of its citizens. The primary community is the family. When several families come together to provide for daily needs and other considerations, the village comes into existence. When several villages are joined together for the common good of their members and become somewhat self-sufficient, the state comes into existence. The state differs from the family and the village qualitatively as well as quantitatively. Only in the state can a person live the good life to the fullest extent possible. Further, because the good life is a person's natural end, the state must be a natural society.[19]

The practice of Athenian democracy was the foundation from which Aristotle drew his qualifications for citizenship. This type of democracy is very similar

⤸ Selected Reading 3.2

Politics
Aristotle (384–322 B.C.E.)

The next thing to investigate after what we have just discussed is whether the virtue of a good man and of a good citizen should be regarded as the same, or not the same. But surely if we should indeed investigate this, the virtue of a citizen must first be grasped in some sort of outline.

Just as a sailor is one of a number of members of a community, so, we say, is a citizen. And though sailors differ in their capacities (for one is an oarsman, another a captain, another a lookout, and others have other sorts of titles), it is clear both that the most exact account of the virtue of each sort of sailor will be peculiar to him, and similarly that there will also be some common account that fits them all. For the safety of the voyage is a task of all of them since this is what each of the sailors strives for. In the same way, then, the citizens too, even though they are dissimilar, have the safety of the community as their task. But the community is the constitution. Consequently, if indeed there are several kinds of constitution, it is clear that there cannot be a single virtue that is the virtue—the complete virtue—of a good citizen. But the good man, we say, does express a single virtue: the complete one. Evidently, then, it is possible for someone to be a good citizen without having acquired the virtue expressed by a good man.

By going through problems in a different way, the same argument can be made about the best constitution. If it is impossible for a city-state to consist entirely of good people, and if each must at least perform his own task well, and this requires virtue, and if it is impossible for all the citizens to be similar, then the virtue of a citizen and that of a good man cannot be a single virtue. For that of the good citizen must be had by all (since this is necessary if the city-state is to be best), but the virtue of a good man cannot be had by all, unless all the citizens of a good city-state are necessarily good men. Again since a city-state consists of dissimilar elements (I mean that just as an animal consists in the first instance of soul and body, a soul of reason and desire, a household of man and woman, and property of master and slave, so a city-state, too, consists of all these, and of other dissimilar kinds in addition), then the citizens cannot all have one virtue, any more than can the leader of a chorus and one of its ordinary members.

It is evident from these things, therefore, that the virtue of a man and of a citizen cannot be unqualifiedly the same.

But will there, then, be anyone whose virtue is the same both as a good citizen and as a good man? We say, indeed, that an excellent ruler is good and possesses practical wisdom, but that a citizen need not possess practical wisdom. Some say, too, that the education of a ruler is different right from the beginning, as is evident, indeed, from the sons of kings being educated in horsemanship and warfare, and from Euripides "No subtleties for me . . . but what the city-state needs," (since this implies that rulers should get a special sort of education). But if the virtue of a good ruler is the same as that of a good man, and if the man who is ruled is also a citizen, then the virtue of a citizen would not be unqualifiedly the same as the virtue of a man (although that of a certain sort of citizen would be), since the virtue of a ruler and that of a citizen would not be the same. Perhaps this is why Jason said that he went hungry except when he was a tyrant. He meant that he did not know how to be a private individual.

Yet the capacity to rule and be ruled is at any rate praised, and being able to do both well is held to be the virtue of a citizen. So if we take a good man's virtue to be that of a ruler, but a citizen's to consist in both, then the two virtues would not be equally praiseworthy.

Since, then, both these views are sometimes accepted, that ruler and ruled should learn different things and not the same ones, and that a citizen should know and share in both, we may see what follows from that. For there is rule by a master, by which we mean the kind concerned with the necessities. The ruler does not need to know how to produce these, but rather how to make use of those who do. In fact, the former is servile. (By "the former" I mean actually knowing how to perform the actions of a servant.) But there are several kinds of slaves, we say, since their tasks vary. One part consists of those tasks performed by manual laborers. As their very name implies, these are people who work with their hands. VULGAR CRAFTSMEN are included among them. That is why among some peoples in the distant past craftsmen did not participate in office until extreme democracy arose. Accordingly, the tasks performed by people ruled in this way should not be learned by a good person, nor by a statesman, nor by a good citizen, except perhaps to satisfy some personal need of his own (for then it is no longer a case of one person becoming master and the other slave).

But there is also a kind of rule exercised over those who are similar in birth and free. This we call "political" rule. A ruler must learn it by being ruled, just as one learns to be a cavalry commander by serving under a cavalry commander, or to be a general by serving under a general, or under a major or a company commander to learn to occupy the office. Hence this too is rightly said, that one cannot rule well without having been ruled. And whereas the virtues of these *are* different, a good citizen must have the knowledge and ability both to be ruled and to rule, and this is the virtue of a citizen, to know the rule of free people from both sides.

In fact a good man too possesses both, even if a ruler does have a different kind of justice and temperance. For if a good person is ruled, but is a free citizen, his virtue (justice, for example) will clearly not be of one kind, but includes one kind for ruling and another for being ruled, just as a man's and a woman's courage and temperance differ. For a man would seem a coward if he had the courage of a woman, and a woman would seem garrulous if she had the temperance of a good man, since even household management differs for the two of them (for his task is to acquire property and hers to preserve it). Practical wisdom is the only virtue peculiar to a ruler; for the others, it would seem, must be common to both rulers and ruled. At any rate, practical wisdom is not the virtue of one who is ruled, but true opinion is. For those ruled are like makers of flutes whereas rulers are like the flute players who use them.

So then, whether the virtue of a good man is the same as of an excellent citizen or different, and how they are the same and how different, is evident from the preceding.

---

to the contemporary concept of the representative form of government. Citizens are both rulers and ruled and are vested with the rights to participate in making laws and administering justice.[20]

Aristotle questioned whether the virtues of a good person are the same as the virtues of a good citizen. Even though citizens differ from one another, they all have the same common goal, the preservation of the state. Hence the unifying dimension is the common good of the state and not the virtues of individual citizens.

In relation to the tenet of governing, Aristotle made a significant observation about human nature: the person who has never learned how to obey cannot know how to command. It is admirable, then, for a person to learn both how to rule and how to obey. Indeed, the good citizen must know how to do both, which Aristotle considered virtues of a citizen.

In Aristotle's view the family is the primary unit. Principals and superintendents also understand the primary position of the family as the basic unit within the educational community. If the family is considered an entity outside the school community, both the school and the family will be unable to collaborate at the level necessary for the best educational practice. The relationship is integral, but also poses difficulties that may not be easily addressed. The time commitment that must be given to interacting with parents by teachers, staff members, and administrators can present a tremendous challenge when enrollments are large and staffing ratios inadequate. The quality of the relationship is also dependent on the human-relations skills of the teachers and staff members and on the organizational skills of the administrators.

All those who work in collaboration for the welfare of children must assume different roles depending on a given situation. This is true of all the professionals who work in schools. The term *educational leader* is certainly not restricted to educational administrators. Teachers, librarians, guidance counselors, and other staff members are called upon to lead students and, at times, colleagues. Because schools and school districts are organizations, administrators assume the formal position of leadership, but the informal exercise of leadership is required of all professional members of the educational community.

Aristotle's notion of citizenship is of particular importance. The preparation of citizens in terms of leadership according to Aristotle revolves around experiential knowledge. A person cannot know how to lead people unless he or she has learned how to follow a leader. This is sometimes painfully apparent when a person first enters the field of educational leadership. The principal who has an inflated ego and declined to accept the leadership of his or her principal when he or she was a teacher may find it difficult to trust the leadership capabilities of teachers. Learning how to trust and how to rely on the abilities of others is not an abstraction, but an acquired attitude honed through experience. People in leadership positions who lack this attitude will probably not convey the proper attitude of leadership to those whom they supervise. Some people do rise to the occasion, of course, and either quickly or through trial and error learn the nuances of leadership. However, it can be a painful process for both the leader and the followers.

The Meditations of Marcus Aurelius Antoninus. Born in Rome in 121 C.E., during the reign of the emperor Hadrian, Marcus Aurelius was named Marcus Annius Verus by his parents. After their death, when Marcus was very young, he was adopted by his grandfather. Marcus's grandfather understood the importance of education and provided Marcus with a number of excellent tutors. At the age of seventeen, Marcus was adopted by Aurelius Antoninus, an uncle by marriage, who had recently become emperor. Antoninus had no son of his own and wanted an heir. He changed Marcus's name to his own and maneuvered him into marrying his daughter, Faustina. They had five children, but only one, Commodus, survived, and he later succeeded Marcus as emperor.

On the death of Antoninus in 161 C.E., Marcus became emperor and did something unheard of in Roman history. He appointed another adopted son of Aurelius Antoninus, Lucius Verus, co-emperor, and both men jointly ruled the Roman Empire. At that time the empire was experiencing the natural disasters of famine, floods, and plague in addition to the invasions of the barbarians. Verus died in 167, when Marcus was leaving Rome to join the legions on the Danube. During this period Marcus composed his reflections, entitled simply *To Himself*. Later these writings became known as the *Meditations*. Marcus died in 180 C.E.[21]

Marcus was schooled in the Stoic tradition and was a person of great humanity, which is amply demonstrated in his writings. The Stoic philosophy was originated in the Middle Eastern part of the world by Zeno, a native of Citium in Cyprus. He taught and discoursed in Athens at the colonnade, or *stoa*, from which his philosophy received its name. The Stoic philosophy is based on three concepts: (1) everything in the universe, even time and thought, is composed of physical matter; (2) everything can ultimately be reduced to a single, unifying principle; and (3) everything is in the process of becoming something else.[22]

The reflections of Marcus do not contain a connecting theme as is commonly found in philosophical literature; they are the private meditations of a great person. Their content, however, is philosophical and has been of great assistance to many people. A value of the format is that a reader can take up or put down the book at any point without sacrificing the coherent understanding of its content. It is helpful to remember that according to Marcus, philosophy was the medium that could rightfully expound on the unseen powers behind creation, on the purpose and nature of human existence, and on how people should live their lives.

The meditations of Marcus were included in this chapter because he was a dutiful person whose reflections on life must have been influenced not only by Stoicism, but also by his experience as a civil leader. Historians and philosophers have given recognition to his great humanity, which validates the quality of his leadership and gives credibility to his ideas.

Selected Reading 3.3 contains four meditations; the headings were inserted by this author. In the first meditation, Marcus states that leading a moral life can give a person self-control and courage in the pursuit of truth and justice through the use of reason. He also recognizes that this approach will give a person peace when he or she is faced with a destiny that is beyond his or her control. For Marcus, destiny is synonymous with duty.

The second meditation reinforces this perspective. Adhering to destiny with zeal and energy through the use of reason and being armed with a fearless truthfulness will give a person such purpose in life that no one will have the power to divert that person from fulfilling his or her duty.

The third meditation sets forth Marcus's understanding of the role reason plays in human relations. Human reason is the common bond that unites all people in the pursuit of goodness. Reason establishes universal laws of conduct that all people are required to obey. This theme can be seen in the fourth meditation, in which Marcus explains that rational beings by their very nature are required to help each other and in no way harm one another. Further, Marcus posits that truthfulness is required by reason and that to lie deliberately is impious; even an involuntary lie brings discord to that nature which is the source of reason and gives order to the entire universe.

Marcus further expounds on the perennial enigma, why bad things happen to good people and good things happen to bad people. Nature makes no distinction between good and inferior people when bestowing pain or pleasure, death or life, fame or dishonor. According to Marcus, it behooves a person to live with this same type of disinterest and to pursue duty without regard to these conditions of nature.

Educational administrators who are constantly measuring their personal worth or the value of their professional performance against such criteria as fame, honor, and happiness are certain to encounter depression and despair. The safeguard against this pitfall is the rational approach to duty, which places a high priority on courage, self-control, truthfulness, and trustfulness. Principals, superintendents, and other administrators can also benefit from the perspective of Marcus in regard to the acceptance of duty as destiny, implying a healthy indifference to the whims of others and a steadfast adherence to ethical standards. Finally, within the tradition of Marcus Aurelius Antoninus, administrators are charged with the dictum of human reason, Do no harm.

Duty in the Discourse Ethics of Jürgen Habermas.   The contemporary philosopher Habermas is a member of the Frankfurt school movement, which promotes the philosophical method commonly referred to as critical theory. This approach originated in Germany during the 1930s. Habermas's chief concern is with instrumental reason in industrial societies, which deals with the relation between means and ends.

The uniqueness of Habermas's theorizing lies in his attempt to shift the philosophical emphasis from the subjective-objective relationship to intersubjective communication. From this base he argued that the existence of society requires two types of action: labor, which is instrumental action, and social interaction, which is communicative action. These types of action are endemic to the human social phenomenon and establish different categories of knowledge derived from hermeneutic and critical modes of inquiry. Communicative action is directed toward a deeper understanding of others by uncovering unconscious compulsions. Instrumental action is directed toward empirical-analytic enquiry for the purpose of controlling and predicting objective processes.[23]

Habermas's later works reflect his attempt to identify the normative commitments that are established through linguistic communication. Habermas referred to these normative commitments as universal pragmatics. In public dis-

Selected Reading 3.3

Meditations

Marcus Aurelius Antoninus (121–180 C.E.)

Choosing the Better Way

If you find in human life something better than justice, truth, self-control, courage, something better, in a word, than that your mind should be contented with itself when it makes you act according to the rule of Reason and contented with your destiny in what is allotted to you without any choice—if, I say, you see something better than this, then turn to it with all your soul and enjoy this best which you have found. But if nothing is shown to be better than the divine spirit itself which is established within you, the spirit which brings your private impulses under its dominion, scrutinizes your impressions and, as Socrates said, withdraws itself from the emotions of sense; a spirit which subordinates itself to the service of the gods and takes thought for men; if then you find all other things unimportant and paltry in comparison, then give no place to anything else in your thoughts, for if you incline and lean toward anything else you will no longer be able without distraction to give the place of honor to that good which is peculiarly your own.

It is not lawful for anything different—be it the praise of men, offices of power, wealth, or the enjoyment of pleasures—to stand in the way of what is reasonable and for the common good. All these things, even if for a while they seem to accord with the good life, suddenly overwhelm one and lead one astray. Do you, I say, in freedom and simplicity choose the better part and cling to it. "But the better is the advantageous." If you mean to your advantage as a reasonable being, give heed to it, but if you mean to your advantage as an animal creature, say so, and keep to your decision without vanity. Only see to it that your examination of the question be without danger to yourself. . . .

Inner Strength

If you perform the task before you and follow the right rule of reason steadfastly, vigorously, with kindness; if you allow no distraction but preserve the

spirit within you in its pure state as if you had to surrender it at any moment; if you concentrate on this, expecting nothing and shirking nothing, content to do any natural action which is at hand, heroically truthful in every word you utter, you will lead the good life. There is no one who could prevent you. . . .

The Common Bond

If we have intelligence in common, so we have reason which makes us reasoning beings, and that practical reason which orders what we must or must not do; then the law too is common to us and, if so, we are citizens; if so, we share a common government; if so, the universe is, as it were, a city—for what other common government could one say is shared by all mankind?

From this, the common city, we derive our intelligence, our reason and our law—from what else? Just as the dry earth-element in me has been portioned off from earth somewhere, and the water in me from the other element, the air or breath from some other source and the dry and fiery from a source of its own (for nothing comes from what does not exist or returns to it), so also then the intelligence comes from somewhere. . . .

Nature's Guidance

Wrongdoing is impious, for the nature of the Whole has fashioned rational creatures for each other's sake, so that they should benefit each other as they deserve but never injure one another. The man who transgresses its intention is clearly guilty of impiety toward the oldest of divinities, for the universal nature is the nature of ultimate realities, and these are closely related to all that now exists.

The man who speaks untruth is impious toward the same goddess, for her name is Truth and she is the first cause of all that is true. The deliberate liar is therefore impious insofar as he wrongs people by deceiving them, and the involuntary liar is also impious insofar as he is out of tune with the nature of the Whole and brings disorder as he struggles against the nature of the orderly universe. He who on his own initiative is carried towards the opposite of what is true does struggle against this. He received his original impulses from nature, and it is through neglecting them that he is no longer able to distinguish the false from the true.

And indeed the man who pursues pleasure as good, and avoids pain as evil, is impious also. He must needs reproach the common nature frequently for distributing something unfairly between inferior and good men, since inferior men often enjoy pleasures and possess the means to attain them, while good men are often involved in pain and in things that produce pain.

Then again, the man who is afraid of pain will at times be afraid of something that is to happen in the world, and this is already impious. Further, the pleasure seeker will not refrain from wrongdoing, which is obviously impious.

With regard to those things toward which the common nature is indifferent (for she would not create both pains and pleasures if she were not indifferent to both), those who would follow nature and be of like mind with her must also be indifferent. Whoever is not himself indifferent to pain and pleasure or to life and death, or to reputation and the lack of it—things which the nature of the Whole uses indifferently—is clearly impious.

When I say that the common nature uses these things indifferently, I mean that they happen in due sequence and without difference to those who now are living, and to their posterity, and are caused by some long past impulse of Providence. In accordance with this impulse and from a first principle Providence started the process which culminated in the present orderliness of the universe; for Providence had grasped certain rational, creative principles of what was to be, and marked out certain powers generative of substances, changes, and things of the same kind to succeed them.

Source: From Marcus Aurelius Antoninus, *The Meditations,* trans. G. M. A. Grube (Indianapolis: Hackett Publishing Company, Inc., 1983), pp. 21, 23, 26–27, 86–87. Copyright © 1983 by Hackett Publishing Co., Inc. All rights reserved.

course it must be assumed that the conditions necessary to arrive at an unconstrained consensus have already been realized. Thus the discourse situation must be characterized by a sense of equality and reciprocity of participation. This approach makes it possible to formulate a critique of the inequalities of social power that is not based on personal value commitments.[24]

In *The Theory of Communicative Action,* Habermas argues that the problems and issues of contemporary society have occurred through the invasion of the life world by quasi-autonomous systems of bureaucracy and the economy. The life world is the domain of social existence that has been organized through communication. Habermas believes that this invasion of the life world is opposed by all social movements as they attempt to bring solidarity to all forms of social life and to bring the dynamics of money and power under democratic control.[25]

Selected Reading 3.4 contains a selection from Habermas's work in which he identifies the linguistic expressions that characterize morality. Habermas states that obligations have their experiential base in moral feelings that act as a general rule indicating when someone transgresses against his or her duties. Further, feelings of offense and resentment arise in a person from the actions of others that violate his or her personal rights; shame and guilt arise from a person's own transgressions; and outrage and contempt arise as a universal response to certain transgressions when the person is not directly involved in the transgression, but is more than merely an observer. The implication is that everyone belongs to a community in which human interaction should be judged by the norms established through these linguistic expressions. Moreover, these affective responses are often expressed in terms of confessions, condemnations, and so forth, which often lead to accusations, justifications, and excuses. Such is the experiential basis of obligations.

In this selection, Habermas further asserts that norms regulate human interaction by imposing obligations on people as community members. He contrasts mere conventions with duties. Conventions bind by custom, whereas duties bind because they are based on reason. This is an important factor in Habermas's argument; because the norms of duty are based on reason, people can explain why they are recognized as norms. This internal connection between norms and the grounds for their justification constitutes the rational foundation of their validity.

Another key factor in Habermas's argument revolves around his concept of will. Although duties bind the will, they do not compel it as impulses do. According to Habermas, empiricists would disagree with this view because they would hold that norms oblige people only to the extent that they are backed up by sanctions. The empiricist neglects to consider human intuition, which is a non-coercive force that transfers norms into duties and into a feeling-obliged-to-obey response. In Habermas's view, the affective reactions of resentment, outrage, and contempt are all that is really expressed in sanctions.

From this perspective, Habermas initiates a different way of considering duties. They are to be understood only in the following context: act in such a way that everyone has the communicative freedom to take positions on duties. The integrity of the acting subject is the core value. In this context, a person acts truthfully not simply by refraining from deception, but also by acting in a positive manner through recognition of the value and freedom of others as participants in discourse. Thus duties take on a positive rather than a negative connotation.

The person engaged in reciprocal respect and recognition is a symbol of human freedom. The integrity of physical life is not at risk as much as is a person's personality structure, which is reliant on interpersonal relations. For this reason, according to Habermas, some people risk death rather than lose freedom.

Selected Reading 3.4

Discourse Ethics and Duty

Jürgen Habermas

"Ought" sentences expressing obligations are the primary linguistic form in which morality finds expression. Duties prescribe actions or omissions. Prohibitions are the negations of permissions, permissions the negations of prohibitions. Obligations have their experiential basis not in perceptions but, as Strawson has shown, in moral feelings. The latter point as a general rule to violations of duties, transgressions against norms from which duties and rights (i.e., legitimate expectations concerning actions in accordance with duties) can be derived. Feelings of offense and resentment are second-person reactions to violations of our rights by others; feelings of shame and guilt are reactions to our own transgressions; and outrage and contempt are reactions of one present but not directly involved to the violation of a recognized norm by a third person. Thus, these affective states correspond to the perspectives and roles of the participants in interaction—ego and alter—and of a neutral party who is not presently involved but whose perspective should not be confused with that of a mere observer, his view being that of a representative of universality. They all belong to a community in which interpersonal relations and actions are regulated by norms of interaction and can be judged in the light of these norms to be justified or unjustified.

These *affective responses* to violations that find expression in turn in reproaches, confessions, condemnations, and so forth and can lead to accusations, justifications, or excuses constitute the *experiential basis* of obligations, though they do not exhaust their semantic meaning. The normative sentences in which these obligations are expressed point to a background of normatively generalized behavioral expectations. Norms regulate contexts of interaction by imposing practical obligations in a justifiable manner on actors who belong to a shared community. Conventions are norms of interaction that define reciprocal behavioral expectations in such a way that their content does not need to be justified. "Mere" conventions bind, so to speak, in a groundless fashion by custom alone; we do not associate a moral claim with them. Duties, by contrast, derive their binding force from the validity of norms of interaction that claim to rest on good reasons. We feel obligated only by norms of which we believe that, if called upon to do so, we could explain why they both deserve and admit of recognition on the part of their addressees (and of those affected).

The internal connection between norms and justifying grounds constitutes the *rational foundation of normative validity.* This can be confirmed at the phenomenological level by the corresponding sense of obligation. Duties *bind (binden)* the will but do not *bend (beugen)* it. They point the will in a certain direction and give it orientation but do not compel it as impulses do; they motivate through reasons and lack the impulsive force of purely empirical motives. Hence the empiricist notion that norms obligate only to the extent that they are backed up by well-founded expectations of sanctions neglects the fundamental intuition that the noncoercive binding force is transferred from the validity of a valid norm to the duty and the act of feeling obligated. Only the affective reactions to the violation and the perpetrator—resentment, outrage, and contempt—are expressed in the sanctions that result from transgressions of norms. . . .

From this viewpoint the privileged status accorded basic duties such as "You should not lie" can be accounted for in a different way. To these core duties belong only those that can be understood as aspects of the general demand: "Act with an orientation to mutual understanding and allow everyone the communicative freedom to take positions on valid claims." They are fundamental because they are oriented to respect for the integrity of communicatively acting subjects. But these norms do not just have the force of purely negative duties. In behaving truthfully I do not merely *refrain* from deception but at the same time *perform* an act without which the interpersonal relation between performatively engaged participants in interaction dependent on mutual recognition would collapse. The norms that prescribe the fulfillment of the necessary pragmatic presuppositions of communicative action as a duty are strangely different regarding the distinction between negative and positive duties: by showing respect for another person, I at the same time protect the vulnerable core of his person. Hence, it is no coincidence that other norms of this kind (for example, those that oblige us to respect normative validity claims) are formulated in positive terms. Gert's ten rules also include such positive duties:

7. You should keep your promises.
10. You should do your duty.

The fundamental status of the kinds of commands that Gert includes in his catalog of duties cannot be explained in terms of the determinateness of norms prescribing omissions but only in terms of their self-referential character. These duties regulate precisely the necessary pragmatic presuppositions of communicative action from whose normative content discourse ethics derives the basic substance of morality by analyzing the universal and necessary communicative presuppositions of the practice of argumentation—that is, the reflective form of communicative action. Gert's ten rules are concerned immediately with the integrity of the person himself as a symbolic structure that is produced and reproduced through relations of reciprocal recognition; they are concerned mediately with the preservation and development of the bodily existence of the respect-worthy person. The constitutional susceptibility of a personality structure that is at the mercy of interpersonal relations is of even greater moment than the more tangible vulnerability of the integrity of body and life: the symbolic structure can disintegrate while the physical substrate remains intact. For this reason, we sometimes risk death rather than live a life devoid of freedom. This insight is indeed open to ideological misuse, but its truth is not thereby denied as such.

Source: From Jürgen Habermas, *Justification and Application: Remarks on Discourse Ethics*, trans. Ciaran P. Cronin (Cambridge: The MIT Press, 1994), pp. 40–41, 66–67. Reprinted by permission.

Principals and superintendents would be well-advised to consider language as a key to ethical conduct. Linguistic expressions give rise to mental constructs that, in turn, affect conduct. This situation is obvious in the linguistic expressions of gang members who use code words to communicate attitudes and expectations among themselves. This exclusivity and secrecy of expression are necessary tools used by gang leaders to control the behavior of other gang members. Breaking the code makes gang members vulnerable to exposure by mitigating the protection of secrecy.

Because these same concepts apply to everyone, teachers are affected by the linguistic expressions of principals and principals are affected by the linguistic expressions of superintendents. The situation is similar in relation to communicating with all internal and external constituents, including the news media. Obviously, written communication leaves a rather permanent record of expressions that affect ethical behavior.

The connection between linguistic expression and feelings also requires careful attention. Principals, superintendents, and other administrators who are oblivious to the effect of their manner of verbal expression on the attitudes and feelings of others are vulnerable to misunderstanding. Irate parents and teachers may ascribe negative characteristics to these people, which could hinder their professional relationships and their effectiveness as administrators.

Respecting the humanity of other people is a significant dimension of Habermas's approach to duty. This sense of human integrity gives rise to his notion of communicative ethics. But underlying the importance of respecting the integrity of people and the communicative milieu is Habermas's understanding of the significance of membership in the community to the establishment of ethical norms. This membership gives people the right to enter into discourse and is the base from which norms that have universal application can be derived.

The establishment of norms for student rights and responsibilities is certainly in keeping with the ideas of Habermas if they are established through discourse with the students who are to be affected by the norms. Once the norms are established, they become student duties. The process for establishing the norms is of particular importance. Because representatives of the student body may not always truly represent the beliefs and values of the student body at large, it is important for the administration to establish a method whereby all students have an opportunity to participate in some form of discourse. This will ensure that the real issues—and not merely the supposed issues—of student life are uncovered and addressed.

Because norms must be based on reason, according to Habermas, norms established for students must be in concert with the rational norms established by the larger community. Although school communities are composed primarily of young people, these young people tend to reflect the mores of their parents, which, in general, have a basis in rationality.

What is more controversial is the establishment of norms for the professional and support staffs. Again, representatives of these groups may not truly represent the real issues that concern the majority of group members. Consequently, it is important to establish some mechanism whereby these individuals have the opportunity to enter into the discourse. Doing so is particularly challenging when the employees are represented by unions. It is incumbent upon both parties engaged in collective negotiations to make distinctions concerning the ethics of conduct as it relates to working conditions and the ethics of conduct as it relates to universal conditions that transcend what might be considered working conditions.

OTHER PHILOSOPHICAL APPROACHES TO THE ISSUES IN THIS CHAPTER

The issue of power was also treated by Thomas Hobbes and Friedrich Nietzsche, both of whom proposed strong leaders who would take control of the institutions of government and do what was best for all the people. They favored raw power.

Much more can be found in philosophical writings in relation to duty from an ethical obligation perspective. Epictetus was a Stoic philosopher who lived during the latter half of the first century and who believed in living a life of austerity in order to learn the true meaning of life's obligations. Joseph Butler (1692–1752) proposed that people are psychological beings who are motivated to act according to many principles, the most important of which is conscience. F. H. Bradley was a British philosopher who wrote *My Station and Its Duties*. Although his philosophy was later distorted by others, it nonetheless made a significant contribution to ethics. Bradley viewed the individual not as an isolated person, but as part of a larger whole that alone made his or her existence meaningful. W. D. Ross urged people to do what they perceived to be their duty even though another action could promote a better consequence.

Others whose views might be consulted in relation to duty are Ruth Benedict, David Hume, Derek Parafit, Louis P. Pojman, Josiah Royce, Henry Sidgwick, and Plato.

CROSSWALK TO ISLLC STANDARD FIVE

The contents of this chapter support the following dimensions of ISLLC Standard Five:

Knowledge

The administrator has knowledge and understanding of:

♦ the purpose of education and the role of leadership in modern society

♦ various ethical frameworks and perspectives on ethics

Dispositions

The administrator believes in, values, and is committed to:

♦ subordinating one's own interest to the good of the school community

Performances

The administrator:

♦ examines personal and professional values

♦ demonstrates values, beliefs, and attitudes that inspire others to higher levels of performance

♦ accepts responsibility for school operations

♦ uses the influence of the office to enhance the educational program rather than for personal gain

♦ treats people fairly, equitably, and with dignity and respect

- recognizes and respects the legitimate authority of others
- expects that others in the school community will demonstrate integrity and exercise ethical behavior
- applies laws and procedures fairly, wisely, and considerately

ETHICAL CONSIDERATIONS PRESENTED IN THIS CHAPTER

- How a principal or superintendent exercises the power of office will have a significant effect on other staff members. The actions of powerful people are never neutral in terms of consequences.
- The culture of a given school or school district is directly affected by the manner in which a principal or superintendent yields the power of office.
- The manner in which an educational leader exercises the power of office is an indication of his or her inner life and the true measure of who he or she is as a person.
- A good method for carrying out educational leadership responsibilities is to act from a principle that the person wishes everyone would use.
- The educational leader must strive to do what is right in relation to the welfare of others regardless of the consequences; this is the only defensible way of acting.
- A principal or superintendent will better understand duty if he or she learned how to follow the leadership of others as a teacher or staff member.
- Integrity is the core value of every educational leader.
- The obligations of duty are founded on reflective human reason, which is one of the most effective tools in leading a person through the maze of professional life.
- Human reason is the basis for asserting that norms of conduct have universal applicability.
- In a real sense, the performance of duty is a solitary responsibility through which a principal or superintendent comes to terms with his or her freedom.
- Performance of duty always entails a social dimension and usually a public dimension in the practice of educational leadership.
- The duty of the educational leader is founded on recognizing the value and integrity of others and in respecting their freedom to communicate positions on what constitutes professional duty.

◯ SUMMARY

All professional relationships that include a supervisor-employee dimension intrinsically involve power. In the practice of educational leadership the question of ethics must be considered in relation to power, particularly the power of office. The six aspects of the power of office are inspirational, charismatic, expert, persuasive, knowledge, and coercive. When administrators use assertiveness or sanctions, dependent employees often try to counterbalance these power strategies through strategies for making a favorable impression, such as conformity, excuses, apologies, acclaiming, flattery, and favors.

Power is exercised because people have freedom to conform or not to conform. The consequences of power struggles can have a significant effect on the morale of other staff members.

Schools and school districts as institutions have a culture, which is in a constant state of fluctuation. The degree to which a school or school district's administration supports the following characteristics is an indication of its culture: members' identification with the school and school district, group emphasis, people focus, unit integration, minimal control mechanisms, risk tolerance, favorable reward criteria, conflict tolerance, means-end orientation, and open-system focus. The motives and behavior of individuals within a school or school district, and especially of educational leaders in relation to their power of office, can affect the culture of the organization positively or negatively.

The charisma of leadership refers to viewing leadership not as a job or even as a profession, but as a lifelong process of discerning how to be of service to the academic community. This charisma liberates the educational leader from the constraints of fragmentation and unifies the person in the search for transcendental meaning. The inner life gives meaning to the outer life. Living an ethical live is therefore much more than adherence to a code; it is a way of thinking and acting that reflects the person's innermost being.

Duties can generally be classified into duties to self, family, friends, colleagues, neighbors, and acquaintances; and duties to employer, employees, and the profession.

Immanuel Kant's treatment of duty synthesized ideas from two philosophical approaches, rationalism and empiricism. Kant's view of duty originated in his categorical imperative: Act only according to that maxim whereby you can at the same time will that it should become a universal law. He proceeded from this principle to identifying duty with a willed universal law; Kant intended the categorical imperative to be applicable in all situations. The key to utilizing the categorical imperative is the practice of reflection in the decision-making process.

Another approach to duty is found in the philosophy of Georg Wilhelm Friedrich Hegel. His notion of duty is transcendental in the sense that it is abstract and universal. Accordingly, people are liberated from performing their duty in order to obtain a particular end, but are admonished to carry out their duty for its own sake. Hegel's universal principle is: Do what is right and strive after welfare. Here, welfare refers to the welfare of other people. Duty is the essence of moral self-consciousness; and striving after welfare implies that people must decide for themselves the goodness aspect of welfare. Further, Hegel believed that only in the exercise of duty would a person comes to understand his or her freedom. Finally, private rights are subordinate to the rights of the state, but the state is responsible for enacting laws that provide for the well-being and happiness of individuals and to provide services for them.

The philosophy of Aristotle speaks to the duty of citizens. The purpose of the state is the fostering of the supreme good: the moral and intellectual development of its citizens. A key to Aristotle's political philosophy is his idea that citizens are both rulers and subjects vested with the right to participate in making laws and the right to participate in the administration of justice. According to Aristotle, the virtues of a good person and the virtues of a good citizen may intersect, but the virtues of a good ruler differ from those of a good citizen. Further, the person who has never learned how to obey cannot know how to command.

For Marcus Aurelius Antoninus, destiny is synonymous with duty. Thus, a person may not have the luxury of determining his or her duty but may have it thrust on him or her. Marcus's basic principle appears to be that leading a moral life will give a person self-control and courage in the pursuit of truth and justice. The tool for this pursuit is reason. If a person channels his or her zeal and energy with truthfulness toward fulfilling his or her duty, no other power will be able to divert him or her from this purpose. Through reason, people are capable of establishing universal laws of conduct that serve as a common bond uniting all people in the pursuit of goodness. Marcus held that as nature makes no distinction between good and bad people when bestowing pain or pleasure, life or death, fame or dishonor, people should live their lives with the same indifference and perform their duty without regard to these conditions.

The uniqueness of Jürgen Habermas's approach to duty lies in his attempt to shift the philosophical emphasis from the subjective-objective relationship to intersubjective communication. He attempted to identify the normative commitments that are established through linguistic communication. Further, a positive assumption must be made concerning the conditions necessary to arrive at an unconstrained consensus, and the discourse situation must be characterized by a sense of equality and reciprocity of participation. In discourse, linguistic expressions characterize morality. Obligations have their experiential base in moral feelings, which act as a general rule indicating when someone transgresses against his or her duties. Norms regulate human interaction by imposing obligations on people as community members; these norms of duty are based on reason and are valid only if people can establish an internal connection between the norms and their justification. In this view, human intuition is a noncoercive force that transfers norms into duties and into a feeling that evokes an obligation to obey them. The basic principle is: Act in such a way that everyone has the communicative freedom to take positions on duties. Finally, the integrity of the acting person is the core value. A person acts truthfully not merely by refraining from deception, but also by acting in a positive manner through recognition of the value and freedom of others as participants in discourse.

↪ DISCUSSION QUESTIONS AND STATEMENTS

1. Explain what is meant by the *power of office* and give an example of how educational leaders yield power.
2. What are the aspects of the power of office and how are they related to educational leadership?
3. Which aspects of the power of office utilize influence and which utilize control?
4. What are techniques for making a favorable impression and why are they used?
5. Explain Michel Foucault's concept of power and how it is related to educational leadership.
6. Explain the meaning of the terms *organization* and *society*.
7. Elucidate the ten characteristics of a positive school and school-district culture.
8. What is meant by the *charisma* of educational leadership?
9. Explain the transcendental dimension of educational leadership.
10. What influence can the concepts of Carl Jung have on the practice of educational leadership?
11. Explain the concept of duty and describe the kinds of duties that most people have.
12. Explain Kant's categorical imperative and how it relates to the practice of educational leadership.
13. What did Hegel mean when he stated that a person comes to understand his or her freedom only in the exercise of duty?
14. In Aristotle's philosophy, what is the relationship between giving a command and obeying a command?
15. What gives credibility to the meditations of Marcus Aurelius Antoninus?
16. Explain what is meant by the shift from subjective-objective relationship to intersubjective communication in the philosophy of Jürgen Habermas.

◡ CASE STUDY 3.1

A Case of Leadership Style

The principal of the middle school is the first Hispanic American woman to became a building principal in the school district. She received her master of arts degree in educational administration four years ago and immediately began searching for her first administrative position. She had been a science teacher for six years at another middle school in the district. Her teaching record was exemplary. She was well liked not only by her students, but also by the staff and parents.

The school district is a large county school district with an enrollment of approximately 12,000 students. There are large concentrations of African, Mexican, and European Americans living in relatively segregated sections of the county. However, the Mexican community is the only one experiencing growth. Most of the administrators in the district are European Americans who were hired before the great influx of Mexican Americans over the last ten years.

The superintendent of schools understands the appropriateness of being proactive in hiring African and Mexican Americans into teaching and administrative positions. He has been the superintendent for nineteen years; when he was hired, the enrollment was approximately half its current number. His administrative style is very directive. He has no qualms about requiring administrators to carry out his directives in precisely the manner in which he prescribes. His concerns tend to center on pupil achievement, and he is most alarmed when he believes that administrators, staff members, and teachers are not continually on task. His perception of what it means to be on task was developed when he was a teacher and later a principal in the school district.

As an educator, this superintendent believes that students must have well-defined learning goals; every student should have the equivalent of an IEP (Individualized Education Program, which is required for students with disabilities).

The principal has a different approach to school leadership. Although she is concerned that each student be challenged to develop his or her abilities to the highest possible degree, educating the whole person is her focus. To this purpose she has instituted in-school suspension. She knows that some students deliberately perform inappropriate actions in order to be suspended; suspension liberates them from supervision during the school day because most of their parents are at work.

Together with the teachers this principal has been able to establish an atmosphere in which students can celebrate their African and Mexican heritages through drama productions and specialized events, in addition to the many ethnic decorations throughout the school building.

Discussion Questions and Statements

1. Compare and contrast the manners in which the principal and the superintendent exercise the power of office.

2. How does the concept of culture influence their administrative practices?

3. How does the principal exhibit the charisma of educational leadership?

4. Explain how the principal's and superintendent's actions could be influenced by the principles of depth psychology.

5. Compare and contrast the actions of the principal and superintendent with the ten characteristics that indicate the cultural quality of a school or school district.

✍ CASE STUDY 3.2

The School District with Inadequate Funding

The school district is experiencing the effects of urban flight. It is located in a county adjacent to a large city. For ten years a combination of factors have resulted in an influx of people from the city: the quality of education in the city school district is poor because of a high pupil-teacher ratio and the loss of highly skilled, experienced teachers to other districts that pay higher salaries; also, housing in the county is relatively inexpensive.

Parents of young children and new families seek out the housing in the county that is sprouting up at the rate of one new subdivision every six months. The cost of renovating older homes in the city is just as high as buying a new home in the county. In addition, the influx of young families reinforces the eagerness of other young people to live in the same area.

The superintendent of the county school district has been in her position for eleven years. The rapid development of the school district caught her by surprise. When she came to the district, it had a rather small pupil enrollment of approximately two thousand students. The district now has twelve thousand students in eight elementary schools, two middle schools, and one high school. All the schools are overcrowded, and the pupil-teacher ratio is ever increasing. The assessed valuation of the school district has not increased in proportion to the financial resources that are needed to accommodate the growing population, because although the number of housing units has significantly increased, there has not been an increase in commercial property, which is assessed at a higher percentage than is residential property and thus brings in more revenue. Furthermore, the younger parents seem to appreciate the need to increase the technology budget at all levels in the educational program. They use computers and other technology at work and fully understand that the future work environment into which their children will enter will be replete with technology.

Some of the same issues that affect the quality of education in the city school district are now beginning to affect the county school district, in particular, the growing pupil-teacher ratio and the loss of teachers to other districts that pay higher salaries.

Many parents have formed advocacy groups to support issues that they believe are critical to the quality of education their children receive. The most vocal groups are those concerned with services to children with disabilities; increasing teacher salaries and benefits; reducing class sizes; increasing the quality of pupil-transportation services; improving technology in the learning process; increasing cocurricular opportunities, especially for high school students; and improving school facilities, particularly those supporting the athletic programs.

The board of education is composed almost entirely of younger parents who are also college graduates. They sympathize with the advocacy groups, but fear that a tax-levy referendum will fail because most young families are significantly in debt. Further, many of the board members are concerned that their constituents will be dissatisfied with their performance if they try to increase taxes. Some of the board members have experienced decreases in their own salaries because of their companies' downsizing and believe that other parents are probably in the same situation.

There is growing dissatisfaction among the board members with the performance of the superintendent. They believe she has done an inadequate job of meeting the challenge brought on by the rapid increase in student enrollment. Further, they think that she and her staff may lack the vision necessary to lead the district into the next decade. Two of the seven board members have even asked for the superintendent's resignation. These two were the most recently elected and were supported in their campaigns by various advocacy groups. They have castigated the other board members for renewing the superintendent's contract two years earlier, stating that most parents have not been satisfied with the superintendent's performance for the last five years.

The superintendent has been trying to meet the challenges of a rapidly increasing pupil population. Three years ago she invited the state association of school board members to work with the local board in devising a procedure to develop a strategic plan that would involve all segments of the community as well as the professional and support staffs of the schools. At that time the superintendent and her staff also developed a community relations program aimed both at informing the entire community of the successes of the academic program and at explaining what financial, human, and equipment resources would be needed to continue to improve the academic program. In this way the super-intendent hoped to prepare the community for the eventual need for a tax-levy referendum. However, the board of education turned down the superinten-dent's request to hire an additional central-office staff member to implement the community relations program. The board felt that the cost of the program was too expensive in relation to the other needs of the school district and pointed out that the salary and benefits needed for the additional staff member could be used to hire two more teachers.

After the board rejected her community relations plan, the superintendent continued to search for ways to convince the board members of the need to pre-pare the public for a possible tax-levy election. The board wanted her to take a more definitive position against salary and benefit increases with the teachers union and the unions representing the support staff. However, the superinten-dent continued to press for approval of reasonable salary and benefit increases for teachers and staff members even though she knew that doing so would prob-ably lead to more dissatisfaction with her performance. The board also did not agree with her recommendation to halt cocurricular and athletic-program development until financial stability could be garnered for the district. Yet the superintendent has publicly stated her opposition to placing a bond-issue pro-posal before the taxpayers for the construction of athletic facilities until a tax-levy increase is approved.

Discussion Questions and Statements

1. In relation to Kant's categorical imperative, how would you assess the actions of the superintendent of schools?

2. How does the rejection by the board of education of the superintendent's community relations plan violate the tenets of Jürgen Habermas's dis-course ethics?

3. From the perspective of Marcus Aurelius Antoninus, how do the actions of the superintendent coincide with the notion of indifference to pain and suffering?

4. How do the actions of the board of education measure up to Aristotle's views concerning the duty of citizens?

5. Using Hegel's ideas, explain how you would bring into question the actions of the board of education and validate the actions of the superin-tendent of schools.

6. Drawing on the various approaches to duty presented in this chapter, develop a plan of action on which the board and the superintendent could agree that could be used to chart the future of the school district.

SELECTED BIBLIOGRAPHY

Ackril, J. L., ed. *A New Aristotle Reader.* Princeton, N.J.: Princeton University Press, 1987.

Antoninus, Marcus Aurelius. *Meditations.* London: Penguin Books, Ltd., 1964.

Aristotle. *Nicomachean Ethics.* Trans. T. Irwin. Indianapolis: Hackett Publishing Company, Inc., 1985.

Beiser, F. C., ed. *The Cambridge Companion to Hegel.* Cambridge: The Cambridge University Press, 1993.

Gordon, G. G. "Industry Determinants of Organizational Culture," *Academy of Management Review* (April 1991): 396–415.

Gratton, Carolyn. *The Art of Spiritual Guidance: A Contemporary Approach to Growing in the Spirit.* New York: The Crossroad Publishing Company, 1995.

Guyer, P., ed. *The Cambridge Companion to Kant.* Cambridge: The Cambridge University Press, 1992.

Habermas, Jürgen. *Justification and Application: Remarks on Discourse Ethics.* Trans. Ciaran P. Cronin. Cambridge: The MIT Press, 1995.

Hegel, Georg Wilhelm Friedrich. *Philosophy of Right.* Trans. T. M. Knox. Oxford, England: Oxford University Press, 1942.

Hitchcock, John. *The Web of the Universe: Jung, the New Physics, and Human Spirituality.* New York: Paulist Press, 1991.

Jung, Carl Gustav. *Modern Man in Search of a Soul.* New York: Harcourt Brace Jovanovich Publishers, 1933.

———. *Psychology and Religion.* New Haven, Conn.: Yale University Press, 1966.

———. *Man and His Symbols.* New York: Dell Publishing, 1968.

———. *Psychology of the Unconscious: A Study of the Transformation and Symbolism of the Libido.* Bollingen Series, vol. 20. Princeton, N.J.: Princeton University Press, 1991.

Kant, Immanuel. *Grounding for the Metaphysics of Morals* with *On a Supposed Right to Lie because of Philanthropic Concerns.* 3d ed. Trans. James W. Ellington. Indianapolis: Hackett Publishing Company, Inc., 1996.

Krackhardt, D. "Assessing the Political Landscape: Structures, Cognition, and Power in Organizations," *Administrative Science Quarterly* (June 1990): 342–369.

MacIntyre, A., ed. *Hegel: A Collection of Critical Essays.* Garden City, N.J.: Anchor Books, 1972.

McKeon, Richard, ed. *Introduction to Aristotle.* New York: Random House, Inc., 1947.

Moore, Robert L., ed. *Carl Jung and Christian Spirituality.* New York: Paulist Press, 1988.

O'Sullivan, R. *An Introduction to Kant's Ethics.* Cambridge: The Cambridge University Press, 1991.

Paton, H. *The Categorical Imperative: A Study in Kant's Moral Philosophy.* London: Hutcheson Press, 1947.

Rabinow, Paul, ed. *The Foucault Reader.* New York: Pantheon Books, 1984.

Rist, J. M., ed. *The Stoics.* Berkeley: University of California Press, 1978.

Robbins, Stephen P. *Organizational Behavior: Concepts, Controversies, and Applications.* 6th ed. Upper Saddle River, N.J.: Prentice Hall, 1993.

Ross, W. D., ed. *The Works of Aristotle.* Oxford, England: Clarendon Press, 1925.

Saunders, C. S. "The Strategic Contingencies Theory of Power: Multiple Perspectives," *Journal of Management Studies* (January 1990): 1–18.

Schneider, G. *Organizational Climate and Culture.* San Francisco: Jossey-Bass, 1991.

Singer, June. *Boundaries of the Soul: The Practice of Jung's Psychology.* Revised and updated. New York: Doubleday, Anchor Books, 1994.

PART TWO

The Ethical Practice of Educational Leadership

4

Ethical Considerations in Leadership at the School-District Level

This chapter treats the ethics of district-level leadership under three aspects: contractarianism, as exemplified by Jean-Jacques Rousseau's notion of the social contract and Jean-François Lyotard's concept of the social bond; utilitarianism, as set forth by John Stuart Mill; and the professionalism of school-district leadership.

The ethical issues covered in the section on contractarianism center on creating a vision and goals for a school district through community cultural assessment, school-reform expectations, the debureaucratization of school districts, empowerment, and the privatization movements. In the section on utilitarianism, ethical considerations focus on assessment and reporting of student achievement, curriculum development, human-resource leadership, fiscal accountability, and stress in the superintendency. The final section, on professionalism in school-district leadership, reviews and analyzes the ethical statements of the American Association of School Administrators, the Association of School Business Officials International, the Association for Supervision and Curriculum Development, and the National School Boards Association.

SCHOOL-DISTRICT LEADERSHIP AS A SOCIAL CONTRACT

Theories of leadership and, specifically, of educational leadership abound in the professional and popular literature. The position on leadership set forth in this section relating to ethics is embedded in the very foundation of the U.S. government. It is historical and cultural. Both founding ancestors and contemporary leaders in U.S. government and education have utilized the ideas of the philosophers presented in this section to make decisions that continue to affect the lives of people in U.S. society.

The Social Contract Theory of Jean-Jacques Rousseau

Jean-Jacques Rousseau (1712–1778) was born a citizen of the *free* city of Geneva, Switzerland. The concept of freedom had a significant influence on his life and ultimately resulted in the legacy of *citizenship* that Rousseau bequeathed to Western civilization. He was an impassioned yet unsystematic philosopher. His writings gained influence because of his passion and rhetorical style. He launched one of the first attacks against eighteenth-century rationalism, and his thought helped develop the intellectual movements of romanticism in literature and idealism in philosophy.

Rousseau led a rather unpleasant existence. He was constantly moving from one country to another in search of the good life. Although he spent most of his life in France, he also lived in Switzerland, northern Italy, and England. Rousseau's mother died during his birth, and his father abandoned him when he was eleven years old. He was a very emotional person, who suffered not only from ill health, but also from emotional excesses. He argued and quarreled with many of the intellectuals of his time, including Diderot, Hume, and Voltaire.[1]

Although this presentation will deal with Rousseau's book *On the Social Contract,* it should be remembered that his book *Emile* had a similarly profound effect on the people of his times. In *Emile* he set forth an educational philosophy that was revolutionary. Rousseau held that the process of education should promote and encourage the natural creativity of children rather than act as a curb and hindrance to their natural tendencies. He emphasized the importance of the direct involvement of children with other people and in situations as a method of learning, and he deemphasized verbal instruction. Further, Rousseau recognized that parents are the natural teachers of their children and that their effectiveness as teachers will be significantly greater if they approach learning with love and sympathy for their children rather than with rules and punishment.[2]

On the Social Contract, written by Rousseau in Bourbon, France, but published in Holland, served as both manifesto and chronicler of the revolutionary change from the old to the new order in Western society. It prophesied popular democracy. *On the Social Contract* was not a synthesis, but an original work from which developed much of contemporary social and moral thought. The book called for the beginning of a new era, championing the cause of the common person and government by the people.[3]

Rousseau developed his approach from many sources, including Calvinism; classical literature; the work of Machiavelli concerning the popular government of the Roman Republic; Montesquieu's study of social institutions; the political thought of Plato and Aristotle; philosophical rationalism; late-medieval experience of self-governing cities in Germany, Italy, and Switzerland; and the social customs of the North American Indian tribes.[4]

The subtitle of *On the Social Contract, Principles of Political Right*, illustrates the difference between Rousseau and other political writers. In his *Second Treatise of Civil Government*, John Locke appears to have accepted the social contract as a historical fact. But there is no historical evidence that any society was established by a contract; even if such a phenomenon did occur, it did not *have* to happen. Further, Locke believed that society was only an aggregate of independent and sovereign individuals. Thus, each person has certain specific rights, which he or she seeks to protect through the establishment of a society. These individual rights have a priority over the notion of the common good.[5]

Rousseau proceeded from a statement of principle and not from a historical event. He used the deductive-reasoning approach developed by René Descartes (1596–1650), Gottfried Wilhelm Leibniz (1646–1716), and Benedict de Spinoza (1632–1677) in setting forth his position. Rousseau was searching for a first principle, which would be logical and incontrovertible, by which people could defend their actions. His first principle is embodied in the opening statement in part 1 of book 1 of *On the Social Contract*, "Man is born free." The absolutist societies of Rousseau's time presented evidence to the contrary. Indeed, as he stated, "Everywhere he is in chains." Thus, Rousseau's first principle is not predicated on empirical evidence; rather, he believed it to be a metaphysical truth. Rousseau's major objective was not to analyze the social conditions under which people lived, but to establish principles that could be used by people to determine what is right or wrong and what should be the right course of future actions.[6] A significant concept of Rousseau's is that each person places his or her personal will and all his or her options under the direction of the general will of the collective majority through acceptance of the process by which people in the aggregate make decisions. Thus arises the concept of the *public person* who is formed by the will of all other persons and who embodies the sovereignty of the public institution. This sovereignty is exercised through a representative form of government in which the people elect those who will carry out the general will. In education, this sovereignty is implemented through the election of citizens to the board of education.

Of even greater significance is Rousseau's idea that when a person gives over his or her will to the general will, in reality he or she gives this personal attribute to no one person. Further, individuals lose nothing that they do not gain over others through this same process. From this frame of reference, it must be recognized that what the majority wants may not always be good and just. However, it is the process that is important, and the process tends to be self-correcting. When the representative of the majority makes bad decisions, he or she will eventually be replaced in a subsequent election.

Selected Reading 4.1 contains an excerpt from Rousseau's *Social Contract* in which he establishes the importance of his concepts concerning the general will and the place of the individual in society.

Selected Reading 4.1

On the Social Contract

Jean-Jacques Rousseau (1712–1778)

I suppose that men have reached the point where obstacles that are harmful to their maintenance in the state of nature gain the upper hand by their resistance to the forces that each individual can bring to bear to maintain himself in that state. Such being the case, that original state cannot subsist any longer, and the human race would perish if it did not alter its mode of existence.

For since men cannot engender new forces, but merely unite and direct existing ones, they have no other means of maintaining themselves but to form by aggregation a sum of forces that could gain the upper hand over the resistance, so that their forces are directed by means of a single moving power and made to act in concert.

This sum of forces cannot come into being without the cooperation of many. But since each man's force and liberty are the primary instruments of his maintenance, how is he going to engage them without hurting himself and without neglecting the care that he owes himself? This difficulty, seen in terms of my subject, can be stated in the following terms:

"Find a form of association which defends and protects with all common forces the person and goods of each associate, and by means of which each one, while uniting with all, nevertheless obeys only himself and remains as free as before." This is the fundamental problem for which the social contract provides the solution.

The clauses of this contract are so determined by the nature of the act that the least modification renders them vain and ineffectual, that, although perhaps they have never been formally promulgated, they are everywhere the same, everywhere tacitly accepted and acknowledged. Once the social compact is violated, each person then regains his first rights and resumes his natural liberty, while losing the conventional liberty for which he renounced it.

These clauses, properly understood, are all reducible to a single one, namely the total alienation of each associate, together with all of his rights, to the entire community. For first of all, since each person gives himself whole and entire, the condition is equal for everyone; and since the condition is equal for everyone, no one has an interest in making it burdensome for the others.

Moreover, since the alienation is made without reservation, the union is as perfect as possible, and no associate has anything further to demand. For if some rights remained with private individuals, in the absence of any common superior who could decide between them and the public, each person would eventually claim to be his own judge in all things, since he is on some point his own judge. The state of nature would subsist and the association would necessarily become tyrannical or hollow.

Finally, in giving himself to all, each person gives himself to no one. And since there is no associate over whom he does not acquire the same right that he would grant others over himself, he gains the equivalent of everything he loses, along with a greater amount of force to preserve what he has.

If, therefore, one eliminates from the social compact whatever is not essential to it, one will find that it is reducible to the following terms. *Each of us places his person and all his power in common under the supreme direction of the general will; and as one we receive each member as an indivisible part of the whole.*

At once, in place of the individual person of each contracting party, this act of association produces a moral and collective body composed of as many members as there are voices in the assembly, which receives from this same act its unity, its common *self*, its life and its will. This public person, formed thus by union of all the others formerly took the name *city*, and at present takes the name *republic* or *body politic*, which is called *state* by its members when it is passive, *sovereign* when it is active, *power* when compared to others like itself. As to the associates, they collectively take the name *people*; individually they are called *citizens*, insofar as participants in the sovereign authority, and *subjects*, insofar as they are subjected to the laws of the state. But these terms are often confused and mistaken for one another. It is enough to know how to distinguish them when they are used with absolute precision.

Source: From Jean-Jacques Rousseau, *On the Social Contract*, trans. and ed. by Donald A. Cress (Indianapolis: Hackett Publishing Company, Inc., 1987), pp. 23–25. Copyright © 1987 by Hackett Publishing Co., Inc. All rights reserved.

The implications of Rousseau's social-contract theory for educational leadership stems from his notion of human freedom. Government receives its validation from the will of the people as conceptualized through an agreement that preserves their freedom while entrusting to government certain responsibilities that foster the common good of all people. School districts are state-government agencies operating within a limited geographical area for the purpose of providing educational services. School districts exist for the general welfare of the citizenry and as such have an obligation not only to provide the best possible education to children, but also to involve the entire community in developing educational policy if the compact is to be fully realized. This implies that public discourse should be an ongoing method of fulfilling the compact. Administrators are thus charged with developing methods of two-way communication with all constituents.

Jean-François Lyotard's Perceptions About the Current State of the Social Bond

In 1979, Lyotard presented his report concerning the problems of the postmodern period to the education community in the province of Quebec. He viewed the current milieu as producing discontinuity, plurality, and logically unjustified conclusions. The reason for this state of affairs lay in the unprecedented desire in society for expediency, which had seriously lessened the requirement of legitimization in decision making by those in positions of authority.

Thus the current dilemma for all governmental agencies, including school districts, is that the function of regulating and, therefore, of growth and development is being placed under the mindless control of technology. Such technology stores enormous amounts of information, much of which concerns the private lives of people. This information can be manipulated in ways that further invade the privacy of people and can be used by the relatively few individuals who have access to it to make decisions that can affect not only individuals, but society in general.

Further, there is concern that contemporary society is so complex that a common understanding of what people are trying to communicate is virtually impossible. Although the words may be the same, the concepts transmitted by the words may be diverse. Thus, what one person means when he or she states that education must prepare people to make a living in U.S. society can be quite different from what another person means by the same statement. Although such divergence has always existed to a certain extent, today's society contains many more options and these alternatives bring with them countless variations. This situation leads to consideration of certain ethical issues that arise within the context of how the social contract functions in contemporary educational leadership.[7]

Ethical Issues and Contractarianism

Creating a Vision and Goals.   The importance of creating a vision and goals for a school district cannot be overstated. History testifies to this importance in relation to how people achieve change in American society. Consider the intensity of vision that was necessary to bring about equal educational opportunities for members of minority groups, for women, and for people with disabilities. The responsibility for creating the process for developing the vision and goals for a school district rests with the board of education and the superintendent of schools.

The operative phrase here is "creating the process," not "developing the vision and goals." In keeping with the social-contract concept, the board and the superintendent must acknowledge the necessity of involving all stakeholders in the process of developing the vision and goals. Although it would be easier and faster for the board and superintendent to create the vision and set the goals, even if the vision and goals were appropriate the fact that the stakeholders were not involved would mitigate against the very notion of the social contract. The board of education, acting on the recommendation of the superintendent of schools, does have the operative responsibility for the vision and goals, but stakeholders must have the opportunity to provide input.

Establishing the vision and creating the goals of a school district are best carried out through a strategic planning process involving all stakeholders: parents, students, community members, teachers, staff members, and administrators. Although all members of these groups can be given the opportunity to answer questionnaires and attend public forums, efficiency and effectiveness require that the number of strategic-planning-committee members be limited. The best procedure for selecting representatives from the various stakeholder groups is an election, which allows people to choose those by whom they want to be represented.

The process of strategic planning has many models. However, whichever model it follows, the board of education, on the recommendation of the superintendent of schools, should incorporate the following elements into the process:

- Allocate necessary funds
- Initiate the participant-selection process
- Evaluate student-achievement data
- Analyze the culture of the communities in which the children live
- Set deadlines for the planning process
- Conduct a future-instructional-program needs assessment
- Determine the human, financial, materials, and facilities requirements to accomplish the future instructional program

- Set the instructional-program vision and goals based on the culture or cultures of the school district, the needs of the instructional program, and the resources that are or will be available
- Establish benchmarks that will indicate significant progress in reaching the instructional-program vision and goals
- Devise a method for communicating the strategic plan to all stakeholders in the school district
- Set a time for reconvening the strategic-planning committee to evaluate the effectiveness of the strategic plan

It should be clear from this strategic-planning model that the central issue is the instructional program: everything revolves around it, and nothing should take priority over it. From the perspective of educational leadership, implementation of a school district's vision and goals is of primary concern to the superintendent of schools. In all but the smallest school districts, this responsibility is shared by the superintendent with an administrative team composed of assistant superintendents, other central-office administrators, and school principals. In turn, each of these administrators is responsible for implementing the vision and goals with his or her respective staff members. Thus, the assistant superintendent for business who supervises the transportation and food-service programs is responsible for communicating, implementing, and supporting the vision and goals with the bus drivers and cooks. The building principal is responsible for communicating, implementing, and supporting the vision and goals with parents, students, teachers, and staff members in his or her school.

Shared governance in the establishment of a vision and goals for a school district, then, requires shared educational leadership in communicating, implementing, and supporting the vision and goals of the school district. The social contract requires such collaboration to ensure that the implementation will be effective. The notion set forth by Lyotard in terms of the legitimation of decision making is also addressed through shared governance and shared leadership.

Within this context, shared leadership requires certain dispositions exemplified in the following statements:

- All children can learn
- All students should be included in the school community
- High standards of achievement must be held for students, teachers, and staff members
- Children learn in a variety of ways
- Learning is a lifelong process
- Professional development is required for school improvement
- Diversity of cultures is beneficial to the school
- Schools should be safe havens from violence and intimidation
- Schools should prepare students to be contributing members of society

- ◆ Leadership involves taking personal risks to improve schools
- ◆ Leadership involves trusting the judgments of others
- ◆ Families are partners with teachers, staff members, and administrators in the education of children
- ◆ Dialogue with business and political leaders is crucial to the enhancement of educational opportunities for children
- ◆ Members of the community at large should be involved with the schools in the education of children[8]

Community Cultural Assessment.   No school operates in a vacuum. Successful ethical leadership requires administrators to blend the school culture with the culture of the community from which the children come. In some schools this will require the blending of many cultures. Significant numbers of new immigrants have settled in large urban areas as well as in many suburban and rural areas. These people have brought with them cultures that are quite different from those of the immigrants of past generations. This issue is addressed in detail in Chapter 7.

Cultural analysis is the process of trying to identify the history, values, visions, storytellers, rituals, traditions, beliefs, heroes, and heroines of a given culture. This knowledge helps teachers, staff members, and administrators design the curriculum and establish instructional strategies in relation to student learning patterns and interests. Some school districts have established community culture committees charged with providing information about the ethnic populations in the school community. Such information may include a history of the ethnic groups as well as artifacts and literature about their rituals, traditions, and celebrations. Instructional materials for students and parents are also helpful in breaking down barriers that may isolate some people from others in the population.

Information, artifacts, and literature provide a foundation to understanding diversity, but will only be an abstraction unless they are enhanced by regularly bringing into the school community artists, musicians, poets, athletes, artisans, business and industrial leaders, medical specialists, and others from different ethnic backgrounds. Such programs help students develop a positive self-image and ultimately could affect their choice of a career.

A further refinement of the attempt to meld the culture of the community with the culture of the school centers on the notion of celebration. There are two ways to act on this notion. First, celebrating the traditional feasts or holidays of the various ethnic groups can further the appreciation of others for the richness of their culture. Second, celebrating the successes of members of the school community who are from different cultures is another way of acknowledging the importance of everyone and the equality of every culture. The accomplishments of community leaders, parents, teachers, staff members, and administrators, in addition to those of students, should be celebrated.[9] In this way the bond of the social contract can be strengthened.

Reform Expectations. *School reform* has been a catchphrase for the last decade. People have a general idea that public education is in need of reform, but there is great confusion as to what specifically can or should be reformed. There is, however, no doubt that the superintendent of schools is a key player in school reform; the tenuousness of life in the superintendency testifies to this observation. This is the seat of the ethical problem. A new superintendent is expected to reform the schools in the district. This generally means making a decision about what needs to be changed. The superintendent must consider such options as service learning, authentic assessment, computerized instruction, incentive-based pay, privatization of services, empowerment, and site-based management, to name but a few of the many reforms that are on the lips of education critics.

Time is also a consideration. If the superintendent does not initiate change in a relatively short period of time, he or she will be viewed as a failure and the search will begin for a replacement. Rapid turnover in the superintendency is a related problem that particularly affects large, urban districts.

As mentioned earlier, the process for establishing the vision and goals of a school district is not only the most effective way to bring about reform, but it is also a way to ensure the integrity of the social-contract philosophy. Without such a process, teachers, staff members, and administrators are placed in a difficult ethical position. Knowing that the superintendent may want to make a mark on the district as quickly as possible in order to retain his or her job, which is critical for his or her career advancement, the educators in the district may not want to spend time and energy initiating the superintendent's agenda, especially if they have seen a number of superintendents come and go within a short period of time. Such a situation causes teachers, staff members, and administrators to become cynical and resistant.

There are five conditions for bringing about school reform in an ethical manner: [10]

1. The stakeholders must view the reform as being educationally sound.
2. The stakeholders must view the reform as being capable of effectively dealing with an important problem.
3. The strategy for carrying out the reform must be viewed by the stakeholders as viable.
4. The educators must believe that the strategy for initiating the reform does not place an unreasonable burden on them given their other responsibilities.
5. The stakeholders must view the superintendent as trustworthy, credible, and willing to carry through with the reform.

Debureaucratization. Much of the restructuring that is taking place in education involves the debureaucratization of school districts, which is a product of the reform movement. Debureaucratization is accomplished primarily through initiating site-based management. The concept is obvious: remove educational responsibilities as much as possible from the central office and assign these responsibilities to the individual schools. The assumption is that the principal, teachers, and staff members of a given school are in a much better position to make informed decisions concerning the education of children than are central-office administrators.

Some aspects of administration, such as business and human-resource functions, should be performed by the central office. Principals have neither the business nor the legal expertise to perform these functions in isolation from the central office. However, the manner in which these functions are performed can enhance or diminish site-based management. The principal and his or her staff must be involved in both functions in a significant way. For example, the hiring of teachers and staff members should be accomplished on the recommendation of the principal with input from the professional staff and parents; making certain that the school is adhering to affirmative-action guidelines and other legal requirements should be the responsibility of the central office.

Only through this type of decentralization can true site-based management be accomplished. The social-contract approach to leadership requires such debureaucratization. The formalized structure of a central office that dictates administrative policy and initiates controlling procedures for the schools blurs the vision of a school district and hinders the accomplishment of school-district goals.

Empowerment.   The notion of empowerment is embedded in the social contract. A contract implies the acceptance by at least two people of an obligation. There is agreement about what each party to the contract will be responsible for carrying out. School-district leadership has been one-sided through much of its history. The superintendent sent forth his or her wishes and others were responsible for carrying them out. By way of example, this treatment of empowerment will focus on the role and function of the building principal.

The social contract with the principal is based on the position that the principal knows what is best for the students, teachers, and staff members in his or her school and that he or she is a capable professional. On one side of the contract, the superintendent will provide psychological and material support; on the other side of the contract, the principal will provide building-level leadership services to the parents, students, teachers, and staff members. The ethical issues arise in the implementation of the contract.

There are three dimensions of the principal's empowerment: autonomy in decision making, opportunity for professional growth, and professional status. Implementation of these dimensions is predicated on the attitudes of the superintendent and the principal. These three dimensions are easily recognized as essential aspects of good leadership. Most administrators would readily agree that principals must be empowered along these lines if they are to be effective principals. However, the manner in which the superintendent supports a principal and the way the principal functions are ethical situations. Neither the superintendent who unreasonably blames the principal for low student test scores nor the principal who avoids making necessary decisions is fulfilling the social contract.

Privatization.   Whereas most reforms deal with restructuring schools and school districts, privatization removes part or all of the educational enterprise from the public sector. Privatization can range from a private business's funding a specialized program to the contracting out of an entire school program. Three variations of the privatization movement are considered here.

Charter schools are a relatively recent phenomenon. The first charter-school law was passed by Minnesota in 1991. Since then many states have followed this course of action; although the specifics differ, the essence of these laws is the same. The rationale behind the charter-school movement is that people should have an alternative to public education. The major difference between other private schools and charter schools is in the way they are financed: charter schools are financed by public monies. The funding was extended to include federal funds by The Goals 2000: Educate America Act.

Charter schools are established by a charter or contract with a local school district, a state education agency, or a state institution of higher education, such as a community college, college, or university. Charters can be given to a group of parents, a group of teachers from an existing school or a proposed school, an institution of higher education, or any other group that has a particular philosophy of education. The purposes of a charter school are to increase accountability and to give greater autonomy to individual schools. Thus, charter schools are another aspect of the reform movement. To some people, the charter-school approach seems to be an extreme measure. However, if the social-contract philosophy is accepted, charter schools are a legitimate extension of the will of the people as expressed through state and federal legislation.

Performance contracting for specialized services has a rather long history in public education. Private, for-profit companies have been providing bus transportation, food service, and custodial services to school districts for many years. However, another phenomenon, which began in the 1970s, has experienced rapid growth in the last decade—the privatization of instruction. The Sylvan Learning Systems contracted with the Baltimore school district to provide remedial mathematics and reading services to approximately eight hundred students. Other providers of instructional services include the Huntington Learning Centers, Britannica Learning Centers, and the Kaplan Educational Centers.

The most extensive privatization projects are those in which a private company is contracted to operate a school or even an entire school district. For example, in Wichita, Kansas, the for-profit Edison Project contracted to operate two elementary schools; and the Hartford, Connecticut, school district contracted with Education Alternatives Incorporated to operate the entire school system.

If the ethical issue centers on how education can best be delivered to children, then the privatization movement should be appreciated as an alternative approach to education. It meets all the requirements of social-contract philosophy because it is expressed through the legislative vote of the elected representatives of the people.[11]

SCHOOL-DISTRICT LEADERSHIP AND UTILITARIANISM

Utilitarianism is concerned with two basic concepts. First, an action is right if it increases human happiness or if it decreases human misery. Because ethical validity rests on this principle, all actions and institutions are judged accordingly. Second, pleasure is the only good in itself and pain the only evil in itself. Thus, happiness consists of pleasure and freedom from pain.

The origins of utilitarianism lie in Greek thought and captured the imagination of many modern philosophers. In this section the philosophy of John Stuart Mill will be presented. Mill's utilitarianism is rather complicated; he used his ideas to attack the economic, legal, political, and social problems of his time.[12]

The Utilitarianism of John Stuart Mill

In general and in a very simplistic way, the rightness or wrongness of an action can be considered from two points of view: either in the nature of the act itself or in the consequences of the action. School violence, therefore, would be considered wrong because it both violates the principle of self-integrity and produces undesirable consequences. John Stuart Mill (1806–1873) was a proponent of the consequence-oriented approach and set forth the notion that the defining consequence is happiness. Mill believed that people should always choose the actions that bring the most happiness or the least unhappiness to the greatest number of people. He further believed that people should consider both short- and long-term consequences of their actions and should consider the happiness of others as equal in importance to their own.

The concept of utilitarianism appeared in the writings of many philosophers, including those of the English social reformer Jeremy Bentham. Through Bentham, utilitarianism captured the attention of the philosopher and economist James Mill, the father of John Stuart. The elder Mill incorporated the ideas of utilitarianism into the education of his son, who was born in London in 1806. John Stuart was an extremely intelligent child. He studied Greek at the age of three and began learning Latin at age eight. His education included the classics, history, logic, mathematics, and philosophy. Learning was his passion and his legacy. His writings in the areas of epistemology, ethics, logic, the philosophy of science, and social philosophy continue to educate students in many disciplines.

The popularity of his treatise, *Utilitarianism*, probably lies not only in its depth, but also in its brevity. In five short chapters, Mill sets forth the principles of utilitarianism and demonstrates how it is connected to other theories and how it is grounded in human nature. Further, the treatise responds to a number of objections to the concept of utilitarianism. However, what has captured the imagination of many readers is the treatise's relevance to the ordinary moral framework of everyday life.

Some of the objections to utilitarianism will be discussed as a prelude to reading the selection from Mill's work. First, how can people know what will maximize their happiness? This is a practical consideration in the implementation of utilitarianism. It leads to further questions. How can we know who, in the present and in the future, will be affected by a given action? How can we know what will be the effect on each person? How can we know the degree of happiness or unhappiness each individual will experience because of these effects?

Also, there is some doubt about the ethics of following the greatest-happiness principle in certain circumstances. For example, it is not clear that lying will bring less happiness than telling the truth. Since telling the truth is so ingrained in our Western religious tradition, it is difficult to consider lying as a possible alternative to truthfulness.

Mill's reply to these objections is characteristic of his genius. To the objection that the utilitarian approach requires the extensive gathering of information about who will be affected, what the effect will be, and what might be the level of happiness of those affected, Mill stated that the information-gathering process need not begin anew for every decision. Because the past is a highly reliable guide to present situations, the entire past experience of humanity constitutes the information gathering. Thus, according to utilitarianism, the human aversion to lying is explained through past experience, which indicates that truthfulness maximizes happiness.

Although this explanation is satisfactory for most situations, it does seem possible for there to be a situation in which lying would bring the most happiness to the most people. Mill's position, however, insists that lying would bring a general weakening of trust, which ultimately would have disastrous social consequences.

The question of right and wrong is treated in the final chapter of *Utilitarianism*. The argument proceeds as follows: Right and wrong are not simply equivalent to what does or does not maximize happiness; an act that fails to maximize happiness is called wrong only if a person should be punished for doing it; the punishment may be rendered by law, by the opinion of others, or by the reproach of the person's conscience. Further, acts that are unjust are a subset of acts that are wrong. For an act to be unjust, it must violate the rights of a particular person in the sense that it interferes with a valid claim that the person has on society. The claim is that society has an obligation to protect the person in the possession of something through the force of law, the force of education, or the force of opinion. The claim to social protection is determined by general utility; thus, the whole structure of society rests on a utilitarian base.

In the consequence approach of Mill, the most happiness or least unhappiness to the greatest number of people becomes the defining principle. On first consideration this principle may appear to be unrelated to contemporary educational leadership. However, when considered from the vantage point of human experience, the quest for happiness is a primary motivator in most human enterprises. For this reason, it is a most relevant principle for educational administrators. For example, when developing a student rights and responsibilities policy, it can be used as a guiding principle. The happiness of the student body is an important variable when administrators and teachers are trying to create an atmosphere within a school that is conducive to learning. The misunderstanding that often accompanies the idea of utilitarianism is that it is synonymous with license, which is absolutely contrary to the facts. Mill's argument concerning lying illustrates this point: human experience has shown that lying cannot ultimately maximize human happiness.

The orientation toward happiness is important for educational leaders. Too often the negative effects of human interaction can create a mind-set that mitigates a positive point of view. The tenets of utilitarianism can act as a safeguard against negativism.[13]

Ethical Issues and Utilitarianism

Student Achievement.   No issue evokes more controversy than student achievement. Boards of education, parents, and the business community are all extremely interested in the academic progress of students. Teachers, staff members, and administrators are also eager to know the results of standardized-test scores. What some educators fear is the blame that is sometimes laid at their feet for the failure of students to achieve expected results. The issue is very complicated, because test scores by themselves exemplify very little. Some students are so affected by the environment in their homes and neighborhoods that they are distracted from the learning process. Other students consider attaining high test scores the only objective to be reached in school and neglect other aspects of their personal development.

Superintendents must be cognizant of the role test scores play in the development of attitudes about the various schools and the school district. Test scores are important in community relations, especially when a board of education decides to place before the voters a tax-levy increase or a bond issue. Many states require school districts to publish aggregate scores, and in almost every instance the public media compare a school district's test scores with those of other districts. Thus, superintendents must be able to explain how and why the test scores of their students differ from the test scores of students in other districts. Further, they must be able to give an explanation as to why test scores vary from one year to another.

When setting standards of achievement, the superintendent, along with the administrative team, faculty, and staff, must be results orientated. There is no

Selected Reading 4.2

Utilitarianism
John Stuart Mill (1806–1873)

Most of the maxims of justice current in the world, and commonly appealed to in its transactions, are simply instrumental to carrying into effect the principles of justice which we have now spoken of. That a person is only responsible for what he has done voluntarily, or could voluntarily have avoided, that it is unjust to condemn any person unheard; that the punishment ought to be proportioned to the offense, and the like, are maxims intended to prevent the just principle of evil for evil from being perverted to the infliction of evil without that justification. The greater part of these common maxims have come into use from the practice of courts of justice, which have been naturally led to a more complete recognition and elaboration than was likely to suggest itself to others, of the rules necessary to enable them to fulfill their double function, of inflicting punishment when due, and of awarding to each person his right.

The first of judicial virtues, impartiality, is an obligation of justice, partly for the reason last mentioned, as being a necessary condition of the fulfillment of the other obligations of justice. But this is not the only source of the exalted rank, among human obligations, of those maxims of equality and impartiality, which, both in popular estimation and in that of the most enlightened, are included among the precepts of justice. In one point of view, they may be considered as corollaries from the principles already laid down. If it is a duty to do to each according to his deserts, returning good for good, as well as repressing evil by evil, it necessarily follows that we should treat all equally well (when no higher duty forbids) who have deserved equally well of *us*, and that society should treat all equally well who have deserved equally well of *it*, that is, who have deserved equally well absolutely. This is the highest abstract standard of social and distributive justice, towards which all institutions and the efforts of all virtuous citizens should be made in the utmost possible degree to converge. But this great moral duty rests upon a still deeper foundation, being a direct emanation from the first principle of morals, and not a mere logical corollary from secondary or derivative doctrines. It is involved in the very meaning of utility, or the greatest happiness principle. That principle is a mere form of words without rational signification unless one person's happiness, supposed equal in degree (with the proper allowance made for kind), is counted for exactly as much as another's. Those conditions being supplied, Bentham's dictum, "everybody to count for one, nobody for more than one," might be written under the principle of utility as an explanatory commentary. The equal claim of everybody to happiness, in the estimation of the moralist and of the legislator, involves an equal claim to all the means of happiness except in so far as the inevitable conditions of human life and the general interest in which that of every individual is included set limits to the maxim; and those limits ought to be strictly construed. As every other maxim of justice, so this is by no means applied or held applicable universally; on the contrary, as I have already remarked, it bends to every person's ideas of social expediency. But in whatever case it is deemed applicable at all, it is held to be the dictate of justice. All persons are deemed to have a *right* to equality of treatment, except when some recognized social expediency requires the reverse. And hence all social inequalities which have ceased to be considered expedient assume the character, not of simple inexpediency, but of injustice, and appear so tyrannical that people are apt to wonder how they ever could have been tolerated—forgetful that they themselves, perhaps, tolerate other inequalities under an equally mistaken notion of expediency, the correction of which would make that which they approve seem quite as monstrous as what they have at last learned to condemn. The entire history of social improvement has been a series of transitions by which one custom or institution after another, from being a supposed primary necessity of social existence, has passed into the rank of a universally stigmatized injustice and tyranny. So it has been with the distinctions of slaves and freemen, nobles and serfs, patricians and plebeians; and so it will be, and in part already is, with the aristocracies of color, race, and sex.

It appears from what has been said that justice is a name for certain moral requirements which, regarded collectively, stand higher in the scale of social utility, and are therefore of more paramount obligation, than any other, though particular cases may occur in which some other social duty is so important as to overrule any one of the general maxims of justice. Thus, to save a life, it may not only be allowable, but a duty, to steal or take by force the necessary food or medicine, or to kidnap and compel to officiate the only qualified medical practitioner. In such cases, as we do not call anything justice which is not a virtue, we usually say, not that justice must give way to some other moral principle, but that what is just in ordinary cases is, by reason of that other principle, not just in the particular case. By this useful accommodation of language, the character of indefeasibility attributed to justice is kept up, and we are saved from the necessity of maintaining that there can be laudable injustice.

The considerations which have now been adduced resolve, I conceive, the only real difficulty in the utilitarian theory of morals. It has always been evident that all cases of justice are also cases of expediency; the difference is in the peculiar sentiment which attaches to the former, as contradistinguished from the latter. If this characteristic sentiment has been sufficiently accounted for; if there is no necessity to assume for it any peculiarity of origin; if it is simply the natural feeling of resentment, moralized by being made co-extensive with the demands of social good; and if this feeling not only does but ought to exist in all the classes of cases to which the idea of justice corresponds—that idea no longer presents itself as a stumbling block to the utilitarian ethics. Justice remains the appropriate name for certain social utilities which are vastly more important, and therefore more absolute and imperative, than any others are as a class (though not more so than others may be in particular cases); and which, therefore, ought to be, as well as naturally are, guarded by a sentiment, not only different in degree, but also in kind; distinguished from the milder feeling which attaches to the mere idea of promoting human pleasure or convenience at once by the more definite nature of its commands and by the sterner character of its sanctions.

other justifiable way to proceed. However, the use of standardized-test scores is only one measure of success. Criterion-referenced test scores, pupil observations, and student grades are also measures of success. Establishing a benchmark for continual progress toward success is the key to all authentic assessment.[14]

The use of student achievement as the criterion on which decisions can be made concerning the quality of the instructional program and subsequently making changes that will benefit students based on that achievement is utilitarian in nature. The objective is to enhance the future happiness of students by providing them with the best possible education. Parents, teachers, staff members, administrators, and members of the community also experience an increase in their happiness because of successful student achievement, and their future happiness will be increased because the students are on their way to becoming contributing members of society.

Curriculum Development.   The process used to design, deliver, and evaluate the curriculum can be either beneficial or detrimental to students. The primary goal for a school district is to offer a sequential curriculum, preschool through twelfth grade, that will prepare students to be well-rounded, knowledgeable, capable of self-determination, and capable of being productive members of society. This goal implies that students will be given the opportunity to develop their intellectual, emotional, physical, and psychological capabilities.

The issue of individual differences is an important variable in the curriculum-development process. Not all students learn in the same way; not all students can learn the same amount of material; and not all students can develop their capabilities to the same level. Thus, the curriculum must resemble a continuum rather than a fixed standard. However, each student must be given the opportunity to grow and develop to the fullest extent possible. Therefore, implementing the curriculum must include services to assist students in making full use of their educational opportunities. From this perspective, counseling, social work, and other support services become necessary to the delivery of the curriculum.

In like manner, implementing the curriculum must include support services for teachers and other staff members who have curricular responsibilities. Staff-development programs are the usual vehicles for helping teachers adapt and strategize on curriculum delivery.

As with student achievement, the design, delivery, and improvement of the curriculum based on effective program evaluation contributes to the happiness of the students, of the professional staff, and of the community in general. Student happiness is significantly increased when the curriculum is focused on the development of the entire person and when the intention is to maximize development of each person's capabilities. Utilitarianism is an appropriate philosophy for the educational leader to use as a guide in carrying out his or her academic responsibilities.

Human-Resource Leadership.   From the perspective of the central office, the human-resources function is concerned with recruiting, selecting, placing, appraising, retaining, and compensating administrators, teachers, and staff members. This is perhaps the most important central-office function because the quality of the instructional program is directly related to the quality of the professional educators employed by the school district. Further, these professional educators could not perform their responsibilities in the most effective way without quality support staff. As personnel needs are directly related to the instructional program, the human-resources function usually begins with a master planning process during which present and future personnel needs are identified.

Three of the most important ethical issues with regard to human resources are affirmative action and equal employment opportunity, personnel evaluation and due process, and fair and equitable compensation.

Affirmative action and equal employment opportunity are mandates of all civil rights legislation that affect employment. Affirmative action requires school districts to evaluate and take corrective measures that ensure the representation of women and minorities in the workforce. The usual criterion is the makeup of the community served by the school district. If 60 percent of the people in a community are Hispanic, the school district should try to have a workforce that is 60 percent Hispanic. To achieve the goal of affirmative action, a school district must devise a recruitment process that will encourage qualified women and members of minority groups to apply for all categories of positions.

Equal employment opportunity means eliminating bias in the hiring and promotion processes. All qualified people should be considered for positions based solely on their qualifications. Age, disability, ethnic origin, religion, and all other designations should have no influence in hiring and promoting people.

Personnel evaluation is an extremely important process in a school district. Because the business of a district is providing human services, the purpose of evaluation is to improve the service. The manner in which the evaluation process is conducted is critical. Fairness and objectivity on the part of the evaluator are concerns of teachers, staff members, and administrators. Further, the due process provided to a person who receives an unsatisfactory evaluation can make the difference between making successful improvements or failing. Mentoring and other types of staff-development opportunities could help marginal employees become proficient in carrying out their responsibilities.

Although salary and fringe benefits have been improving, the education profession still falls short of other professions in relation to compensation. Competition between school districts is keen for special-education teachers, teachers of English as a second language, and guidance counselors. School districts that pay higher salaries and provide good benefits can usually attract good teachers in general as well as teachers with special skills that are in short supply.

The utilitarian philosophy can be employed to set the direction in human-resource administration. Because every ethnic group can be a minority, depending on the makeup of the community, because everyone can at some time fall short of performance expectations, and because U.S. society is based on the free-market approach, fair and equitable human-resource policies and procedures will provide happiness to most of the people most of the time.

Fiscal Accountability.   Some superintendents have been fired because they did not pay attention to the financial condition of their school districts. The fiscal integrity of a district is always a consideration. Some parents, teachers, staff members, administrators, boards of education, and communities in general are probably more concerned with the fiscal condition of their school district than with any other function. Indeed, the quality of the instructional program will be significantly affected by the financial health of a school district. A financially distressed district may lack supplies, materials, adequate facilities, and the best employees. This does not mean that a district with inadequate financing will not have good employees, but it does mean that such a district will have difficulty attracting and keeping employees if neighboring districts pay higher salaries and provide better benefits. Of course, there will always be some teachers, staff members, and administrators who will remain with a district even when salary increases are not forthcoming.

Fiscal integrity is usually exemplified through an ongoing process of revenue projecting, expenditure budgeting, budget monitoring, and auditing. The process is cyclic and its components overlap. The only effective way for a superintendent to monitor the financial function of a school district when that function is managed by an assistant superintendent or business manager is through a monthly budget operating report. The proper objective check on the financial function occurs through the hiring of an independent auditing firm to conduct a yearly audit.

The importance of the monthly budget operating report and the independent audit resides in the trust that these procedures generate. Employees and taxpayers will have confidence in a superintendent who understands the necessity of financial integrity. This confidence could be the reason that voters approve an increase in their tax levy when the school district needs additional revenue.

In a financially sound school district, students will have the quantity and quality of supplies and materials they need, along with adequate facilities. Further, school-district employees will receive a compensation package that allows them to remain with the district. What emanates from the ethical response of the superintendent in relation to the fiscal health of the school district is the increased happiness of all stakeholders.

Stress in the Superintendency.   The milieu within which educational leadership is practiced today is quite different from what it was even a decade age. A hallmark of this milieu is stress. In educational leadership stress is fostered by the fact that contemporary educational problems and issues seldom lend themselves to simple solutions. Complexity brings ambiguity and uncertainty. Yes or no answers have given way to *maybe*. What was once certain is now questionable. This is particularly true in relation to both pupil and employee issues and problems. The proper response to an issue involving student discipline can differ according to the circumstances surrounding a given event. Further, drug abuse and student violence prompt problems that require educational administrators to engage in profound deliberation before making a decision, for any decision not only could be injurious to the people involved, but also could have legal implications for the administrator and the school district.

Even seemingly noncontroversial actions, such as purchasing supplies and materials, might have political implications in the business community that are not readily apparent. The rights and responsibilities of taxpayers, parents, students, and employees seem to be open to interpretation on almost every issue.

Further, the time and energy required to deal with all these issues often seem to extend far beyond what is reasonable.

The utilitarian approach of making decisions that will produce the greatest happiness for the greatest number of people applies to the life of the superintendent and all central-office administrators. Implementing this approach is the problem. The first requirement is the happiness of the administrator. An unhappy person will have a higher level of stress than will a happy person.

There are several ways in which superintendents can reduce stress. Most important is for the superintendent to build and maintain a support system of family members and friends. The stoic approach does not help reduce stress and ultimately can affect a person's mental and physical well-being. This support system can extend to people in the business and professional communities who can provide feedback and help when the superintendent is faced with situations that require an unusual amount of critical consideration. Superintendents need to develop an approach to criticism that enables them to draw a distinction between criticism that is personal and criticism that is aimed at the office. Most criticism is aimed at the office.

Continually upgrading management and organizational skills is also key. Much can be learned through a personalized self-improvement strategy that incorporates attendance at conferences and workshops. Spending time away from the school district and engaging in activities and interests that are not work related can help alleviate stress in addition to helping develop a balanced perspective on life. Finally, good physical health habits are extremely important. Exercise, healthy eating, adequate sleep, and responsible use of alcohol, along with engaging in entertainment activities, make work-related problems and issues less onerous.[15]

PROFESSIONALISM IN SCHOOL-DISTRICT LEADERSHIP

The codes of ethics for four professional organizations are included as appendices for this chapter:

Appendix 4.1: The Code of Ethics of the American Association of School Administrators

Appendix 4.2: The Standards of Conduct of the Association of School Business Officials International

Appendix 4.3: Belief Statements of the Association for Supervision and Curriculum Development

Appendix 4.4: Code of Ethics for School Board Members

The codes differ in some respects but are identical in others. The people for whom the codes were developed have different responsibilities in the educational enterprise, and this is reflected in the content and tone of each code's tenets.

The code of the American Association of School Administrators (AASA) begins by acknowledging that it was written for all administrators and has as its purpose the establishment of both idealistic and practical guidelines for administrator conduct. The code further establishes that the schools belong to the public and that the administrator is called upon to provide leadership in both the school and the community. This obligation of leadership to the community is an important component of this code. The introduction to the various tenets of the code ends with a clear statement about the responsibility of the administrator to exhibit exemplary professional conduct. The tenets of AASA's code speak to student well-being as the fundamental value in all decision making and support honesty and fairness in carrying out all responsibilities. There are also proactive tenets, which challenge the administrator to change laws, policies, and procedures that are not consistent with sound educational goals; and the administrator is admonished to seek improvement of the profession through research and continuing professional development.

The Association of School Business Officials International (ASBO) has adopted both a code of ethics and standards of conduct. The code of ethics is identical to AASA's code. The standards of conduct are more specific to the business function of school districts and are directed to satisfying some concerns of the movement toward accountability. The standards deal with the school business official's relationships within the school district, his or her conduct in carrying out business responsibilities, and his or her relationships with colleagues in other districts and in professional associations. Within the district, the school business official is expected to give complete support to district goals and objectives and to carry out his or her responsibilities in a fair and objective manner while supporting other employees. In conducting business, the official must act in such a way that there will be no question about his or her honesty and integrity. Finally, in relation to colleagues in other districts and in professional associations, the school business official is to be supportive and collaborative and is to avoid any situation that could indicate that he or she is motivated by personal gain.

In its belief statements the Association for Supervision and Curriculum Development (ASCD) asserts that the intrinsic worth and dignity of the person are the guiding principle in all educational endeavors. Further, diversity of cultures enriches and strengthens society and thus is crucial to the democratic way of life. ASCD challenges organizations such as school districts to recognize that organizational health is predicated on self-renewal and that the culture of an organization contributes to appropriate individual attitudes and behaviors. This culture is shaped by shared values and common goals.

The code of ethics of the National School Boards Association (NSBA) is concerned with the responsibility of board members to create policies for school districts that are fair and equitable to all students and employees and have been fashioned after informed discussion and debate. Certain tenets deal with the role and function of the board of education in relation to the role and function of the superintendent of schools. The code of ethics certainly supports the importance of educational administration and the ethical statements of associations of administrators. The code of ethics has been included in this chapter because of the significant impact that boards of education have on educational leadership.

OTHER PHILOSOPHICAL APPROACHES TO THE ISSUES IN THIS CHAPTER

When Bertrand Russell published *Principia Mathematica* in collaboration with Alfred North Whitehead, the analytical movement in philosophy took a giant leap forward. The movement split into two schools: the formalists, represented by Russell, and the linguists, represented by Ludwig Wittgenstein.

The formalists utilized the scientific method in philosophical analysis and developed a modern logical technique that was couched in very technical language. In applying the scientific method to problems of philosophy, Russell began with the results or consequences of an issue and then worked backward to uncover the premises that had caused the phenomenon. Thus, data are complex but interrelated; the philosopher formulates the data into propositions, which are then arranged into a deductive chain of propositions. The propositions are more precise and simpler than the data.

In using the analytical approach to ethics, a superintendent would develop a series of propositions about issues that require his or her support or decision. In essence, the propositions become the guidelines that the superintendent applies when confronted with an ethical problem or dilemma.

The linguistic branch, of course, believes that ethical problems and issues emanate from the nuances of language and that they can be cleared up by a careful examination of language. Wittgenstein held the position that language is an activity in which a person uses part of his or her experience, such as words and images, to represent other dimensions of experience. Thus, language and thought are inseparable but are capable of being clarified. The limits of language constitute the limits of what is knowable. In educational leadership the ethics of an action are thus predicated on the superintendent's understanding of what people are saying about a situation.

CROSSWALK TO ISLLC STANDARD FIVE

The contents of this chapter support the following dimensions of ISLLC Standard Five:

Knowledge

The administrator has knowledge and understanding of:

♦ various ethical frameworks and perspectives on ethics

♦ professional codes of ethics

Dispositions

The administrator believes in, values, and is committed to:

♦ the principles in the Bill of Rights

♦ the right of every student to a free, quality education

♦ using the influence of one's office constructively and productively in the service of all students and their families

♦ development of a caring school community

Performances

The administrator:

♦ demonstrates a personal and professional code of ethics

♦ serves as a role model

♦ accepts responsibility for school operations

♦ uses the influence of the office to enhance the educational program rather than for personal gain

♦ treats people fairly, equitably, and with dignity and respect

♦ protects the rights and confidentiality of students and staff

♦ expects that others in the school community will demonstrate integrity and exercise ethical behavior

♦ opens the school to public scrutiny

♦ fulfills legal and contractual obligations

♦ applies laws and procedures fairly, wisely, and considerately

ETHICAL CONSIDERATIONS PRESENTED IN THIS CHAPTER

♦ In school-district governance the general will of the people in the district as expressed through the decisions of their elected representatives constitutes the social contract under which the district operates.

♦ Expediency has produced a pervasive state of affairs in which the legitimation of some decisions is called into question.

- ◆ In school districts the storage and manipulation of data through technology can be a threat to the confidentiality of information concerning students and employees.

- ◆ The contemporary school district is so complex that it is difficult to have a common understanding of what people are trying to communicate.

- ◆ Creating a vision for a school district based on community cultural assessment is necessary in order to bring about change in the school district.

- ◆ The debureaucratization of a school district and the empowerment of stakeholders can strengthen the social bond within the school district.

- ◆ In making decisions, educational leaders should attempt to bring the most happiness to the greatest number of people without violating the rights of individuals.

∽ SUMMARY

The contractarian approach is embedded in the writings of many philosophers, each with a slightly different perspective on the notion of the social contract.

John Locke accepted the social contract as a historical fact, although there is no evidence that any society was established by a contract. Locke believed that society is only an aggregate of independent and sovereign individuals and that the role of society is to protect the rights of these individuals. The notion that individual rights have priority over the common good is prevalent in Locke's works.

The writing of Jean-Jacques Rousseau is of particular interest. His *On the Social Contract* serves as the base for much of contemporary social and ethical thought. In this work, Rousseau champions the cause of the common person and government by the people. Rousseau proceeded from a statement of principle and not from a historical event. He was searching for a first, logical and incontrovertible, principle by which people could defend their actions. That principle can be simply stated as People are born free. Rousseau's objective was to establish a principle that could be used by people in determining what is right or wrong and what will be the correct course for future actions.

Another key notion is that each person places his or her personal will and all his or her options under the direction of the general will of the collective majority through acceptance of the process by which people in the aggregate make decisions. From this arises Rousseau's concept of the public person who is formed by the will of all other persons and who embodies the sovereignty of the public institution. This sovereignty is exercised through a representative form of government. Finally, when a person gives over his or her will to the general will, he or she gives this personal attribute to no one person. From this perspective the individual loses nothing that he or she does not gain over others through this same process.

Because school districts are state-government agencies, they exist for the general welfare of the citizenry and as such have an obligation not only to provide the best possible education to children, but also to involve the entire community in developing educational policy if the social contract is to be fully realized.

The concept of the social contract was further refined by Jean-François Lyotard through a report given in 1979 to the education community in Quebec, Canada. In Lyotard's view, the current milieu is producing discontinuity, plurality, and logically unjustified conclusions. The unprecedented societal desire for expediency has seriously lessened the requirement of legitimation in decision making by those in positions of authority. This situation is a direct outgrowth of the extensive use of technology in decision making and of the lack of true communication among people owing to the complexity of modern society.

An important issue for educational leaders is creating a vision and goals for a school district. Devising the process for creating the vision and goals is the responsibility of the board of education and the superintendent of schools and is best accomplished through a strategic-planning process that involves all school-district stakeholders. The superintendent of schools must share leadership with others in communicating, implementing, and supporting the vision and goals of the school district.

Community cultural assessment is played out through melding the cultures of the community with the culture of the school district. A very diversified community strengthens and enriches the culture of individual schools and of the school district.

School reform is another area that requires ethical consideration. The superintendent of schools is key in bringing about reform, but can be successful only if the stakeholders trust him or her and believe that he or she will be there to see the reform come to a conclusion.

Debureaucratization is a specific school reform that is best understood from the perspective of site-based management. The assumption is that the principal, teachers, and staff members of a given school are in a much better position to make informed decisions concerning the education of students than are central-office administrators. In consort with site-based management is the notion of empowerment, through which principals recognize that they have autonomy in making decisions. Further, the superintendent must support the professional growth of principals and must find ways to enhance their professional status. Privatization of services to students can mean the contracting out of transportation or instruction or even of management of an entire school or school district. When privatization of education is carried out through the expressed vote of the elected representatives of the people, it meets the requirements of the social contract.

The utilitarian principle that an action is right if it increases human happiness or if it decreases human misery can be an effective guiding principle in educational leadership. John Stuart Mill took a consequence-oriented approach to utilitarianism. Simply stated, people should always choose those actions that bring the most happiness to the greatest number of people. This principle should be operationalized in the context of both short- and long-term consequences. Further, a person should consider the happiness of others as equal in importance to his or her own happiness.

Mill believed that people can know what will maximize their happiness and who will be affected by decisions because the process for understanding these considerations does not need to begin anew with every situation. The entire past experience of humanity constitutes reliable information that can be used to make decisions.

Because the quest for happiness is a primary motivator in most human enterprises, it can be an extremely helpful guideline for educational leaders as they carry out their responsibilities. Certain ethical issues in educational leadership are particularly well-suited to solution through exercising of the utilitarian principle. The role of student achievement in setting instructional standards that ultimately will benefit the future happiness of students and gain the approval of taxpayers and the business community is validated through the utilitarian principle. When the school curriculum is focused on the development of the entire person and the intention is to maximize each person's capabilities, educational leaders are increasing the happiness of most students.

The human-resources function is concerned with the recruitment, selection, placement, appraisal, retention, and compensation of all school-district employees. It is key to a quality instructional program because the instructional program is dependent on the quality of the people who are hired to provide direct educational services to students and to support the educators. Three specific issues that concern human resources are affirmative action and equal employment opportunity, personnel evaluation and due process, and fair and equitable compensation. These three issues can be effectively managed through the exercise of the utilitarian principle.

Fiscal accountability means that taxpayers and other stakeholders are able to have confidence that the superintendent of schools and other administrators are managing the financial resources of the school district in an effective and efficient manner. This confidence on the part of taxpayers and stakeholders could be very important to the future happiness of students and employees should the district seek an increase in tax revenue.

The attitude of the superintendent of schools must be considered because the superintendent is responsible for the proper functioning of the entire school district. The contemporary milieu within which educational leadership is exercised is complex and stressful. The utilitarian principle can be an important guide to the superintendent as he or she considers how to maintain a balance between personal life and professional responsibilities.

The codes of ethics for the American Association of School Administrators, the Association of School Business Officials International, the Association for Supervision and Curriculum Development, and the National School Boards Association support the integrity and dignity of professional educators, the value of public education, the centrality of student welfare, and the importance of educational opportunity.

~ DISCUSSION QUESTIONS AND STATEMENTS

1. Compare the social-contract ideas of Jean-Jacques Rousseau and John Locke.
2. Explain how Rousseau's notion of the social contract relates to school-district leadership.
3. How does Jean-François Lyotard's analysis of contemporary society apply to school-district leadership?
4. What is an effective way to create a vision and goals for a school district?
5. Describe the elements that should go into a strategic-planning process.
6. List some leadership dispositions that an administrator should possess in order to be a visionary leader.
7. Explain the importance of initiating community cultural assessment.
8. How can a superintendent of schools effectively bring about change in a school district?
9. Explain the relationship between debureaucratization and empowerment.
10. Is the privatization of education in consort with the concept of the social contract?
11. Explain John Stuart Mill's utilitarian principle.
12. What are the implications of the greatest-happiness principle for school-district leadership?
13. How does the utilitarian philosophy relate to the issues of student achievement and curriculum development?
14. How does the utilitarian philosophy relate to the issues of human resources and fiscal accountability?
15. Explain how utilitarian principles can help superintendents deal with stress.
16. Discuss the tenets of the ethics statements of the American Association of School Administrators, the Association of School Business Officials International, the Association for Supervision and Curriculum Development, and the National School Boards Association.

∽ CASE STUDY 4.1

A Collective Negotiations Impasse

It is the fourth year of a five-year agreement between the board of education and the teachers' union. The provision for renegotiation of the master contract calls for the process to begin the year before the contract expires. The board's team consists of three principals; one each from an elementary school, a middle school, and the high school. The assistant superintendent for business and financial services and the director of human resources have been appointed by the superintendent of schools to the negotiating team. The director of human resources is the chairperson of the board's team and also the spokesperson for the team at the negotiating table.

The teachers' union took a similar approach in selecting three teachers; one each from an elementary school, a middle school, and the high school. The local teachers' union president appointed a special-education teacher to the team, and the regional office of the union assigned a consultant to the team who has had extensive experience in negotiations. The consultant will assume the role of spokesperson for the union at the negotiating table and will act as the chairperson of the teachers' team.

In preparation for negotiations, both the board's representatives and the union's representatives have polled their respective constituents about issues and concerns that have arisen since the present contract was negotiated. The board's team was particularly interested in the opinions of building principals, who identified two major issues: the need to assign extra duty to teachers because of a hiring freeze due to budget constraints and more required staff development for teachers who need to upgrade their instructional skills. The union's team, of course, was interested in the opinions of the teachers, who identified three areas of concern: the need for a salary increase large enough to make the teacher salary schedule comparable and competitive with the salary schedules of surrounding school districts; the need for more security in schools, particularly in relation to gang activities; and the need for more class preparation time.

The chairpersons met in order to establish the ground rules for at-the-table negotiating and agreed that the union would present its proposals first, with a brief rationale and explanation. The board's team could then ask clarifying questions. The board's team would follow the same procedure of presenting proposals with a brief rationale and explanation. The union could then ask clarifying questions.

It was believed that having experienced negotiators on both sides would help bring the process to a speedy conclusion. Both the board and the union also knew that the necessary mechanism for success was a willingness to compromise, and both sides were ready to do just that. The negotiations proceeded as planned until the issue of extra duty reached the table. The board's team tried to convince the union's team that budgetary constraints were so severe that it was impossible even to hire replacements for some positions that had become vacant during the school year. These positions included teacher assistants, who were used to supervise the playground, the cafeteria, and the loading and unloading of children on and off the school buses. The most important use of teacher assistants, however, was as substitute teachers, because of the difficulty in getting qualified substitutes to work for the lower rate of pay than that offered by surrounding school districts. This practice of using assistants as substitutes meant that teachers were left to handle large classes of approximately thirty students without assistants.

The two spokespersons had discussed impasse procedures during their preliminary discussion about procedures. They had agreed on mediation and fact finding, in that order. Arbitration was rejected because both felt that this procedure subverted the decision-making responsibilities of both the board and the union. After repeated attempts to arrive at a compromise, negotiations broke off, and both sides decided to wait a few days before returning to the table. The board's team met with the superintendent and the board of education to seek clarification about the district's position on this issue; the union's team met with representatives of the membership in order to get their reaction to the impasse. Both sides were adamant in their positions. The board's and union's spokespersons met briefly before the negotiations session as a courtesy and to discuss how the impasse procedures would be implemented.

There were no surprises. Both sides agreed to disagree and acknowledged that an impasse had occurred, which was the official requirement for beginning the impasse procedure. Because mediation was the agreed-upon first step, each team submitted the names of three potential mediators to the other team. The teams ranked the names, and then the spokespersons attempted to reach a consensus as to who would be the best mediator. A university professor of educational leadership with expertise in collective negotiations in terms of experience, research, and teaching was selected as the mediator.

However, the issue was more significant and emotional than had previously been understood by the negotiating teams and the mediator. The teachers believed that it was more than a time-on-task issue; they felt that the administration and the board of education did not understand or care about the demands of teaching. They considered it an insult that they were paid less and expected to do more than their colleagues in neighboring school districts.

The executive committee of the teachers' union called a general meeting of the teachers to allow them to vent their frustrations with the mediator. This was not the mediator's usual procedure, but it was obvious that he had to have a better understanding of the emotional reaction of the teachers. The meeting was not very productive, and several vocal members threatened to lead the teachers into a strike over the issue. The executive committee authorized informational picketing as a method of bringing the teachers' concern to the attention of the parents and other citizens of the district.

The mediator was extremely frustrated and suggested that a fact-finding committee be established to verify the information the two negotiating teams had been using at the table. The financial information in particular was questioned. Before a committee could be chosen and convened, however, the teachers voted to go on strike and immediately walked. It was a dramatic and drastic measure, and completely unexpected by both teams.

The board of education quickly met in executive session to develop a strategy for action. The board's attorney outlined the legal position of the district, explaining that it was in violation of a state statute for teachers to strike. The board unanimously voted to seek an injunction against the union that would require teachers to return to the classrooms. An injunction was obtained, and the state circuit court ordered the union officials to have the teachers return to work. The penalty for disobeying the injunction was a five-hundred-dollar-a-day fine against the union, and possible jailing of the union officials if the strike did not end.

The teachers were also beginning to feel the disfavor of the parents, who had little sympathy for the teachers. After three days of discussion with influential teacher representatives, the union officials were able to convince the teachers that the best course of action was to end the strike, which they did.

Obviously, mediation had not worked. The two chairpersons discussed the possibility of returning to the table with the hope of arriving at some workable solution to the issue before the taxpayers and parents completely lost confidence not only in the board but also in the administration and teachers. They decided to present as a joint proposal the following: the board would agree to lift the hiring freeze, and the union would set aside the salary issue for a period of six months, during which preparations would be made to present a tax-increase referendum to the taxpayers. The expectation was that the board, administration, and teachers would support and work toward passage of the tax increase. Meanwhile, the negotiations would continue. After the referendum, both teams would meet to negotiate the salary issue.

Discussion Questions and Statements

1. Compare and contrast the collective-negotiations process from both contractarian and utilitarian perspectives.

2. Is the collective-negotiations process compatible with strategic planning?

3. Did the board of education act in accordance with the code of ethics for school board members?

4. How does the agreement between the board and the union to seek a tax increase meet the requirements of contractarianism?

5. Explain how John Stuart Mill's idea of the most happiness for the greatest number of people is operationalized through collective negotiations.

6. How does the sanction set forth in the court-ordered injunction conform to utilitarian principles?

7. Explain how the actions of the administrators on the board's team were in conformity with the code of ethics of the American Association of School Administrators.

8. How is Jean-Jacques Rousseau's principle that people are born free reflected in the collective-negotiations process?

SELECTED BIBLIOGRAPHY

Council of Chief State School Officers. *Interstate School Leaders Licensure Consortium: Standards for School Leaders.* Washington, D.C.: Council of Chief State School Officers, 1996.

Fullan, Michael. *Change Forces: The Sequel.* Philadelphia: Falmer Press, 1999.

Galbraith, J. *The Good Society.* Boston: Houghton Mifflin Co., 1996.

Johnson, Susan Moore. *Leading to Change: The Challenge of the New Superintendency.* San Francisco: Jossey-Bass Publishers, 1996.

Lutz, Frank W., ed. "Peabody Journal of Education." *The American Superintendency and the Vulnerability Thesis,* vol. 71, no. 2 (1996).

Lyotard, Jean-François. *The Postmodern Condition: A Report on Knowledge.* Trans. Geoff Bennington and Brian Masumi. Minneapolis: University of Minnesota Press, 1984.

Mill, John Stuart. *Utilitarianism.* Ed. George Sher. Indianapolis: Hackett Publishing Company, Inc., 1979.

Norton, M. Scott, L. Deal Webb, Larry L. Dlugosh, and Ward Sybouts. *The School Superintendency: New Responsibilities, New Leadership.* Needham Heights, Mass.: Allyn & Bacon, 1996.

Pojman, Louis. *Ethics: Discovering Right and Wrong.* Belmont, Calif.: Wadsworth Publishing Company, 1990.

Rousseau, Jean-Jacques. *On the Social Contract, or Principles of Political Right.* Ed. and trans. Charles M. Sherover. New York: New American Library, 1974.

Sharp, William L. *The School Superintendent: The Profession and the Person.* Lancaster, Pa.: Technomic Publishing Company, Inc., 1997.

Statement of Ethics of the American
Association of School Administrators

An educational administrator's professional behavior must conform to an ethical code. The code must be idealistic and at the same time practical so that it can apply reasonably to all educational administrators. The administrator acknowledges that the schools belong to the public they serve for the purpose of providing educational opportunities to all. However, the administrator assumes responsibility for providing professional leadership in the school and community. This responsibility requires the administrator to maintain standards of exemplary professional conduct. It must be recognized that the administrator's actions will be viewed and appraised by the community, professional associates and students. To these ends, the administrator subscribes to the following statements of standards.

The educational administrator:

1. Makes the well-being of students the fundamental value in all decision making and actions.

2. Fulfills professional responsibilities with honesty and integrity.

3. Supports the principle of due process and protects the civil and human rights of all individuals.

4. Obeys local, state and national laws and does not knowingly join or support organizations that advocate, directly or indirectly, the overthrow of the government.

5. Implements the governing board of education's policies and administrative rules and regulations.

6. Pursues appropriate measures to correct those laws, policies and regulations that are not consistent with sound educational goals.

7. Avoids using positions for personal gain through political, social, religious, economic or other influence.

8. Accepts academic degrees or professional certification only from duly accredited institutions.

9. Maintains the standards and seeks to improve the effectiveness of the profession through research and continuing professional development.

10. Honors all contracts until fulfillment or release.

Source: American Association of School Administrators, *Statement of Ethics* (Arlington, Va.: American Association of School Administrators, 1996). Reprinted by permission.

Standards of Conduct for the Association of School Business Officials International

Now, especially in this age of accountability, when the activities and conduct of school business officials are subject to greater scrutiny and more severe criticism than ever before, Standards of Conduct are in order. The Association cannot fully discharge its obligation of leadership and service to its members short of establishing appropriate standards of behavior.

In relationships within the school district it is expected that the school business official will:

1. Support the goals and objectives of the employing school system.
2. Interpret the policies and practices of the district to subordinates and to the community fairly and objectively.
3. Implement, to the best of the official's ability, the policies and administrative regulations of the district.
4. Assist fellow administrators as appropriate in fulfilling their obligations.
5. Build the best possible image of the school district.
6. Refrain from publicly criticizing board members, administrators or other employees.
7. Help subordinates achieve their maximum potential through fair and just treatment.

In the conduct of business and the discharge of responsibilities, the school business official will:

1. Conduct business honestly, openly, and with integrity.
2. Avoid conflict of interest situations by not conducting business with a company or firm in which the official or any member of the official's family has a vested interest.
3. Avoid preferential treatment of one outside interest group, company or individual over another.
4. Uphold the dignity and decorum of the office in every way.
5. Avoid using the position for personal gain.

6. Never accept or offer illegal payment for services rendered.

7. Refrain from accepting gifts, free services, or anything of value for or because of any act performed or withheld.

8. Permit the use of school property only for official authorized activities.

9. Refrain from soliciting contributions from subordinates or outside sources for gifts or donations to a superior.

In relationships with colleagues in other districts and professional associations, it is expected that the school business official will:

1. Support the actions of a colleague whenever possible, never publicly criticizing or censuring the official.

2. Offer assistance and/or guidance to a colleague when such help is requested or when the need is obvious.

3. Actively support appropriate professional associations aimed at improving school business management, and encourage colleagues to do likewise.

4. Accept leadership roles and responsibilities when appropriate, but refrain from "taking over" any association.

5. Refrain from using any organization or position of leadership in it for personal gain.

Source: Association of School Business Officials International, *Standards of Conduct* (Reston, Va.: Association of School Business Officials International, 1996). Reprinted by permission.

Belief Statements of the Association for Supervision and Curriculum Development

Fundamental to ASCD is our concern for people, both individually and collectively.

♦ We believe that the individual has intrinsic worth.

♦ We believe that all people have the ability and the need to learn.

♦ We believe that all children have a right to safety, love, and learning.

♦ We believe that a high-quality, public system of education open to all is imperative for society to flourish.

♦ We believe that diversity strengthens society and should be honored and protected.

♦ We believe that broad, informed participation committed to a common good is critical to democracy.

♦ We believe that humanity prospers when people work together.

ASCD also recognizes the potential and power of a healthy organization.

♦ We believe that healthy organizations purposefully provide for self-renewal.

♦ We believe that the culture of an organization is a major factor shaping individual attitudes and behaviors.

♦ We believe that shared values and common goals shape and change the culture of healthy organizations.

Source: From *Belief Statements* by the Association for Supervision and Curriculum Development. Alexandria, Va.: Association for Supervision and Curriculum Development. Copyright © 1996 ASCD. Reprinted by permission. All rights reserved.

Appendix 4.4

Code of Ethics for School Board Members

As a member of my local Board of Education, I will strive to improve public education, and to that end I will:

Attend all regularly scheduled board meetings insofar as possible, and become informed concerning the issues to be considered at those meetings;

Recognize that I should endeavor to make policy decisions only after full discussion at publicly held board meetings;

Render all decisions based on the available facts and my independent judgment, and refuse to surrender that judgment to individuals or special interest groups;

Encourage the free expression of opinion by all board members, and seek systematic communications between the board and students, staff, and all elements of the community;

Work with other board members to establish effective board policies and to delegate authority for the administration of the schools to the superintendent;

Communicate to other board members and the superintendent expressions of public reaction to board policy and school programs;

Inform myself about current educational issues by individual study and through participation in programs providing needed information, such as those sponsored by my state and national school boards association;

Support the employment of those persons best qualified to serve as school staff, and insist on a regular and impartial evaluation of all staff;

Avoid being placed in a position of conflict of interest;

Take no private action that will compromise the board or administration, and respect the confidentiality of information that is privileged under applicable law; and

Remember always that my first and greatest concern must be the educational welfare of the students attending the public schools.

Member Signature:

Source: National School Boards Association, *Code of Ethics for School Board Members* (Alexandria, Va.: National School Boards Association, 1999). All rights reserved. Reprinted by permission.

CHAPTER 5

Ethical Considerations in School-Building Leadership

This chapter treats the ethics of school-building leadership under four aspects: contractarianism, as exemplified by the social covenant idea of Thomas Hobbes; utilitarianism, as set forth by Jeremy Bentham; pragmatism, as treated by John Dewey; and the professionalism of school leadership.

The ethical issues covered in the section on the social covenant center on creating a positive school culture and participative leadership. In the section on utilitarianism, ethical considerations focus on student behavior. Certain humane dimensions of education are the focus of the ethical issues covered in the section on pragmatism. Finally, the section on professionalism reviews and analyzes the ethical statements of the National Association of Elementary School Principals, the National Association of Secondary School Principals, the American Federation of Teachers, the National Education Association, and the American School Counselor Association.

THE SOCIAL COVENANT IDEA OF THOMAS HOBBES

The political philosophy of Thomas Hobbes (1588–1679) is set forth in *Leviathan*, considered by many scholars to be the defining work of English political thought. This work influenced other writers from the late seventeenth century to the early twentieth century, yet when it appeared in the bookstores of England in 1651, *Leviathan* offended and shocked many of its readers. Even some of Hobbes's old friends felt betrayed by his account of political power and his view of the role religion played in society.[1]

Hobbes was recognized throughout his life as an intellectual; he was particularly adept in the Renaissance curriculum, the study of languages. His first published work was a translation of Thucydides, and one of his last was a translation of Homer. He wrote in English and in Latin and could read French, Greek, and Italian. These skills were much in demand in Hobbes's time. He spent much of his life assisting public figures and educating their older children in preparation for their entry into public life. He was particularly involved in assisting William Cavendish, the first earl of Devonshire and one of the wealthiest people in England. Public figures of the time envisioned themselves in the line of Cicero. A citizen of ancient Rome, Cicero had actively engaged in fighting to preserve the freedom to which the republic had given birth; through his oratory, Cicero continually attempted to persuade other citizens to join his noble cause.[2]

In *Leviathan*, Hobbes sets forth his fundamental law of nature, which is a general rule of reason by which every person naturally seeks peace. A second dimension of this law is that all people have a right to protect their personal interests. Hobbes's second law of nature acknowledges that a person may put aside his or her right to something; in so doing, the person divests himself or herself of a liberty in order not to hinder others from enjoying the same right to which he or she has a claim. A person does this only when it is advantageous. Thus, there are some rights a person cannot set aside, such as the right to self-protection, because setting aside such rights would not be advantageous.[3]

Hobbes defined a *contract* as entailing the delivery of something by one person, leaving the other to perform his or her part of the contract at a later determined time. This definition calls for an element of trust, which elevates the contract to the status of a *pact,* or *covenant.* This is an important notion for Hobbes; it is the foundation for his idea of commonwealth as a social covenant.

Hobbes's third law is that people must perform their covenants. This is the basis of justice. If no covenant exists, there can be no unjust action, and what is not unjust, is just. Thus, injustice is the nonperformance of a covenant. In *Leviathan*, Hobbes lists nineteen laws, followed by an extremely important assertion: these laws bind in conscience. Hobbes's ethical theory, therefore, rests on reason and the human desire for security.[4]

The title *Leviathan*, taken from the Hebrew Scriptures, represents a sea monster who is defeated by Yahweh in various accounts. For Hobbes, the totalitarian state is the Leviathan.

Hobbes's concept of covenant enhances Rousseau's social-contract theory in relation to educational leadership. The word *covenant* highlights the notion of trust and assumes that the parties to the covenant will perform their respective responsibilities at the appropriate time. When a school district is in need of additional property-tax revenue in order to preserve a quality educational program, it becomes the responsibility of the citizenry to provide the needed funds.

Of course, the mere request by educational administrators will never suffice to convince the public that additional revenue is needed. Documentation through ongoing communication and public discourse is required before most citizens will approve a tax increase. However, it is a violation of the covenant for

Selected Reading 5.1

Leviathan

Thomas Hobbes (1588–1679)

To this warre of every man against every man, this also is consequent; that nothing can be Unjust. The notions of Right and Wrong, Justice and Injustice have there no place. Where there is no common Power; there is no Law: where no Law, no Injustice. Force, and Fraud, are in warre the two Cardinall vertues. Justice, and Injustice are none of the Faculties neither of the Body, nor Mind. If they were, they might be in a man that were alone in the world, as well as his Senses, and Passions. They are Qualities, that relate to men in Society, not in Solitude. It is consequent also to the same condition, that there be no Propriety, no Dominion, no *Mine* and *Thine* distinct; but onely that to be every mans, that he can get; and for so long, as he can keep it. And thus much for the ill condition, which man by meer Nature is actually placed in; though with a possibility to come out of it, consisting partly in the Passions, partly in his Reason. . . .

From that law of Nature, by which we are obliged to transferre to another, such Rights, as being retained, hinder the peace of Mankind, there followeth a Third; which is this, *That men performe their Covenants made:* without which, Covenants are in vain, and but Empty words; and the Right of all men to all things remaining, wee are still in the condition of Warre.

And in this law of Nature, consisteth the Fountain and Originall of JUSTICE. For where no Covenant hath preceded, there hath no Right been transferred, and every man has right to every thing; and consequently, no action can be Unjust. But when a Covenant is made, then to break it is *Unjust:* And the definition of INJUSTICE, is no other than *the not Performance of Covenant.* And whatsoever is not Unjust, is *Just.* But because Covenant of mutuall trust, where there is a feare of not performance on either part, (as hath been said in the former Chapter,) are invalid; though the Originally of Justice be the making of Covenants; yet Injustice actually there can be none, till the cause of such feare be taken away; which while men are in the naturally condition of Warre, cannot be done. Therefore before the names of Just, and Unjust can have place, there must be some coercive Power, to compell men equally to the performance of their Covenants, by the terrour of some punishment, greater than the benefit they expect by the breach of their Covenant; and to make good that Propriety, which by mutuall Contract men acquire, in recompence of the universal of a Common-wealth. And this is also to be gathered out of the ordinary definition of Justice in the Schooles: For they say, that *Justice is the constant Will of giving to every man his own.* And therefore where there is no *Own*, that is, no Propriety, there is no Injustice; and where there is no coerceive Power erected, that is, where there is no Common-wealth, there is no Propriety; all men having Right to all things: Therefore where there is no Commonwealth, there nothing is Unjust. So that the nature of Justice, consisteth in keeping of valid Covenants: but the Validity of Covenants begins not but with the Constitution of a Civill Power, sufficient to compell men to keep them: And then it is also that Propriety begins. . . .

The names of Just, and Injust, when they are attributed to Men, signifie one thing; and when they are attributed to Actions, another. When they are attributed to Men, signifie Conformity, or Inconformity of Manners, to Reason. But when they are attributed to Actions, they signifie the Conformity, or Inconformity to Reason, not of Manners, or manner of life, but of particular Actions. A Just man therefore, is he that taketh all the care he can, that his Actions may be all Just: and an Unjust man, is he that neglecteth it. . . .

Justice of Actions, is by Writers divided into *Commutative*, and *Distributive:* and the former they say consisteth in proportion Arithmeticall; the later in proportion Geometricall. Commutative therefore, they place in the equality of value of the things contracted for; And Distributive, in the distribution of equally benefit, to men of equall merit. As if it were Injustice to sell dearer than we buy; or to give more to a man than he merits. The value of all things contracted for, is measured by the Appetite of the Contractors: and therefore the just value, is that which they be contented to give. And Merit (besides that which is by Covenant, where the performance on one part, meriteth the performance of the other part, and falls under Justice Commutative, not Distributive,) is not due by Justice; but is rewarded of Grace onely. And therefore this distinction, in the sense wherein it useth to be expounded, is not right. To speak properly, Commutative Justice, is the Justice of a Contractor; that is, a Performance of Covenant, in Buying, and Selling; Hiring, and Letting to Hire; Lending, and Borrowing; Exchanging, Bartering, and other acts of Contract.

Source: Excerpts from Thomas Hobbes, *Leviathan,* revised student ed., ed. Richard Tuck (Cambridge: Cambridge University Press, 1996), pp. 90, 100–101, 103–104, 105. Reprinted by permission.

a citizen to refuse support for the schools because he or she does not have children or has children who are no longer in school. The quality of life in communities is enhanced through public education because the U.S. economic and political systems require an educated citizenry. Further, people without children or without children in school paid for the schools and their programs in past generations; thus, current childless people and empty nesters have the same obligation to preserve the educational system for future generations.

Ethical Issues and the Social Covenant

Creation of a Positive School Culture. All school activities are influenced by the culture of the school. This fact is certainly obvious to anyone in education. However, the real issue centers on the kind of culture that is created and the process that initiates cultural change. The operative word in discussing school culture is *positive*. There is a reciprocal relationship between a positive school culture and the method that is used to sustain such a culture. It is impossible to have a positive school culture if the parents, students, teachers, and staff members do not have a sense of ownership of the school.

A positive school culture has four dimensions: values, norms, expectations and sanctions, and symbolic activities.[5] The social-covenant approach to building-level leadership embodies fundamental principles of human nature that can be used to initiate and develop a positive school culture. The values dimension is especially well suited to the social-covenant idea. If Hobbes's fundamental law is that the rule of reason prompts everyone to seek peace, it behooves parents, mature students, principals, teachers, and staff members to set forth as a primary school value the respect that is due to everyone because of his or her humanity. Respect for other human beings as human beings makes irrelevant categorizations such as gender, age, ethnicity, and disability. Everyone is entitled to respect simply because he or she is a human being.

A second school value that emanates from the social-covenant approach is that a person can divest himself or herself from certain human rights for the common good. A relevant example concerns the rights and responsibilities of students. Certainly students have a right to defend themselves against the insults and aggressive behavior of other students. Passive resistance, coupled with seeking the assistance of administrators, counselors, and teachers, in a sense divests the individual student from the right to defend himself or herself directly; yet the student is following a course of action that is necessary not only to his or her well-being, but also to the well-being of all the other students in the school.

A third school value is that each person will perform his or her responsibilities at all appropriate times. This is the covenant in the sense that it calls for trust among all members of the school community. Each person is bound to every other person through a pact whereby people agree that when called upon they will perform their responsibilities.

The notion of a positive school culture is thus predicated on certain values, which form the basis on which the other three dimensions can be operationalized. Values tend to be useful only if they are converted into norms—rules and regulations that control behavior. When the values of individual parents, students, administrators, teachers, and staff members are congruent with the norms of a school, there is greater personal satisfaction and easier compliance.

When the norms of a school are applied to a specific situation, they constitute expectations. Thus, when students accept the value that they will permit the professional staff to protect their humanity by not directly defending themselves against the insults and aggressive behavior of other students and when this value is codified into a rule, there is an expectation that the administrators, teachers, and staff members will intervene on behalf of individual students who are harassed.

When expectations are not met, sanctions must be applied, or the covenantal relationship among members of the school community will deteriorate. If the student who is being harassed by other students decides to take matters into his or her own hands and counters the harassment with aggressive behavior, then that student is breaking the covenant. If members of the professional staff do not intervene and search for ways effectively to alleviate the harassment, then they are breaking the covenant. Either situation requires sanctions. The student might be assigned to in-school suspension for fighting; professional staff members might be reprimanded for not intervening in a timely manner.

In this situation, sanctions are punitive; such is the purpose of sanctions. However, the better course of action in terms of educational leadership is to use symbolic activities to reinforce expectations. Symbolic activities are limited only by the imagination of the members of the school community. Recognition ceremonies, awards assemblies, and positive school slogans and campaigns are some of the more traditional approaches to creating high expectations for students. More refined reinforcement should be used for professional educators; examples include a word of thanks, a formal letter recognizing an achievement, elevation to the status of master teacher, or even financial compensation.

An effective way for principals and teachers to engender expectations is through modeling positive behaviors. In a school in which many students have reading difficulties, the principal might encourage the professional staff to be visibly engaged in reading activities. A principal who never has a kind or positive comment for students or staff should not be surprised when others do not either.

Participative Leadership.   Developing a positive school culture involves active participation in making decisions about the values, norms, expectations and sanctions, and symbolic activities of a school. Sharing decision making is an effective way to develop ownership in a school. It is a requirement for the social-covenant approach to school leadership because covenant implies agreement, which cannot be reached without active participation. Participation in the decision-making process may take different forms, but the most frequently used approach is to engage representatives of the various stakeholders. One way of implementing this approach is for the principal to ask various groups to select a person or persons to serve on committees that will be charged with tasks related to the establishment and development of the school culture.

There are other benefits to participative decision making in addition to fulfilling the covenantal requirement. Involving more people increases the number of different ideas and thus may expand the alternatives to a given issue. Shared decision making also draws on the expertise that exists in all school communities. Further, it is easier and more effective to implement a decision if those affected by it or those responsible for its implementation are the decision makers. Finally, participative decision making enhances the morale in a school because it demonstrates to people that they are valued members of the school community.[6]

THE UTILITARIAN IDEA OF JEREMY BENTHAM

Jeremy Bentham (1748–1832) was a precocious child who studied Latin at the age of four and could write in French more easily than he could in English at the age of twelve. Following in the footsteps of both his father and his grandfather, he entered Oxford to study law at the age of twelve and graduated at age fifteen. He was disenchanted with what he considered to be the evils of the legal and political systems in society, and because of this attitude the ordinary practice of law was closed to him.

On reading the *Treatise of Human Nature* by David Hume, Bentham became convinced that *utility* was the foundation for what he had observed in the motives and behavior of people. This philosophical notion occupied Bentham's study and writings with a consistency seldom found in the history of philosophy. The modifications he made in his approach to utilitarianism were primarily for the sake of clarification rather than because of developments in his thought. Bentham's best-known works are *A Fragment on Government* and *Introduction to the Principle of Morals and Legislation*.

Bentham took the name for the general principle from which he proceeded to analyze human behavior from the term used by Hume, *utility*. Bentham held the position that the ethical value of every action must be judged by the degree to which it contributes to happiness. Many intellectuals living during the time Bentham wrote questioned this position, arguing that when something is valued for what it produces, its value is secondary.

Bentham began to emphasize the happiness aspect of his principle, rather than the means for producing happiness. Eventually, he refined his terminology and called his principle "the greatest happiness of the greatest number." Accord-

Selected Reading 5.2

An Introduction to the Principle of Morals and Legislation
Jeremy Bentham (1748–1832)

We have seen that the general object of all laws is to prevent mischief; that is to say, when it is worth while; but that, where there are no other means of doing this than punishment, there are four cases in which it is not worth while.

When it *is* worth while, there are four subordinate designs or objects, which, in the course of his endeavours to compass, as far as may be, that one general object, a legislator, whose views are governed by the principle of utility, comes naturally to propose to himself.

1. His first, most extensive, and most eligible object, is to prevent, in as far as possible, and worth while, all sorts of offences whatsoever: in other words, so to manage, that no offence whatsoever may be committed.

2. But if a man must needs commit an offence of some kind or other, the next object is to induce him to commit an offence *less* mischievous, *rather* than one *more* mischievous: in other words, to choose always the *least* mischievous, or two offences that will either of them suit his purpose.

3. When a man has resolved upon a particular offence, the next object is to dispose him to do *no more* mischief than is *necessary* to his purpose: in other words, to do as little mischief as is consistent with the benefit he has in view.

4. The last object is, whatever the mischief be, which it is proposed to prevent, to prevent it at as cheap a rate as possible.

Subservient to these four objects, or purposes, must be the rules or canons by which the proportion of punishments to offences is to be governed.

Rule 1. The first object, it has been seen, is to prevent, in as far as it is worth while, all sorts of offences; therefore,

The value of the punishment must not be less in any case than what is sufficient to outweigh that of the profit of the offence. . . .

Rule 2. But whether a given offence shall be prevented in a given degree by a given quantity of punishment, is never any thing better than a chance; for the purchase of which, whatever punishment is employed, is so much expended in advance. However, for the sake of giving it the better chance of outweighing the profit of the offence,

The greater the mischief of the offence, the greater is the expense, which it may be worth while to be at, in the way of punishment.

Rule 3. The next object is, to induce a man to choose always the least mischievous of two offences; therefore

Where two offences come in competition, the punishment for the greater offence must be sufficient to induce a man to prefer the less.

Rule 4. When a man has resolved upon a particular offence, the next object is, to induce him to do no more mischief than what is necessary for his purpose: therefore

The punishment should be adjusted in such manner to each particular offence, that for every part of the mischief there may be a motive to restrain the offender from giving birth to it.

Rule 5. The last object is, whatever mischief is guarded against, to guard against it at as cheap a rate as possible: therefore

The punishment ought in no case to be more than what is necessary to bring it into conformity with the rules here given.

Rule 6. It is further to be observed, that owing to the different manners and degrees in which persons under different circumstances are affected by the same exciting cause, a punishment which is the same in name will not always either really produce, or even so much as appear to others to produce, in two different persons the same degree of pain: therefore

That the quantity actually inflicted on each individual offender may correspond to the quantity intended for similar offenders in general, the several circumstances influencing sensibility ought always to be taken into account. . . .

Rule 7. These things being considered, the three following rules may be laid down by way of supplement and explanation to Rule 1.

To enable the value of the punishment to outweigh that of the profit of the offence, it must be increased, in point of magnitude, in proportion as it falls short in point of certainty.

Rule 8. *Punishment must be further increased in point of magnitude, in proportion as it falls short in point of proximity.*

Rule 9. *Where the act is conclusively indicative of a habit, such an increase must be given to the punishment as may enable it to outweigh the profit not only of the individual offence, but of such other like offences as are likely to have been committed with impunity by the same offender.*

There may be a few other circumstances or considerations which may influence, in some small degree, the demand for punishment: but as the propriety of these is either not so demonstrable, or not so constant, or the application of them not so determinate, as that of the foregoing, it may be doubted whether they be worth putting on a level with the others.

Rule 10. When a punishment, which in point of quality is particularly well calculated to answer its intention, cannot exist in less than a certain quantity, it may sometimes be of use, for the sake of employing it, to stretch a little beyond that quantity which, on other accounts, would be strictly necessary.

Rule 11. In particular, this may sometimes be the case, where the punishment proposed is of such a nature as to be particularly well calculated to answer the purpose of a moral lesson.

Rule 12. The tendency of the above considerations is to dictate an augmentation in the punishment: the following rule operates in the way of diminution. There are certain cases (it has been seen) in which, by the influence of the accidental circumstances, punishment may be rendered unprofitable in the whole: in the same cases it may chance to be rendered unprofitable as to a part only. Accordingly,

In adjusting the quantum of punishment, the circumstances, by which all punishment may be rendered unprofitable, ought to be attended to.

Rule 13. It is to be observed, that the more various and minute any set of provisions are, the greater the chance is that any given article in them will not be borne in mind: without which, no benefit can ensue from it. Distinctions, which are more complex than what the conception of those whose conduct it is designed to influence can take in, will even be worse than useless. The whole system will present a confused appearance: and thus the effect, not only of the proportions established by the articles in question, but of whatever is connected with them, will be destroyed. To draw a precise line of direction in such cases seems impossible. However, by way of memento, it may be of some use to subjoin the following rule.

Among provisions designed to perfect the proportion between punishments and offences, if any occur, which by their own particular good effect, would not make up for the harm they would do by adding to the intricacy of the Code, they should be omitted.

Source: Excerpted with permission of Simon & Schuster, Inc. from *An Introduction to the Principles of Morals and Legislation* by Jeremy Bentham. Intro. by Laurence J. LaFleur. Copyright © 1948 by Hafner Publishing Company. Excerpts from pages 178–185.

ing to Bentham, the greatest-happiness principle must be understood as a significant mass of happiness experienced by a large mass of people and not as the intense happiness of only a few people.

Bentham admitted that the greatest-happiness principle could not be proven, but he firmly held to the position that it is neither arbitrary nor arbitrarily held. He recognized that some people professed the antithetical principle of asceticism and others held to the principle of caprice, based on personal preference or liking, but he believed that such people would eventually be converted to his position if they genuinely sought the truth.

Bentham also held the position that human pleasure, in principle, can be treated mathematically, because people are capable of quantifying their experiences through introspection. From an evaluation perspective, a person can enjoy a discussion with a friend more than playing a game of tennis or could have enjoyed the discussion last evening more than a current discussion. A person can individually quantify an enjoyment: a person may enjoy opera very much but only slightly enjoy jazz music. Further, the differences between enjoyments can be quantified: a person's preference for Mary over John may be very pronounced, whereas the person may feel indifferent toward two other people. Much of this reasoning applies to comparisons people make about others, such as John enjoys playing tennis much more than Tom does. Bentham's position is that happiness can be quantified even though people lack knowledge about the quality of happiness and do not possess an accurate way of measuring it.

Bentham's greatest-happiness principle rests on the premise that there is no conflict between the happiness of an individual person and the happiness of all. His reasoning centers on the idea that happiness is not a commodity whereby some receive more than others. However, Bentham recognized that certain forces in society tend to bring a person's individual happiness in accord with public happiness; these forces are called *sanctions.*

Bentham's observation that a person's behavior can be controlled by other human beings led to his notion of sanctions. Sanctions help people understand that their personal greatest happiness coincides with the greatest happiness of others. This principle can be demonstrated and understood only if a person's happiness is increased when the happiness of others is increased (reward) or if a person's happiness is decreased when the happiness of others is not attained (punishment). Punishment is operationalized through various types of sanctions dealt out by various entities. Popular sanctions are issued by society at large; political sanctions are issued by governments; and religious sanction are issued by churches.

According to Bentham, political sanctions refer to those imposed by law with the primary purpose of removing hindrances to increasing the happiness of the greatest number of people rather than interfering with the happiness of individuals. From Bentham's perspective, sanctions are meant to deter rather than to reform. Because punishment brings about pain and thus a corresponding diminution of pleasure, legislators should not attach a penalty to the infraction of a law that is not strictly required in order to obtain the desired effect.[7]

The utilitarianism of Bentham rests on his conviction that there is no conflict between the happiness of an individual person and the happiness of all people. However, his contribution to educational administration lies in his concept of sanctions. His understanding that an individual's happiness can be brought into accord with the happiness of all through the use of sanctions is certainly applicable to educational leadership. Students are particularly adept at the use of popular sanctions, which sometimes evolve into the extreme without justification, for example, when students ostracize other students for unjustified reasons. When used by administrators and teachers, sanctions are not only helpful, but may also be necessary to preserve order in the schools. The challenge is to use sanctions properly, and Bentham's rules constitute a reasonable guide to this end.

Bentham's understanding of the purpose for sanctions is also important in the practice of educational leadership. Sanctions are meant to deter rather than to reform. In schools the reform of student behavior is brought about through the intervention of administrators, teachers, and staff members with students and their parents on an individual basis. Thus, sanctions are only one aspect of dealing with inappropriate student behavior; the individual counseling of students and consultation with parents must always accompany the use of sanctions.

Ethical Issues and Utilitarianism

Every school district is constantly balancing the behavior of individual students against the welfare of the entire student body. The need for this balance is particularly acute in schools that have experienced violent student behavior. Parents, students, community leaders, administrators, teachers, and staff members have a vested interest in student behavior, both because disruptive behavior has a negative effect on school climate and because laudatory behavior has a positive effect on school climate. There is no question that student and family services provided by the school can mitigate much negative behavior, but the eradication of all disruptive behavior is improbable. Thus arises the need to develop a program of student rights and responsibilities.

The philosophy of Jeremy Bentham is particularly useful in developing the rationale for such a program. His overall principle of the greatest happiness of the greatest number speaks to the need for a program that considers the common good as the ultimate criterion. Specifically related to the development of sanctions is his perception that both human happiness and human displeasure can be treated quantitatively. Table 5.1 presents a series of guidelines for discipline for middle school or high school students that recognizes that some sanctions are more undesirable than others.

The justification for sanctions, and particularly for sanctions that deprive a person of the right to attend school, must be understood within the context of Bentham's two principles: human behavior can be controlled by other people;

TABLE 5.1
Discipline Guidelines

Event	Minimum Response	Maximum Response
Absence from class	Conference with student	Removal from class
Cheating	Grade reduction	Course failure
Defiance of authority	Conference	Suspension from school
Destruction of property	Restitution	Suspension from school
Disorderly conduct	Conference with student	In-school suspension
Drug and alcohol use at school	Suspension from school	Expulsion from school
Fighting	Suspension from school	Expulsion from school
Harassment	Conference	Suspension from school
Improper dress	Conference with student	Conference with parents
Theft	Restitution	Suspension from school
Truancy	Parent involvement	In-school suspension
Having weapons at school	Suspension from school	Expulsion from school

and a person's greatest happiness coincides with the greatest happiness of others. Students who are not called to task because of their inappropriate behavior in school will certainly be in jeopardy of more serious behavior that could eventuate in more severe sanctions later in their lives. A student who decreases the happiness of other students through harassment should have his or her happiness decreased through a sanction that could deter him or her from performing such behavior in the future, either as a student at school or as an employee in the workplace, where the consequence could be loss of a job.

Developing a code of student rights and responsibilities will be ineffective unless it is developed with input from all members of the school community. Teachers, administrators, parents, students, and community leaders must be actively involved in the research and formulation process. If a code is created solely by the administration and mandated to the students, there is a good possibility that students will neither understand nor voluntarily adhere to the tenets of the code. The following process will help ensure the effective creation of a code of student rights and responsibilities.

First, a committee of students (middle and high school levels), parents, teachers, administrators, and community leaders should be commissioned by the building principal to study the need to develop a code or to update an existing code. The community representative could be a police officer, a representative from the mayor's office, or a business leader. Each segment of the school community could be allowed to choose its own representative for membership on the committee. For example, the student council could appoint the student representative, the PTA could select the parent representative, the faculty could choose the teacher, and so on. Since very large committees tend to be ineffective, a committee of five, seven, or nine members would be desirable.

Second, the committee should conduct a review of the literature dealing with student rights and responsibilities. Other schools could be contacted for information about their codes. State and federal agencies, along with educational associations and advocacy groups, also could provide valuable information. Questionnaires and other techniques, such as interviews and focus groups, could be used to gather the perceptions of students, parents, teachers, staff members, and administrators about student rights and responsibilities.

After the committee has developed or modified the code, a public hearing could be held to receive comments and suggestions from stakeholders in the school community. The input could then be formulated into a draft to be presented for final approval to the building principal, superintendent of schools, or board of education, depending on the political expectations in the school district.[8]

THE PRAGMATISM OF JOHN DEWEY

John Dewey (1859–1952) was one of the most important philosophers of the pragmatism movement in American education. Other contributors to this movement include Francis W. Parker, William James, and William H. Kilpatrick. The movement was very influential around the first half of the twentieth century and has many ethical implications for the current educational leadership milieu.

Dewey produced a significant body of literature that included several hundred articles and approximately forty books. He advocated for schools to recognize the importance of the psychological and social dimensions of child growth and development on the instructional process. Further, he understood the importance of the cultural context of education and the need to convey the fundamental principles of American democracy through the schools. Thus, in Dewey's view, the three pillars of education are the child, society, and subject matter. His two books that clearly set forth this philosophy are *Democracy and Education* and *Experience and Education*.

Dewey's redefinition of democracy calls for the active participation of students in the schools. Students have to assume leadership roles in school if they are to understand the requirements of citizenship. Further, even though the majority rules in American democracy, it is endemic to democracy that the majority does not nullify the rights of minorities. According to Dewey, truth is relative to time and place; for example, educational programs that are effective during a certain time period in particular schools may become ineffective at a later time. To foster active student participation, educators must be cautious in how they handle disciplinary issues, for being overly restrictive will nullify participation. This notion of being wary of being overly restrictive is what Dewey meant by being permissive.

Dewey viewed education as a lifelong process; he believed that no child's future should be predetermined by the educational system. Every child should thus be considered in his or her totality with intellectual, social, physical, and emotional needs. Good schools and an appropriate education must address all these needs.

Dewey further believed that the content of instruction and the instructional approach to teaching should be developed with significant input from students. From this perspective it is easy to see why Dewey believed that instruction should be developed on a thematic and problem-solving base. The curriculum should not only meet general education requirements, but should also include vocational and practical arts courses. Dewey advocated a comprehensive education, which he believed would have great appeal given the diverse interests of students.[9]

Ethical Issues and Pragmatism

One of the most important implications of the pragmatism movement for educational leadership is empowerment, the empowerment of parents, students, teachers, staff members, and administrators. True empowerment must extend to all members of the school community. It is ineffective to empower one segment and not the others.

However, only two groups will be highlighted in this presentation, teachers and students. The work of teaching is most complex in the contemporary school. This complexity often brings a sense of isolation, especially because many teachers have little meaningful contact with colleagues and other professionals. Further, as the focus of a teacher's day is on the instructional program, many teachers have little input into school policy and procedural issues. The range of issues can be as mundane as making suggestions about supplies and materials or as profound as the vision and mission of the school.

Empowerment can mean different things in different schools. However, in all cases it means at the minimum recognizing that members of the school community have the right to direct their own lives and seeing that they are provided with the means and opportunity to solve their own problems, to make short- and long-term plans, and to direct their growth and development.

Implementing the tenets of this definition for teachers involves allowing them to make decisions that have an impact and to have autonomy in providing professional services. Within the school organization, administrators should be charged with providing the structure that will allow teachers to participate in the decision-making process. There are two dimensions to empowerment through decision making. First, teachers must be allowed to make decisions about important matters; this means policy and procedural issues that affect the entire school community. Second, the mechanism for making decisions must ensure that teachers have the time and information they need to make informed decisions. Lack of information is a key reason that some teachers make inappropriate decisions. When administrators recognize this as a problem, usually they can get the information for the teachers. Constructing the building budget is an example of the type of important issue in which teachers should participate. For participation in this process to be effective, it must go beyond merely making suggestions about the budget and should involve setting priorities and making allocations.

Policies and procedures that affect the delivery of services are of primary concern to teachers. Imposing such policies and procedures that were developed without significant participation by teachers will undoubtedly elicit an unfavorable response from teachers because such an action implies that the administration does not value the dignity and expertise of the faculty. In addition, without teacher involvement, such policies and procedures most likely will not address the real concerns of those involved in the delivery of services.

The empowerment of students has some of the same dimensions as the empowerment of teachers. The level of involvement of students will of course depend on their maturity. It is important, however, to begin the process of empowerment in elementary school in order to prepare students to assume their rightful responsibilities in middle school and high school.

Perhaps the most effective way to help students recognize that they are valued members of the school community with responsibilities for self-determination and for the success of the school emanates from a given school's culture. Some of the elements in a school's culture that support student empowerment are an intense focus on students, flexibility and resourcefulness, and risk taking and experimentation.[10]

A school culture that views students as team members rather than as the products of the educational enterprise will permit the empowerment of students. To implement their empowerment, students must understand that they have a stake in the success of the school. Having a sense of ownership in the school generally increases students' awareness of their responsibilities both to other students and to the professional educators. Participation in decision making about important issues is the key to helping students realize their importance to the school community. This participation will influence both the instructional program and the organizational structure of the school. It may also increase the overall participation of students in school activities as well as in planning and policy making.

Concurrent with the focus on participation is the necessity of developing problem-solving and leadership skills in students. These skills are usually incorporated into the goals and objectives of the instructional program, yet their development will also require specific courses, workshops, and the mentoring of students by faculty members. Academic and self-evaluation skills are also necessary, both for students' overall well-being and to enable them to exercise their leadership responsibilities successfully.

Flexibility and resourcefulness are important elements in the process of creating a school culture that supports student empowerment. Flexibility is not a common characteristic in most contemporary schools because of the enormous number of requirements and tasks that are imposed on schools by local, state, and federal mandates. Such mandates make it more difficult to involve students in decision making. Further, it is extremely difficult but necessary to schedule time in the school day for students, faculty, and staff members to be engaged in meaningful discourse.

Local communities tend to have many members who are willing to become resource people to schools. For example, people from the business community can provide valuable assistance in developing students' leadership skills, enhancing the efforts of professional educators.

Endemic to the fuller empowerment of students is an understanding within the school that students, faculty, and staff members can and will make mistakes when they experiment with new ideas. This outlook fosters risk taking and encourages both professional educators and students to become involved in leadership activities. This attitude can exist only if it is practiced by the principal and teachers in their classrooms. Students will not feel comfortable in becoming involved with leadership activities unless they are convinced that the professional educators value their involvement and will not be critical if they fail.[11]

The empowerment of students will be incomplete unless students with disabilities are included in school decision making. The federal mandates concerning the rights of students with disabilities do not insure that all students will be given equal opportunity to participate in school leadership. However, if empowerment does not extend to all students, the basic idea is abrogated. The empowerment of all students means that even those students who are underachieving or who exhibit unusual behavior are provided with the opportunity and encouragement to become active members of the school community. If all are not empowered than none are truly empowered.

PROFESSIONALISM IN SCHOOL-BUILDING LEADERSHIP

Ethical statements from three professional organizations have been included in this chapter:

Appendix 5.1: A Bill of Rights and Responsibilities for Learning: Standards of Conduct, Standards of Achievement of the American Federation of Teachers

Appendix 5.2: Code of Ethics of the Education Profession of the National Education Association

Appendix 5.3: Ethical Standards for School Counselors of the American School Counselor Association

Not included are the codes of ethics of the National Association of Elementary School Principals and the National Association of Secondary School Principals. These codes mirror that of the American Association of School Administrators, which is found in Appendix 4.1. All three of these associations and the Association of School Business Officials sponsored the development of AASA's code. From the perspective of building-level leadership, this code establishes student well-being as the primary criterion for all decision making and actions. Further, the code clearly supports the importance of the administrator's being involved in the community. The administrator is viewed as a public person who is expected to exhibit exemplary conduct that will be favorably viewed not only by colleagues, but also by students and members of the community. The administrator is admonished to be a protector of civil and human rights, to exhibit the traits of good citizenship, and to be a person of honesty and integrity. He or she is expected to support the policies and administrative rules and regulations of the school district.

The American Federation of Teachers (AFT) has a unique approach to the issue of professional ethics. This association has melded the rights and responsibilities of learning with standards of conduct and standards for achievement. The association begins with a reaffirmation of the mission of public education, which is to prepare the nation's young people for equal and responsible citizenship and productive adulthood. The statement clarifies that this goal can be attained by promoting high standards of conduct and achievement.

An important aspect of AFT's Bill of Rights and Responsibilities is the equality it gives student and staff rights. For example, both students and staff members have a right to a school that is safe, orderly, and drug free. This approach effectively emphasizes that the welfare of students is an integral part of the welfare of teachers. A school cannot be concerned about students and neglect teachers; the learning process will not be effective under such circumstances. The manner in which these rights are set forth admonishes administrators to consider the inseparable relationship between the rights of students and the rights of teachers. Further, it serves as a model for the importance of administrator welfare, which itself is directly related to student and teacher welfare. A school district that neglects the rights of administrators will not have the proper disposition to protect the rights of students and teachers.

The code of ethics of the National Education Association (NEA) contains a preamble and two major principles. The preamble sets the tone for the entire code and does an excellent job of establishing a base for the two principles. It begins with an affirmation of the worth and dignity of human beings and the importance of the pursuit of truth in the context of striving for excellence within a democracy. Essential to these goals is equal educational opportunity and academic freedom. The preamble further sets forth the tremendous importance of the teaching process and within this context highlights this sometimes neglected fact.

Principle I deals with commitment to the student. It is organized around the responsibility of the teacher to stimulate students to learn, to acquire knowledge and understanding. It reinforces the equality of all students, regardless of race, color, creed, sex, national origin, marital status, political or religious beliefs, family, social or cultural background, or sexual orientation. This principle supports the position that quality teaching should be available to all and that there is no place in teaching for prejudice or bias.

Principle II deals with commitment to the profession. It reaffirms the importance of teaching and from this position establishes a series of obligations that are endemic to the profession, such as not deliberately making false statements on applications. A further significant aspect of Principle II is its position that every educator has a responsibility to raise professional standards and to prevent the practice of teaching by unqualified persons.

The tenets of NEA's code can provide educational administrators with guidelines that support excellence in teaching, which, of course, is the fundamental purpose of education.

The ethical standards for school counselors set forth by the American School Counselor Association (ASCA) is more extensive than the other codes because of the unique professional relationship that counselors have with students. In the preamble the association states that the counselor should use his or her specialized skills to protect the interests of the counselee within the structure of the school. In this context the counselor becomes an advocate for students. Also in the preamble, the association reinforces the dignity and equality of all people, the right each person has to self-determination, and the right of every person to privacy. Further, the preamble states that ethical standards can be used by a counselor for the purpose of self-appraisal and as an instrument for peer evaluation.

The ethical standards of ASCA are divided into seven main sections, most with a number of subparts. Section A deals with the ethical issues related to confidentiality; the counseling plan developed by a counselor and student; dual relationships, such as when a counselor is working with a student and another member of the student's family; making referrals; counselees who are dangerous to themselves and other; student records; the evaluation, assessment, and interpretation of assessment measures; the use of computer technology; and peer-helper programs. Section B addresses the counselor's relationship to parents and their responsibilities. Section C sets forth the ethical responsibilities of the counselor to colleagues and other professional associates. Section D deals with the ethical responsibilities of the counselor to the school and the community, and section E is concerned with the responsibilities the counselor has to himself or herself. Multicultural skills are addressed in section F, and the code ends with section G, which deals with maintenance of standards.

This very detailed and extensive code presents standards that are important not only for counselors, but also for all professionals who work with children. Knowledge of the ethical standards and codes of professional associations is important for administrators. It helps them understand the ethical point of reference from which these professionals carry out their responsibilities.

OTHER PHILOSOPHICAL APPROACHES
TO THE ISSUES IN THIS CHAPTER

The most well known philosopher from the school of thought called realism is Alfred North Whitehead. He focused on the objective reality that exists apart from a person's consciousness. In his view, what a person perceives is true to the extent that it corresponds to the actual facts of reality. The final objective of knowledge is to discover the laws of nature through scientific investigation. Ethical laws are knowable because they are a part of nature and can be uncovered through observation.

Whitehead used the phrase *really real things* to underscore the objectivity of philosophical inquiry. He viewed engagement in activities as the actualization of potentiality. This process of actualization is a self-creative activity, which is the proper function of life. By intentionally actualizing the data presented by the world, there is an immediacy of self-enjoyment because of the creative nature of the actualization. Whitehead called this the *doctrine of the creative advance*.

Whitehead's concept of *aim* is also important to understanding his philosophy. Aim is the exclusion of alternative potentialities in the process of unification that occurs with actualization. One of the aims of education is the self-actualization of human potentiality that is exemplified through developing people as experts in some specific direction.[12]

In terms of building leadership, realism tends to support the establishment of rules and regulations that are definite and universal. The principal who follows this approach will make decisions from universal principles that are valid for all situations at all times.

CROSSWALK TO ISLLC STANDARD FIVE

The contents of this chapter support the following dimensions of ISLLC Standard Five:

Knowledge
The administrator has knowledge and understanding of:
◆ various ethical frameworks and perspectives on ethics
◆ professional codes of ethics

Dispositions
The administrator believes in, values, and is committed to:
◆ the principles in the Bill of Rights

- the right of every student to a free, quality education
- using the influence of one's office constructively and productively in the service of all students and their families
- development of a caring school community

Performances

The administrator:

- demonstrates a personal and professional code of ethics
- serves as a role model
- accepts responsibility for school operations
- uses the influence of the office to enhance the educational program rather than for personal gain
- treats people fairly, equitably, and with dignity and respect
- protects the rights and confidentiality of students and staff
- expects that others in the school community will demonstrate integrity and exercise ethical behavior
- opens the school to public scrutiny
- fulfills legal and contractual obligations

ETHICAL CONSIDERATIONS PRESENTED IN THIS CHAPTER

- Schools are communities and as such function according to the concept of the social covenant, which calls for the fulfillment of responsibilities that are endemic to the role of each member.
- The effective implementation of the social covenant requires a trusting relationship among all members of the school community: parents, students, teachers, staff members, and administrators.
- The culture of a school will determine the extent and effectiveness of the social covenant under which it is organized.
- There is no conflict between the happiness of each individual and the happiness of all other members of a school community.
- Participative leadership is in agreement with the notion of the social covenant.
- Participative leadership requires the empowerment of all members of the school community so that they can have the opportunity to direct their own lives and solve their own problems.

∽ SUMMARY

In his book *Leviathan,* Thomas Hobbes established his fundamental law of nature, which is a general rule of reason by which every person naturally seeks peace. Even though people have a right to self-promotion, Hobbes's second law holds that a person may put aside his or her right to something; in so doing the person divests himself or herself of a liberty in order not to hinder others from enjoying the same right to which he or she has a claim. When people set aside a right, they do so for an advantageous reason; thus, in essence, they are safe-guarding their right.

Hobbes's definition of a contract entails the delivery of something by one person, leaving the other person to perform his or her part of the contract at a later, determined time. This definition calls for an element of trust that elevates the contract to the status of a covenant. This is Hobbes's fundamental concept in relation to the social contract. Hobbes's last law is that people must perform their covenants, which is basic justice. However, if no covenant exists, there can be no unjust action and what is not unjust, is just.

Directly related to the notion of the social covenant are certain ethical issues pertaining to educational leadership. As a community of learners, professional educators and students are brought together through an agreement whereby each has a set of responsibilities that must be fulfilled for the welfare of the entire community. Further, from the social covenant emanates the need to create a positive school climate. The process for establishing a positive school culture must involve all stakeholders: parents, students, teachers, and staff members. There are four dimensions to creating a positive school culture: values, norms, expectations and sanctions, and symbolic activities. Values include the funda-mental value that all members of the school community are due respect simply because they are human beings. Other values are that a person can divest him-self or herself of certain rights for the common good; and, when called upon to do so, each person must perform his or her responsibilities.

Values are useful only if they are converted into norms—rules and regula-tions that control behavior. When the values of individual parents, students, administrators, teachers, and staff members are congruent with the norms of a school, there is usually greater personal satisfaction and easier compliance with regulations. When norms are applied to a specific situation, they constitute expectations. When expectations are not met there must be sanctions. However, symbolic activities can reinforce expectations and mitigate against the need to use sanctions.

A second ethical issue related to the social covenant is participative leader-ship, active involvement in making decisions about the values, norms, expecta-tions and sanctions, and symbolic activities of a school.

Because all schools are focused on behavior, it is most advantageous for school administrators to have a basis on which to make ethical decisions about behavior. The utilitarian philosophy of Jeremy Bentham provides such a basis. According to Bentham's principle of the greatest happiness of the greatest number, the ethical value of every action must be judged by the degree to which it contributes to happiness. Bentham also believed that human happiness can be mathematically treated because people are capable of quantifying their experiences through introspection. Bentham's greatest-happiness principle rests on the premise that there is no conflict between the happiness of an individual person and the happiness of all.

Bentham's position that people can be controlled by other human beings led to his notion of sanction. Sanctions are imposed for the purpose of removing hindrances to increasing the happiness of the greatest number of people rather than as an interference with the happiness of individuals.

The contribution of Bentham's utilitarianism to the ethical practice of educational leadership can be easily seen in relation to student behavior. Every school district is constantly balancing the behavior of individual students against the welfare of the entire student body. The greatest-happiness principle speaks to the need for a program that considers the common good as the ultimate criterion.

Another approach to dealing with ethical issues is pragmatism, particularly the strand developed by John Dewey. Dewey considered the psychological and social dimensions of child growth and development important aspects of the learning and instructional process. He recognized the importance of the cultural context of education and the need to convey the fundamental principles of American democracy through the schools. He called for students to participate actively in school, believing that by assuming leadership roles in school they would better understand the requirements of citizenship. In addition, Dewey cautioned that the rights of minorities must not be nullified through the rule of the majority.

Dewey supported change through his belief that truth is relative to time and place. He advocated for a permissive approach to discipline. Dewey believed that education is a lifelong process and that instruction should be developed along thematic and problem-solving bases. Finally, he was an advocate for the comprehensive educational curriculum.

One of the most important implications of Dewey's philosophy for educational leadership is the need for empowerment of parents, students, teachers, staff members, and administrators. Empowerment of teachers calls for teachers to be active participants in the decision-making processes concerning policy and procedural issues that effect the entire school organization. It also means providing teachers with the means and opportunity to solve their own problems, to make short- and long-term plans, and to direct their own growth and development.

The empowerment of students has some of the same elements as the empowerment of teachers. Student empowerment emanates from a school culture that promotes an intense focus on students, flexibility and resourcefulness, risk taking and experimentation. A school culture that considers students as team members rather than as the products of the educational enterprise will permit the empowerment of students. To be active members of the school community, students must be given the opportunity to develop problem-solving and leadership skills.

True student empowerment will be ineffective unless empowerment opportunities are extended to students with disabilities and to students who do not fit the mainstream model.

⤳ DISCUSSION QUESTIONS AND STATEMENTS

1. Explain the fundamental law of nature as set forth by Thomas Hobbes in *Leviathan*.
2. Describe how Hobbes's concept of the social covenant relates to the practice of educational leadership.
3. What are the four dimensions of a positive school culture?
4. In the context of a positive school culture, explain the relationship among values, norms, expectations and sanctions, and symbolic activities.
5. How does the concept of the social covenant support participative leadership?
6. According to Jeremy Bentham how should people judge the ethical value of an action?
7. Describe how human pleasure can be quantified, according to Bentham.
8. Under what circumstances can there be a conflict between an individual's happiness and the happiness of all?
9. According to Bentham how can a person's behavior be controlled by other human beings?
10. What is the purpose of sanctions in Bentham's theory?
11. Describe how Bentham's theory of sanctions relates to the development of a policy on student rights and responsibilities.
12. What were the major contributions of John Dewey to the contemporary practice of education in general and educational leadership in particular?
13. Define *empowerment* as it relates to both teachers and students.
14. How can the idea of teacher empowerment be implemented by a school principal?

15. How can the idea of student empowerment be implemented by a school principal?

16. Discuss the tenets of the professional ethics statements of the American Federation of Teachers, the National Education Association, and the American School Counselor Association.

CASE STUDY 5.1

The Newly Appointed Principal

The newly appointed principal was hired because she was perceived as a high-energy person with good academic credentials and she had very good references from the superintendent of the district where she had served as a middle-school principal for eight years. The superintendent described her as a take-charge person who was not afraid of a challenge. The middle school she was hired to lead had had two principals in the past fifteen years. It was a rather difficult school to administer not only because of the diverse student population, but also because the school district was experiencing severe financial problems; teachers and staff members had not received a salary increase in three years.

The real challenge the new principal faced, however, emanated from the leadership style of the two previous principals. Both administrators had concerned themselves primarily with management tasks and had been minimally involved with the instructional process. Both were also strict disciplinarians.

Two years before the new principal arrived at the school, the district had allocated a significant amount of time, energy, and money to developing a master plan, which called for a site-based-management approach to building-level administration. All the principals participated in the development of the master plan, and all received a significant amount of staff-development training in site-based management.

The new principal was a strong proponent of site-based management because she believed that this approach allowed the principal and staff greater latitude in setting building priorities. However, she believed that the principal was really the only person who could possibly have access to all the information necessary to manage not only the school in general, but also the various building-level functions. All issues converged in her office. As a consequence, she was continually calling meetings with the assistant principals, teachers, and staff members so that she could coordinate the various tasks, processes, and procedures that are endemic to middle schools. During her first year as principal she planned to review all the school policies to ascertain whether they needed revision; she intended to initiate any necessary revisions during her second year.

She was especially concerned about the student rights and responsibilities policy and how it related to school safety issues.

Her detractors among the teachers and staff members stated that the principal lacked trust in them to fulfill their professional responsibilities and that her constant interference was counterproductive because she could not possibly understand the issues and problems they encountered in their classrooms. They resented her second-guessing their decisions, especially in relation to issues involving student discipline. During her interview by a team of teachers and staff members as part of the hiring process, the principal had given the distinct impression that she supported teacher autonomy.

Discussion Questions and Statements

1. Compare and contrast the principal's leadership style with Hobbes's concept of the social covenant.

2. What utilitarian principles should be considered when initiating a student rights and responsibilities policy?

3. In relation to the philosophy of John Dewey, describe the process that the principal should initiate to review and update the school's policies.

4. Do you think the principal is capable of leading a school according to the concepts of the social covenant, utilitarianism, and pragmatism?

5. Compare and contrast the leadership style of the principal in relation to the various codes of ethics that are set forth in the appendices.

SELECTED BIBLIOGRAPHY

Beck, L. "Why Ethics? Thoughts on the Moral Challenge Facing Educational Leaders." *The School Administrator*, vol. 9, no. 54 (1996).

Bentham, Jeremy. *An Introduction to the Principles of Morals and Legislation.* New York: Hafner Publishing Company, 1948.

Bowser, John D., and Ross Sherman. *The Principal's Companion: A Workbook for Future School Leaders.* 2d ed. New York: University Press of America, 1996.

Dewey, John. *Democracy and Education.* New York: The Macmillan Company, 1916.

Hobbes, Thomas. *Leviathan.* Ed. Richard Tuck. Cambridge: Cambridge University Press, 1996.

Hoyle, J., and H. Crenshaw. *Interpersonal Sensitivity: The School Leadership Library.* Larchmont, N.Y.: Eye on Education, 1997.

Kidder, R. "Do Values Top Your Agenda?" *The School Administrator*, vol. 9, no. 54 (1996).

Sergiovanni, Thomas J. *Leadership for the Schoolhouse: How Is It Different? Why Is It Important?* San Francisco: Jossey-Bass Publishers, 1996.

Short, Paula M., and John T. Greer. *Leadership in Empowered Schools: Themes from Innovative Efforts.* Upper Saddle River, N.J.: Merrill/Prentice Hall, 1997.

A Bill of Rights and Responsibilities for Learning: Standards of Conduct, Standards for Achievement

The traditional mission of our public schools has been to prepare our nation's young people for equal and responsible citizenship and productive adulthood. Today, we reaffirm that mission by remembering that democratic citizenship and productive adulthood begin with standards of conduct and standards for achievement in our schools. Other education reforms may work; high standards of conduct and achievement do work—and nothing else can work without them.

Recognizing that rights carry responsibilities, we declare that:

1. All students and school staff have a right to schools that are safe, orderly and drug free.

2. All students and school staff have a right to learn and work in school districts and schools that have clear discipline codes with fair and consistently enforced consequences for misbehavior.

3. All students and school staff have a right to lean and work in school districts that have alternative educational placements for violent or chronically disruptive students.

4. All students and school staff have a right to be treated with courtesy and respect.

5. All students and school staff have a right to learn and work in school districts, schools and classrooms that have clearly stated and rigorous academic standards.

6. All students and school staff have a right to lean and work in well-equipped schools that have the instructional materials needed to carry out a rigorous academic program.

7. All students and school staff have a right to learn and work in schools where teachers know their subject matter and how to teach it.

8. All students and school staff have a right to learn and work in school districts, schools and classrooms where high grades stand for high achievement and promotion is earned.

9. All students and school staff have a right to learn and work in school districts and schools where getting a high school diploma means having the knowledge and skill essential for college or a good job.

10. All students and school staff have a right to be supported by parents, the community, public officials and business in their efforts to uphold high standards of conduct and achievement.

Source: American Federation of Teachers, *A Bill of Rights and Responsibilities for Learning: Standards of Conduct, Standards for Achievement* (Washington, D.C.: American Federation of Teachers, 1999). Reprinted by permission.

Code of Ethics of the Education Profession

Preamble

The educator, believing in the worth and dignity of each human being, recognizes the supreme importance of the pursuit of truth, devotion to excellence, and the nurture of the democratic principles. Essential to these goals is the protection of freedom to learn and to teach and the guarantee of equal educational opportunity for all. The educator accepts the responsibility to adhere to the highest ethical standards.

The educator recognizes the magnitude of the responsibility inherent in the teaching process. The desire for the respect and confidence of one's colleagues, of students, of parents, and of the members of the community provides the incentive to attain and maintain the highest possible degree of ethical conduct. The Code of Ethics of the Education Profession indicates the aspiration of all educators and provides standards by which to judge conduct.

The remedies specified by the NEA and/or its affiliates for the violation of any provision of this Code shall be exclusive and no such provision shall be enforceable in any form other than the one specifically designated by the NEA or its affiliates.

Principle I
Commitment to the Student

The educator strives to help each student realize his or her potential as a worthy and effective member of society. The educator therefore works to stimulate the spirit of inquiry, the acquisition of knowledge and understanding, and the thoughtful formulation of worthy goals.

In fulfillment of the obligation to the student, the educator—

1. Shall not unreasonably restrain the student from independent action in the pursuit of learning.
2. Shall not unreasonably deny the student's access to varying points of view.
3. Shall not deliberately suppress or distort subject matter relevant to the student's progress.
4. Shall make reasonable effort to protect the student from conditions harmful to learning or to health and safety.
5. Shall not intentionally expose the student to embarrassment or disparagement.

6. Shall not on the basis of race, color, creed, sex, national origin, marital status, political or religious beliefs, family, social or cultural background, or sexual orientation, unfairly—

   a. Exclude any student from participation in any program

   b. Deny benefits to any student

   c. Grant any advantage to any student

7. Shall not use professional relationships with students for private advantage.

8. Shall not disclose information about students obtained in the course of professional service unless disclosure serves a compelling professional purpose or is required by law.

Principle II
Commitment to the Profession

The education profession is vested by the public with a trust and responsibility requiring the highest ideals of professional service.

In the belief that the quality of the services of the education profession directly influences the nation and its citizens, the educator shall exert every effort to raise professional standards, to promote a climate that encourages the exercise of professional judgment, to achieve conditions that attract persons worthy of the trust to careers in education, and to assist in preventing the practice of the profession by unqualified persons.

In fulfillment of the obligation to the profession, the educator—

1. Shall not in an application for a professional position deliberately make a false statement or fail to disclose a material fact related to competency and qualifications.

2. Shall not misrepresent his/her professional qualifications.

3. Shall not assist any entry into the profession of a person known to be unqualified in respect to character, education, or other relevant attribute.

4. Shall not knowingly make a false statement concerning the qualifications of a candidate for a professional position.

5. Shall not assist a noneducator in the unauthorized practice of teaching.

6. Shall not disclose information about colleagues obtained in the course of professional service unless disclosure serves a compelling professional purpose or is required by law.

7. Shall not knowingly make false or malicious statements about a colleague.

8. Shall not accept any gratuity, gift, or favor that might impair or appear to influence professional decisions or action.

Source: National Education Association, *Code of Ethics of the Education Profession* (Washington, D.C.: National Education Association, 1975). Reprinted by permission.

Ethical Standards for School Counselors

Preamble

The American School Counselor Association (ASCA) is a professional organization whose members have a unique and distinctive preparation grounded in the behavioral sciences, with training in clinical skills adapted to the school setting. The counselor assists in the growth and development of each individual and uses his/her highly specialized skills to protect the interests of the counselee within the structure of the school system. School counselors subscribe to the following basic tenets of the counseling process from which professional responsibilities are derived:

1. Each person has the right to respect and dignity as a human being and to counseling services without prejudice as to person, character, belief or practice, regardless of age, color, disability, ethnic group, gender, race, religion, sexual orientation, marital status or socioeconomic status.
2. Each person has the right to self-direction and self-development.
3. Each person has the right of choice and the responsibility for goals reached.
4. Each person has the right to privacy and thereby the right to expect the counselor-counselee relationship to comply with all laws, policies, and ethical standards pertaining to confidentiality.

In this document the American School Counselor Association has specified the principles of ethical behavior necessary to maintain and regulate the high standards of integrity, leadership, and professionalism among its members. The Ethical Standards for School Counselors were developed to clarify the nature of ethical responsibilities held in common by its members. As the code of ethics of the association, this document establishes principles that define the ethical behavior of its members. The purposes of this document are to:

1. Serve as a guide for the ethical practices of all professional school counselors, regardless of level, areas, population served, or membership in this professional association.
2. Provide benchmarks for both self-appraisal and peer evaluations regarding counselor responsibilities to counselees, parents, colleagues and professional associates, schools and community, self, and the counseling profession.

3. Inform those served by the school counselor of acceptable counselor practices and expected professional behavior.

A. Responsibilities to Students

The professional school counselor:

a.   Has a primary obligation to the counselee who is to be treated with respect as a unique individual.

b.   Is concerned with the educational, career, emotional, and behavior needs and encourages the maximum development of each counselee.

c.   Refrains from consciously encouraging the counselee's acceptance of values, lifestyles, plans, decisions, and beliefs that represent the counselor's personal orientation.

d.   Is responsible for keeping informed of laws, regulations or policies relating to counselees and strives to ensure that the rights of counselees are adequately provided for and protected.

A2. Confidentiality

The professional school counselor:

a.   Informs the counselee of the purposes, goals, techniques and rules of procedure under which she/he may receive counseling at or before the time when the counseling relationship is entered. Notice includes confidentiality issues such as the possible necessity for counseling with other professionals, privileged communication, and legal or authoritative restraints. The meaning and limits of confidentiality are clearly defined to counselees through a written and shared statement of disclosure.

b.   Keeps information confidential unless disclosure is required to prevent clear and imminent danger to the counselee or others or when legal requirements demand that confidential information be revealed. Counselors will consult with other professionals when in doubt as to the validity of an exception.

c.   Discloses information to an identified third party, who by his or her relationship with the counselee is at a high risk of contracting a disease that is commonly known to be both communicable and fatal. Prior to disclosure, the counselor will ascertain that the counselee has not already informed the third party about his or her disease and that he/she is not intending to inform the third party in the immediate future.

d.   Requests from the court that disclosure not be required when the release of confidential information without a counselee's permission may lead to potential harm to the counselee.

e. Protects the confidentiality of counselee's records and releases personal data only according to prescribed laws and school policies. Student information maintained in computers is treated with the same care as traditional student records.

f. Protects the confidentiality of information received in the counseling relationship as specified by federal and state laws, written policies and applicable ethical standards. Such information is only to be revealed to others with the informed consent of the counselee, consistent with the obligation of the counselor as a professional person. In a group setting, the counselor sets norm of confidentiality and stresses its importance, yet clearly states that confidentiality in group counseling cannot be guaranteed.

A3. Counseling Plans

The professional school counselor:

works jointly with the counselee in developing integrated and effective counseling plans, consistent with both the abilities and circumstances of the counselee and counselor. Such plans will be regularly reviewed to ensure continued viability and effectiveness, respecting the counselee's freedom of choice.

A4. Dual Relationships

The professional school counselor:

avoids dual relationships which might impair his/her objectivity and increase the risk of harm to the client (e.g., counseling one's family members, close friends or associates). If a dual relationship is unavoidable, the counselor is responsible for taking action to eliminate or reduce the potential for harm. Such safeguards might include informed consent, consultation, supervision and documentation.

A5. Appropriate Referrals

The professional school counselor:

makes referrals when necessary or appropriate to outside resources. Appropriate referral necessitates knowledge of available resources, and making appropriate plans for transitions with minimal interruption of services. Counselees retain the right to discontinue the counseling relationship at any time.

A6. Group Work

The professional school counselor:

screens prospective group members and maintains an awareness of participants' needs and goals in relation to the goals of the group. The counselor takes reasonable precautions to protect members from physical or psychological harm resulting from interaction within the group.

A7. Danger to Self or Others

The professional school counselor:

informs appropriate authorities when the counselee's condition indicates a clear and imminent danger to the counselee or others. This is to be done after careful deliberation and, where possible, after consultation with other counseling professionals. The counselor informs the counselee of actions to be taken so as to minimize his or her confusion and clarify counselee and counselor expectations.

A8. Student Records

The professional school counselor:

maintains and secures records necessary for rendering professional services to the counselee as required by laws, regulations, institutional procedures, and confidentiality guidelines.

A9. Evaluation, Assessment and Interpretation

The professional school counselor:

a. Adheres to all professional standards regarding selection, administration, and interpretation of assessment measures. The counselor recognizes that computer-based testing programs require specific training in administration, scoring and interpretation which may differ from that required in more traditional assessments.

b. Provides explanations of the nature, purposes, and results of assessment/evaluation measures in language that can be understood by counselee(s).

c. Does not misuse assessment results and interpretations and takes reasonable steps to prevent others from misusing the information.

d. Utilizes caution when using assessment techniques, making evaluations, and interpreting the performance of populations not represented in the norm group on which an instrument was standardized.

A10. Computer Technology

The professional counselor:

a. Promotes the benefits of appropriate computer applications and clarifies the limitations of computer technology. The counselor ensures that (1) computer applications are appropriate for the individual needs of the counselee,

(2) the counselee understands how to use the application, and (3) follow-up counseling assistance is provided. Members of under-represented groups are assured equal access to computer technologies and the absence of discriminatory information and values within computer applications.

b. Counselors who communicate with counselees via Internet should follow the NBCC Standards for WebCounseling.

A11. Peer Helper Programs

The professional school counselor:

has unique responsibilities when working with peer helper programs. The school counselor is responsible for the welfare of counselees participating in peer helper programs under his/her direction. School counselors who function in training and supervisory capacities are referred to the preparation and supervision standards of professional counselor associations.

B. Responsibilities to Parents

B1. Parent Rights and Responsibilities

The professional school counselor:

a. Respects the inherent rights and responsibilities of parents for their children and endeavors to establish as appropriate, a collaborative relationship with parents to facilitate the maximum development of the counselee.

b. Adheres to laws and local guidelines when assisting parents experiencing family difficulties which interfere with the counselee's effectiveness and welfare.

c. Is sensitive to the cultural and social diversity among families and recognizes that all parents, custodial and non-custodial, are vested with certain rights and responsibilities for the welfare of their children by virtue of their position and according to law.

B2. Parents and Confidentiality

The professional school counselor:

a. Informs parents of the counselor's role with emphasis on the confidential nature of the counseling relationship between the counselor and counselee.

b. Provides parents with accurate, comprehensive and relevant information in an objective and caring manner, as appropriate and consistent with ethical responsibilities to the counselee.

c. Makes reasonable efforts to honor the wishes of parents and guardians concerning information that he/she may share regarding the counselee.

C. Responsibilities to Colleagues and Professional Associates

C1. *Professional Relationships*

The professional school counselor:

a.   Establishes and maintains a professional relationship with faculty, staff and administration to facilitate the provision of optimum counseling services. The relationship is based on the counselor's definition and description of the parameters and levels of his/her professional roles.

b.   Treats colleagues with respect, courtesy, fairness and in a professional manner. The qualifications, views, and findings of colleagues are represented to accurately reflect the image of competent professionals.

c.   Is aware of and optimally utilizes related professionals and organizations to whom the counselee may be referred.

C2. *Sharing Information with Other Professionals*

The professional school counselor:

a.   Promotes awareness and adherence to appropriate guidelines regarding confidentiality, the distinction between public and private information, and staff consultation.

b.   Provides professional personnel with accurate, objective, concise and meaningful data necessary to adequately evaluate, counsel, and assist the counselee.

c.   If a counselee is receiving services from another counselor or other mental health professional, the counselor, with client consent will inform the other professional and develop clear agreements to avoid confusion and conflict for the counselee.

D. Responsibilities to the School and Community

D1. *Responsibilities to the School*

The professional school counselor:

a.   Supports and protects the educational program against any infringement not in the best interests of counselees.

b.   Informs appropriate officials of conditions that may be potentially disruptive or damaging to the school's mission, personnel and property, while honoring the confidentiality between the counselee and the counselor.

c.   Delineates and promotes the counselor's role and function in meeting the needs of those served. The counselor will notify appropriate officials of conditions which may limit or curtail his/her effectiveness in providing programs and services.

d. Accepts employment only for positions for which he/she is qualified by education, training, supervised experience, state and national professional credentials, and appropriate professional experience. Counselors recommend that administrators hire for professional counseling positions only individuals who are qualified and competent.

e. Assists in the development of (1) curricular and environmental conditions appropriate for the school and community, (2) educational procedures and programs to meet the counselee's developmental needs, and (3) a systematic evaluation process for comprehensive school counseling programs, services and personnel. The counselor is guided by the findings of the evaluation data in planning programs and services.

D2. *Responsibility to the Community*

The professional school counselor:

collaborates with agencies, organizations, and individuals in the school and community in the best interest of counselees and without regard to personal reward or remuneration.

E. Responsibilities to Self

E1. *Professional Competence*

The professional school counselor:

a. Functions within the boundaries of individual professional competence and accepts responsibility for the consequences of his/her actions.

b. Monitors personal functioning and effectiveness and does not participate in any activity which may lead to inadequate professional services or harm to a counselee.

c. Strives through personal initiative to maintain professional competence and keep abreast of scientific and professional information. Professional and personal growth is continuous and ongoing throughout the counselor's career.

E2. *Multicultural Skills*

The professional school counselor:

understands the diverse cultural backgrounds of the counselees with whom he/she works. This includes, but is not limited to, learning how the school counselor's own cultural/ethnic/racial identity impacts his/her values and beliefs about the counseling process.

F. Responsibilities to the Profession

F1. Professionalism

The professional school counselor:

a. Accepts the policies and processes for handling ethical violations as a result of maintaining membership in the American School Counselor Association.

b. Conducts himself/herself in such a manner as to advance individual, ethical practice and the profession.

c. Conducts appropriate research and reports findings in a manner consistent with acceptable educational and psychological research practices. When using client data for research, statistical, or program planning purposes, the counselor ensures protection of the identity of the individual counselees.

d. Adheres to ethical standards of the profession, other official policy statements pertaining to counseling, and relevant statutes established by federal, state and local governments.

e. Clearly distinguishes between statements and actions made as a private individual and as a representative of the school counseling profession.

f. Does not use his/her professional position to recruit or gain clients, consultees for his/her private practice, seek and receive unjustified personal gains, unfair advantage, sexual favors, or unearned goods or services.

F2. Contribution to the Profession

The professional school counselor:

a. Actively participates in local, state and national associations which foster the development and improvement of school counseling.

b. Contributes to the development of the professional through the sharing of skills, ideas, and expertise with colleagues.

G. Maintenance of Standards

Ethical behavior among professional school counselors, Association members, and non members, is expected at all times. When there exists serious doubt as to the ethical behavior of colleagues, or if counselors are forced to work in situations or abide by policies which do not reflect the standards as outlined in the Ethical Standards for School Counselors, the counselor is obligated to take appropriate action to rectify the condition. The following procedure may serve as a guide.

   1. The counselor should consult with a professional colleague to confidentially discuss the nature of the complain to see if he/she views the situation as an ethical violation.

2. When feasible, the counselor should directly approach the colleague whose behavior is in question to discuss the complaint and seek appropriate resolution.

3. If resolution is not forthcoming at the personal level, the counselor shall utilize the channels established within the school, school district, the state SCA and ASCA Ethics Committee.

4. If the matter still remains unresolved, referral for review and appropriate action should be made to the Ethics Committees in the following sequence:

State school counselor association

American School Counselor Association

5. The ASCA Ethics Committee is responsible for educating and consulting with the membership regarding the ethical standards. The Committee periodically reviews and recommends changes in the code as well as the Policies and Procedures for Processing Complaints of Ethical Violations. The Committee will also receive and process questions to clarify the application of such standards. Questions must be submitted in writing to the ASCA Ethics Chair. Finally, the Committee will handle complaints of alleged violations of our ethical standards. Therefore, at the national level, complaints should be submitted in writing to the ASCA Ethics Committee, c/o The Executive Director, American School Counselor Association, 801 North Fairfax Street, Suite 210, Alexandria, Va 22314.

Source: American School Counselor Association, *Ethical Standards for School Counselors* (Alexandria, Va.: American School Counselor Association, 1998). Reprinted by permission.

PART THREE

Equity and
Educational Leadership

⌐ CHAPTER

The Issue of Gender and Educational Leadership

There is no question but that women are underrepresented in positions of educational leadership, particularly in the superintendency. This situation is changing, albeit slowly. Suppression of women has had economic, legal, political, psychological, and social ramifications for both women and men; nonetheless, men have been able to maintain a privileged status in educational leadership.

Gender inequality has roots in both the individual and the collective self-concepts of many men and at least some women. It is an ancient malady. Other types of discrimation are not tied that closely to personal and collective self-concepts.[1] Discrimination in contemporary society based on age, disability, race, or ethnicity arises more from greed and the quest for political influence than from an ontological basis.

This chapter presents segments from the writings of four women who have written extensively about gender issues. Edith Stein and Simone de Beauvoir lived in dangerous times and experienced difficulties that significantly contributed to their perspectives on gender issues. Their works have gained recognition and appreciation in the discipline of philosophy, and their writings have influenced the gender-equity movement in a positive way. Susan Bordo and Sandra Harding are contemporary writers whose active and interesting lives continue to increase their importance as philosophers.

EDITH STEIN: THE FEMALE SPECIES

Born into a rather large Jewish family in 1891 in Breslau, Germany, Edith Stein demonstrated at an early age her disposition for the intellectual life. She devoted most of her professional career to studying and researching gender issues. However, she also contributed to the history of philosophical thought by studying the relationship between Thomism and phenomenology, and she explored the relationship between psychology and philosophy as it impinges upon human empathy.

Stein studied history, German literature, and philosophy at the University of Breslau. During her studies at Breslau, Stein became fascinated with phenomenology, the philosophical method of Edmund Husserl. Eventually, she left Breslau and entered the University of Göttingen so that she could study directly under Husserl. She received her Ph.D. degree, summa cum laude, in 1916.

When Edmund Husserl took a position at the University of Freiburg, Stein moved there and became his teaching assistant and also undertook the task of editing Husserl's manuscripts. Later in her career, she translated into German John Henry Newman's *The Idea of a University* and *Letters and Journals*. Stein became a Roman Catholic in 1922. In the late 1920s and the early 1930s, she discovered the philosophy of Thomas Aquinas, which had a profound effect on her philosophical thought, particularly after she translated his *Disputed Questions on Truth*. Edith Stein is considered to have been a major force in the development of German neo-scholasticism.

In 1928, Stein took another decisive step in her career; she engaged in public speaking on gender issues, which eventually led to her appointment as a lecturer at the Educational Institute of Münster. There she developed a program geared toward the educational needs of women.

On October 14, 1933, Stein entered a religious order. From that date until she was arrested because of her Jewish heritage and executed at Auschwitz in 1942, she devoted herself to further religious and philosophical research and writing. The excerpt from her writings in Selected Reading 6.1 deals with the differences between ontology and philosophical anthropology and is representative of her unique approach to gender equity.[2]

Method

Stein's methodology is phenomenological, following the approach developed by Edmund Husserl. Husserl's approach to reality begins with sense perceptions of real objects. These objects are then submitted to critical analysis through the exercise of reason. The goal of the analysis is to arrive at an intuitional understanding of the essence of the object under investigation. Because Stein believed that *being* is intelligible to the mind, she referred to this understanding as ontological. Thus, truth revealed through the phenomenological method is different from truth reached through empirical science and revelation.

In Selected Reading 6.1, Stein analyzes *woman* in relation to the question of education. Stein concludes that this analysis properly belongs to what she called *philosophical anthropology*. She uses three different aspects in the analysis: the human species, the woman species, and the individual. The *woman species* is

∽ Selected Reading 6.1

Essays on Woman

Edith Stein (1891–1942)

We have now established a whole range of different methods which have attempted or could attempt to discover woman's unique nature. It would now be feasible to summarize once more the potential contribution of each method to our problem according to the means of cognition utilized.

To expound on the *species* is proper to the cognitive function of *philosophy* which alone can achieve a valid explanation. To even begin to explain how I think this problem can be solved, I must integrate it as I see it into the totality of philosophic problems.

As I have already stated in a previous passage, I regard Ontology, i.e., a science of the basic forms of Being (Sein) and of being (Seienden), as a fundamental discipline. It is able to demonstrate that there is a radical division within being: *pure Being* holds nothing of non-being in itself, has neither beginning nor end, and holds in itself all which can be; *finite being* has as its allocation both beginning and end. We call the one uncreated Being, the other created being; the Creator corresponds to the former and creatures to the latter. (These terms are borrowed from the language of theology, but the reality thus signified can be shown by purely philosophical methods.)

Creatures are arranged into grades depending on how they more or less approximate pure Being, for all created being is an analogy to divine Being. However, the *analogia entis* [analogy of being] is different from each grade; each one corresponds to another kind of being and a different basic form of being: material, organic, animal, and rational being.

Inasmuch as all lower grades are contained in man's structure of being, he occupies a place peculiar to him in this graded structure. His body is a *material body*, but not *only* that. Rather, at the same time, it is an *organism with a soul* which, in the sensitive manner peculiar to him, is open to himself and his environment. And, finally, he is a *spiritual* being who is consciously cognizant of himself and others and can act freely to develop himself and others. All this belongs to the *human species*, and whatever does not evidence this structure of being cannot be termed a *human being*. However, this species appears differentiated in individuals: notwithstanding his specific human nature, every person has his own unrepeatable singularity. Philosophy can also demonstrate that *individuality*, in the sense of uniqueness, is proper to the human species. To comprehend respective individuals is not the concern of philosophy; rather, we utilize a specific experiential function in our daily contact with people. Another, simple differentiation cuts across this differentiation of humanity into a limitless multiplicity of individuals: *sexual* differentiation.

I would now like to point out several significant questions regarding the education of girls. Does the difference between man and woman involve the whole structure of the person or only the body and those psychic functions necessarily related to physical organs? Can the mind be considered unaffected by this difference? This view is upheld not only by women but also by many theologians. Should this latter view be valid, education would then strive towards development of the intellect without consideration of sexual difference. If, on the other hand, the difference does involve the person's entire structure, then educational work must consider the specific structure of the masculine and feminine mind. Furthermore, if the nature of each individual contains both masculine and feminine elements and if only one of these elements is predominant in each person, would not individuals of both species then be needed to represent perfectly the human species as a whole? Could it not be fully represented by one individual? This question is also of practical significance because, depending on the answer, education must be geared to either overcoming limitations of the specifically masculine and feminine natures or to developing their potential strengths.

In order to answer this question, we would need to refer to the entire context of *genetic* problems; this has hardly been done so far. It would be feasible to examine at some time the specific existential mode exclusive to the human being: the species does not come about in ready-made form at the beginning of existence; rather, the individual develops progressively in a process dependent on time. This process is not unequivocally predetermined but depends rather on several variable factors, among others, on man's freedom which enables him to work towards his own formation and that of others. The possibility of a diversity of types is rooted in this human characteristic which encourages the formation of the species in changing circumstances. There are also further questions to be considered: The generation of new individuals; the transmission of the species through successive generations; and their modification in a variety of types as sexual evolution advances. In considering these questions, philosophy is not concerned with specific changes either in a particular individual's existence or in the factual course of history but rather with their potentiality for change. The connection of genetic problems to that of the development of the species can be expressed in a further question: Is the concrete development of the species as a whole perhaps possible only in the entire succession of generations in their sexual and individual differentiation?

The concern of philosophy is to investigate the necessary and potential characteristics of being through its specific function of cognition. *Theology* seeks to establish woman's unique nature according to divine revelation. Its direct concern is not to investigate the problem itself but rather to assemble and explain historical records. Generally, Scripture does not deal with natural practical instructions. For instance, philosophy asks whether the world was created in time or whether we may consider it as existing through eternity. But the account of creation tells us that it did begin in time and how it began. The Scriptures do not ask whether the sexual differentiation is necessary or accidental but say: "God created man according to His image. He created them as man and woman." Here we find the expression of the facts of oneness and differentiation. However, this is a terse statement which requires explanation. What is meant by God's image in man? We find the answer in the complete history and doctrine of salvation, and it is summarized briefly in the words of Our Lord: "Be ye perfect as your heavenly Father is perfect?" I will not at this time discuss the nature of this ideal of perfection. I would simply suggest that in the words "Be ye" the image of God is established as a duty, vocation, or destiny of mankind—i.e., of man and of woman. . . . .

. . . I am convinced that the species *humanity* embraces the double species *man* and *woman*; that the essence of the complete *human* being is characterized by this duality; and that the entire structure of the essence demonstrates the specific character. There is a difference, not only in body structure and in particular physiological function, but also in the entire corporeal life. The relationship of soul and body is different in man and woman; the relationship of soul to body differs in their psychic life, as does that of the spiritual faculties to each other. The feminine species expresses a unity and wholeness of the total psychosomatic personality and a harmonious development of faculties. The masculine species strives to enhance individual abilities in order that they may attain their highest achievements. . . .

The species humanity, as well as the species femininity, is revealed differently in different individuals. First of all, they represent the species more or less perfectly; then, they illustrate more or less one or another of its characteristics. Man and woman have the same basic human traits, although this or that trait predominates not only in the sexes but also in individuals. Therefore, women may closely approximate the masculine type, and conversely. This may be connected to their individual vocation. If, on the whole, marriage and motherhood are the primary vocations for the feminine sex, it is not necessarily true for each individual. Women may be called to singular cultural achievements, and their talents may be adapted to these achievement.

This brings us to *feminine types* classed *according to their natural abilities.* Given the finiteness of human nature, the impulse to cultural creativity expresses itself in a multiplicity of vocations. And since human nature is finite, man constantly longs for perfection, to which all human beings are called. . . . The species *humanity* is realized perfectly only in the course of world history in which the great individual, humanity, becomes concrete. And the species *man* and *woman* are also fully realized only in the total course of historical development. Whoever is active in educational work is given the human material which he must help form in order that it may become part of the species to which it is called.

Source: From Edith Stein, "Problems of Women's Education," in *Essays on Women*, trans. Freda Mary Oben, from *The Collected Works of Edith Stein* (Washington, D.C.: ICS Publications, 1987), pp. 173–181. Reprinted by permission.

unique to philosophical analysis; however, the medieval philosopher Duns Scotus (1266–1308) held that individuals are differentiated through their *form,* or *nature,* rather than through their *matter.* Stein held that a species is differentiated through a never-changing *form* and that changes occur through *types.* Therefore, a female grows and develops through childhood into adolescence and, finally, into adulthood. That which changes is the *type,* while that which does not change is the *form.*

The central issues for Stein revolved around the relationship of the soul to the body. She generally accepted the thought of Thomas Aquinas (1225–1274), who held the position that the soul is the form of the body. However, Stein sought an answer to another question, which became the cornerstone of her approach to gender differences. Are the bodily differences between women and men the result of matter? This question has profound implications, because if the answer is yes, then the differences are merely accidental to the essence of women and men. If the answer is no, then there is an essential difference in the souls of women and men. Stein believed that the soul of a woman is a different species from the soul of a man; but she further believed that women and men share the same human soul.

Stein made an additional argument that individuals represent a species in a more or less perfect manner. The implications are that a given person could be more or less fully a woman or a man and more or less fully human. Thus, the education a person receives can either enhance his or her development or block that development, which, in turn, will have an effect on the degree to which he or she shares in masculinity or femininity and in humanity. Finally, Stein set forth that education can reach its full potency only if it is carried out in a dynamic, continuous interaction with other human beings, female and male.

Stein's further articulation of the differences between women and men as species brought forth her idea that women tend toward holistic expressions of personality, whereas men tend toward the perfection of individual abilities. Women, she argued, have a natural tendency toward empathy because they seek to grasp other people as whole persons; the role of feelings in the motivation of women requires an education that will help strike a balance between intellect, will, and emotions.

Stein recognized that some women could be more masculine than feminine in their actions. This phenomenon did not create a problem for her because she viewed it as another type of the woman species. The converse of this is also valid; there are men whose actions appear to be more feminine than masculine. Stereotypes played no part in her philosophy.[3]

Stein's Contribution to the Study of Ethics

Stein's work predated that of Simone de Beauvoir, who is generally identified as the founder of women's studies. Stein offered a unique and powerful argument for gender equality and tried to avoid taking an extreme position.

To fully understand the contribution of Edith Stein and the contributions of other philosophers treated in this chapter, it is necessary briefly to consider her work in a historical context. The early Greek philosophers were the first to reflect on the relationship between women and men. They delineated four fundamental categories dealing with gender identity: opposition, generation, wisdom, and virtue.

Plato (427–347 B.C.E.) followed with a theory that women and men have the same kind of souls and thus they are essentially the same. The genderless soul could be reincarnated into the body of a man, woman, or animal. Plato's devaluation of the body affirmed that people are the same, and therefore they are equal.

On the other side of the issue, Aristotle (384–322 B.C.E.) argued that women and men are significantly different. Basing his argument on the differences in the female and male bodies, he contended that the female was an imperfect representation of the human species.

Augustine of Hippo (354–430 C.E.) was the first to argue for the simultaneous differentiation and equality of women and men. His thoughts on gender equality were prompted more by his theological beliefs than by philosophical argumentation.

Essentially, very little attention was given to the question of gender equality until contemporary times. The reason for this lack of philosophical interest should be obvious; men have dominated most of the societies and cultures that were capable of producing works of philosophy.

Edith Stein's works can be considered as holding to a *gender complementarity* view of the relationship between women and men. She staunchly denied the existence of a natural superiority of the male over the female. Although making such a statement may seem unnecessary, gender equality is a relatively new concept and has not gained complete acceptance in today's society. The number of human rights laws protecting women is an indication that without such monitoring women would be discriminated against in many aspects of contemporary life.

Stein's position, particularly her notion of species, has received much criticism. The traditional definition of *species* includes the ability to reproduce. According to Stein, women constitute a species different from the male species; however, her writings do not treat the issue of reproduction. Stein posits instead that the female and male species are different because they have a *constancy of form*, whereby one differs from the other. Another criticism of Stein's work is that some of her theories are not philosophical in nature and require analysis from one of the empirical sciences. For example, some philosophers claim that Stein's view that women tend toward holistic expressions of personality is better explained through psychological and sociological factors. Stein was moving toward an original theory of gender complementarity when her arrest and death brought an abrupt end to her research.

Stein made it very clear that education is essential for the maturation process of both women and men. Education in this context can be said to include such categories of knowledge as the anatomical and physiological differences between female and male; gender implications in language, culture, and history; psychological and sociological dimensions of gender roles; and the economic implications of career choices for women and men. Further, the individual defines herself or himself as a unique person to the fullest extent possible by entering into relationships with others in the larger community. Gender complementarity in Stein's conception means gender equality.

Stein's philosophy supports those who advocate for single-gender schools. The educational content she outlined in her writings would be difficult to implement in public education because public education is coeducational. Principals and superintendents who tend to agree with Stein's approach face the dilemma of trying to find a way to reconcile gender-laden curricula in schools that are gender integrated. Male as well as female students have gender-related curricular needs.

Stein's philosophy has profound implications for educational leadership. This is not readily understood until it becomes clear that her concept of *species* implies a gap of understanding between women and men that can never be bridged. It is *ontological*. Stein attempts to reconcile this isolation by stating that both women and men belong to the *human species*; this notion, however, cannot fill the gap of understanding, except in the broadest sense of knowing the fact that women and men are different and yet knowing that both species are human.

This gap of understanding is somewhat disturbing because public education has endured great trauma in degenderizing. Female and male students take the same courses in the same programs of study. If Stein's dichotomy is accepted, then the curricula that currently exist in most schools must be gender biased because they were developed by females and males. The question of compromise is always present when two or more people, regardless of gender, must make a decision; consensus produces the same condition. Although traces of other opinions remain, one position must ultimately prevail.[4]

The ethical issue for educational administrators is managing the processes of leadership. Another area that is gender laden is the code of student rights and responsibilities. Every school has such a code, either in writing or simply embedded in its traditions. In the generic formulations of codes that treat all students alike there must be some disparity because the codes were formulated by females and males.

There is no way out of this dilemma except by establishing single-gender schools in which activities, curricula, and codes are geared toward one gender. Realistically, this will not happen in public education. Consequently, the ethical issue for administrators becomes a work in progress; principals, superintendents, and other staff members must continually be sensitive to the gender needs of individual students and of the student body in the aggregate.

SIMONE DE BEAUVOIR: GENDER COEXISTENCE

Simone de Beauvoir was born at Paris in 1908 into a typical bourgeois family. Her father greatly influenced her intellectual development, and her mother tried to instill in her a sense of the spiritual. Beauvoir's life and philosophical orientation were profoundly affected by this dichotomy between human and spiritual affairs.

She had an intense friendship with Zaza (Elizabeth Mabille), whom she met in 1918. This friendship ended in 1921 with the death of Zaza. Both Beauvoir and Zaza had a mutual friend, Merleau Ponty, who later gained renown as a philosopher. Zaza wanted to marry Ponty, but was impeded from doing so by her family, who viewed Ponty as coming from a lower station in life. Beauvoir attributed Zaza's death to the turmoil she experienced because of her family's position against Ponty. This tragic situation was one of a series of events that inspired Beauvoir to write *The Second Sex*.

In her early teenage years, Beauvoir lost her interest in the spiritual. Most likely, this event was the turning point that chartered the course of her future intellectual pursuits. At the age of twenty-one she brilliantly passed a competitive exam, *Agrégation de Philosophie,* which was necessary to embark on a teaching career in France. At that time teaching was a position not worthy of the bourgeois class, and as a result of Beauvoir's desire to become a teacher, her father alienated himself from her. This was a terrible shock to Beauvoir, which resulted in her leaving home.

Around 1929, Beauvoir met the soon-to-be-famous existential philosopher Jean-Paul Sartre, who was to remain her lifelong friend and confidant. The relationship passed through different stages of intensity, but the bond was never broken. With the outbreak of World War II, the brilliant philosopher and writer Albert Camus recruited both Sartre and Beauvoir to work with him in publishing a clandestine newspaper, *Combat*. Eventually, they went into hiding, which lasted until the liberation of Paris.

Both Beauvoir and Sartre developed left-wing tendencies and took unpopular stands in support of both Soviet and Chinese communism. In her later years, Beauvoir took up the issue of aging and particularly the plight of older women who were abandoned by men in search of relationships with younger women. She gave these women a voice through her writings. Having consistently promoted the equality of women with men, Beauvoir in 1972 embarked on an intense campaign in support of women's rights.

Beauvoir wrote novels, essays, and memoirs, all of which reflected her existentialism. It is easy to detect in her writings the great influence of Jean-Paul Sartre on her thinking. Unlike Sartre, though, Beauvoir was not interested in ideas, but in life—the ordinary everyday lives of people. She attempted to live life as a fully human endeavor in order to reveal to others what was most universal about their lives. To Beauvoir, life was an experiment to be studied in the laboratory of society. She herself was the subject of the investigation.

The Second Sex was based on Beauvoir's personal experiences and rooted in her reaction to the way in which her mother had lived her life. Selected Reading 6.2 contains an excerpt from this book. The meaninglessness of life's routine activities and how they rob a person of living a fulfilling life is the message of this significant work. However, Beauvoir retained a sense of idealism in the midst of this deadening ordinariness. Late in life she told an interviewer, F. Jeanson, that all of life is a quest for being, for the absolute, but that people never reach anything except relativity.[5]

Beauvoir's Contribution to the Study of Ethics

Beauvoir's book *The Second Sex* became the manifesto of the feminist movement in the 1950s. It clearly sets forth Beauvoir's philosophy, which asserts that women are humans first and females second. Fundamentally, women and men are the same, and the detrimental conditions within which women find themselves are products of the bad faith of men.

Beauvoir's position was formulated around the concept that both women and men are subjects who are free and capable of transcendence. Through their actions, women and men can appropriate and transform their lives out of the

Selected Reading 6.2

The Second Sex

Simone de Beauvoir (1908–1986)

And it is true that the evolution now in progress threatens more than feminine charm alone: in beginning to exist for herself, woman will relinquish the function as double and mediator to which she owes her privileged place in the masculine universe; to man, caught between the silence of nature and the demanding presence of other free beings, a creature who is at once his like and a passive thing seems a great treasure. The guise in which he conceives his companion may be mythical, but the experiences for which she is the source or the pretext are nonetheless real: There are hardly any more precious, more intimate, more ardent. There is no denying that feminine dependence, inferiority, woe, give women their special character; assuredly woman's autonomy, if it spares men many troubles, will also deny them many conveniences; assuredly there are certain forms of the sexual adventure which will be lost in the world of tomorrow. But this does not mean that love, happiness, poetry, dream, will be banished from it.

Let us forget that our lack of imagination always depopulates the future; for us it is only an abstraction; each one of us secretly deplores the absence there of the one who was himself. But the humanity of tomorrow will be living in its flesh and in its conscious liberty; that time will be its present and it will in turn prefer it. New relations of flesh and sentiments of which we have no conception will arise between the sexes; already, indeed, there have appeared between men and women friendships, rivalries, complicities, comradeship—chaste or sensual—which past centuries could not have conceived. To mention one point, nothing could seem to me more debatable than the opinion that dooms the new world to uniformity and hence to boredom. I fail to see that this present world is free from boredom or that liberty ever creates uniformity.

To begin with, there will always be certain differences between man and woman; her eroticism, and therefore her sexual world, have a special form of their own and therefore cannot fail to engender a sensuality, a sensitivity, of a special nature. This means that her relations to her own body, to that of the male, to the child, will never be identical with those the male bears to his own body, to that of the female, and to the child; those who make much of "equality in difference" could not with good grace refuse to grant me the possible existence of differences in equality. Then again, it is institutions that create uniformity. Young and pretty, the slaves of the harem are always the same in the sultan's embrace; Christianity gave eroticism its savor of sin and legend when it endowed the human female with a soul; if society restores her sovereign individuality to woman, it will not therefore destroy the power of love's embrace to move the heart.

It is nonsense to assert that revelry, vice, ecstasy, passion, would become impossible if man and woman were equal in concrete matters; the contradictions that put the flesh in opposition to the spirit, the instant to time, the swoon of immanence to the challenge of transcendence, the absolute of pleasure to the nothingness of forgetting, will never be resolved; in sexuality will always be materialized the tension, the anguish, the joy, the frustration, and the triumph of existence. To emancipate woman is to refuse to confine her to the relations she bears to man, not to deny them to her; let her have her independent existence and she will continue nonetheless to exist for him also; mutually recognizing each other as subject, each will yet remain for the other an other. The reciprocity of their relations will not do away with the miracles—desire, possession, love, dream, adventure—worked by the division of human beings into two separate categories; and the words that move us—giving, conquering, uniting—will not lose their meaning. On the contrary, when we abolish the slavery of the half of humanity, together with the whole system of hypocrisy that it implies, then the "division" of humanity will reveal its genuine significance and the human couple will find its true form.

Source: From *The Second Sex* by Simone de Beauvoir, trans. H. M. Parshley. Copyright © 1952 and renewed 1980 by Alfred A. Knopf Inc. Reprinted by permission of the publisher. Excerpt from pages 730–732.

passive, objectlike existence within which they have been placed. Thus, women and men must interpret their present situations and project futures that will transform their lives into their own personal creations. Such transcendence demands constant action and change.

Each person has a tendency to conceive of herself or himself as a universe around which all others move and have their being. Other persons are meaningful to an individual only in this position of relativity. However, human authenticity demands that people affirm not only their own autonomy, but also that of others. Each person is self-creating and sovereign. Beauvoir's notion of bad faith consists in accepting a given situation in life as beyond a person's control. Further, it is fallacious to believe in human destiny; there are only limiting situations and circumstances that can and must be transcended if an individual is to become a true human subject.

Beauvoir believed that the tendency in people to relegate others to positions of dependence in order to deemphasize their importance has fostered an attitude in men that views women as inferior. This attitude, along with the physical imperative of giving birth and nurturing children in societies that also deprive women of economic security, is the reason Beauvoir entitled her book *The Second Sex*. She considered this the original condition of women, but by no means their destined future. By taking control of their lives, women are able to progress toward greater freedom and heightened consciousness. Economic security gained through entry into the world of work along with men is the vehicle for reaching this goal.

Existence presents women with many paradoxes. The most relevant are first, a sense of freedom while situated in limiting conditions, and second, the presence of a yearning, transcending spirit, grounded in nature. Beauvoir made a special point of calling into question the male dictum that women are more natural than men; she believed that both women and men are natural beings. The challenge is for both to transcend the constraints of nature and to liberate their selves through creative work, which, at times, will require courage and the taking of risks. Thus, women to a certain degree must detach themselves from everything they possess in order to gain a clear vision of future potentiality. Myths must be debunked, women must persist in the quest for liberation, and women should not look for help outside their personhood.

There is one other major paradox: the need for personal sovereignty within a coexistence situation. From Beauvoir's perspective, each woman is responsible to herself for searching out ways in which she can foster and develop her own coexistence with men. The ultimate goal is for all people, women and men, to retain and strengthen their individual sovereignty through transcendent activities within a milieu that respects all others as subjects and supports them in their quest for sovereignty.

It is easy to see in Beauvoir's writings the beginnings of the feminist movement that has resulted in the many federal laws that support the sovereignty of women. Beauvoir's notion of economic security and its impact on the quest for a personal sovereignty that permits a person to create his or her own destiny is a tremendous insight into human nature. It places the obligation of self-actualization squarely on the shoulders of each individual; blaming others is unacceptable.[6]

This same concept, however, delineates a clear obligation for educational administrators. As self-actualizing persons themselves, principals, superintendents, and other administrators have the responsibility to make decisions that will not hinder the self-actualization of others. This may seem contradictory in that a principal may limit his or her potential for self-actualization if he or she encourages and situates the school environment so that others can develop their own sovereignty and destiny. However, economic security, sovereignty, and destiny cannot be achieved by the suppression of others. History has attested to this over and over again. Suppressing others in order to achieve personal goals leads an individual to self-absorption, and eventually to self-deception and the probable ruination of his or her own career.

When a principal recommends the employment of teachers or assistant principals whom he or she believes will be easy to manipulate and thus not a threat to his or her authority, that principal has placed his or her own distorted view of self-security above the good of students. Eventually, the performance of ineffective teachers and administrators will lead to the dissatisfaction of parents, students, and other colleagues, which may lead ultimately to termination of that principal's employment for lack of leadership ability.

SANDRA HARDING AND SUSAN BORDO: HUMAN COGNITION

Schools and school districts are affected more than most institutions by the trends and currents that underpin contemporary society. The vast majority of employees in school districts, particularly at the teaching level, are women; however, a significant number of women are entering the principalship and superintendency. Women constitute the largest percentage of those attending graduate programs in educational leadership. This situation represents a monumental change that will continue to influence the administration of schools and school districts. The effects on women of the feminist movement continue to shape them; the feminist movement also has had and will continue to have a profound impact on men. The feminist revolution has progressed from militancy into a subtle mechanism, fashioning society through the transformation of American culture.

The contemporary view of feminism tends to see economic independence as the vehicle for changing society, although most women also recognize the importance of continuing to work for change in government and the public media. When women become economically liberated through work, there is a change in the manner in which household activities and the rearing of children are carried out. In turn, this change affects the attitudes of women and men, not only toward these duties, but also toward all aspects of family life and toward the sexual relationship between women and men.[7]

Moral Inquiry

The most fundamental issue in the feminist movement—in any movement—is how its leaders and theoreticians formulate their ideas and argumentation. Sandra Harding, in "From Feminist Empiricism to Feminist Standpoint Epistemologies," excerpted in Selected Reading 6.3, uses the word *feminist* to emphasize her position that women indeed do differ from men in this manner. She uses the

Selected Reading 6.3

From Feminist Empiricism to Feminist Standpoint Epistemologies

Sandra Harding

Finally, it is historical changes that make possible feminist theory and consequently a feminist science and epistemology, as I have argued elsewhere. Here, too, we can learn from the Marxist analysis. Engels believed that "the great thinkers of the Eighteenth Century could, no more than their predecessors, go beyond the limits imposed upon them by their epoch." He thought that only with the emergence in nineteenth-century industrializing societies of a "conflict between productive forces and modes of production"—a conflict that "exists, in fact, objectively, outside us, independently of the will and actions even of the men that have brought it on"—could the class structure of earlier societies be detected in its fullness for the first time. "Modern socialism is nothing but the reflex, in thought, of this conflict in fact; its ideal reflection in the minds, first, of the class directly suffering under it, the working class."

Similarly, only now can we understand the feminism of the eighteenth and nineteenth centuries as but "utopian" feminism. The men and women feminists of those cultures could recognize the misery of women's condition and the unnecessary character of that misery, but both their diagnoses of its causes and their prescriptions for women's emancipation show a failure to grasp the complex and not always obvious mechanisms by which masculine dominance is created and maintained. Liberal feminism, Marxist feminism and perhaps even the more doctrinaire strains of the radical and socialist feminism of the mid-1970s do not have conceptual schemes rich or flexible enough to capture masculine domination's historical and cultural adaptability, nor its chameleon like talents for growing within such other cultural hierarchies as classism and racism. More complex and culture-sensitive (though not unproblematic) analyses had to await the emergence of historical changes in the relations between the genders. These changes have created a massive conflict between the culturally favored forms of producing persons (gendered, raced, classed persons) and the beliefs and actions of increasing numbers of women and some men who do not want to live out mutilated lives within the dangerous and oppressive politics these archaic forms of reproduction encourage.

If we cannot exactly describe this historical moment through an analogy to a "conflict between productive forces and modes of production" (and why should we have to?), we can nevertheless see clearly many aspects of the specific economic, political, and social shifts that have created this moment. There was the development and widespread distribution of cheap and efficient birth control, undertaken for capitalist and imperialist motives of controlling Third World and domestically colonized populations. There was the decline in the industrial sector combined with growth in the service sectors of the economy, which drew women into wage labor and deteriorated the centrality of industrialized "proletariat" labor. There were the emancipatory hopes created by the civil rights movement and the radicalism of the 1960s in both the United States and Europe. There was the rapid increase in divorce and in families headed by females—brought about in part by capitalism's seduction of men out of the family and into a "swinging singles" lifestyle, where they would consume more goods; in part by women's increased, though still severely limited, ability to survive economically outside of marriage; and no doubt in part by an availability of contraceptives that make what in olden days was called "philandering" less expensive. There was the increasing recognition of the feminization of poverty (probably also an actual increase in women's poverty), which combined with the increase in divorce and the drawing of women into wage labor to make women's life prospects look very different from those of their mothers and grandmothers: now women of every class could—and should—plan for lives after or instead of marriage. There was the escalation in international hostilities, revealing the clear overlap between masculine psychic needs for domination and nationalist domination rhetoric and politics. No doubt other significant social changes could be added to this list of preconditions for the emergence of feminism and its successor science and epistemology.

word *epistemologies*, the usual philosophical designation for theories of knowledge, to mean not only the process of rational thought, but also remembering, proving, imagining, inferring, perceiving, and reflecting.

One of Harding's important contributions to understanding the feminist movement is her clear argumentation that the historical milieu within which people are born situates them and erects barriers that will hinder them in their advance toward different understandings. At the same time, however, change is

Thus, to paraphrase Engels, feminist theory is nothing but the reflex in thought of these conflicts in fact, their ideal reflection in the minds first of the class most directly suffering under them—women. Feminist science and epistemology projects are not the products of observation, will power, and intellectual brilliance alone—faculties that Enlightenment science and epistemology hold responsible for advances in knowledge. They are expressions of ways in which nature and social life can be understood by the new kinds of historical persons created by these social changes. Persons whose activities are still characteristically "womanly," yet who also take on what have traditionally been masculine projects in public life, are one such important group of new persons. This "violation" of a traditional (at least, in our recent history) gendered division of labor both provides an epistemically advantaged standpoint for a successor science project and also resists the continuation of the distorting dualities of modernism. Why should we be loath to attribute a certain degree of, if not historical inevitability, at least historical possibility to the kinds of understandings arrived at in feminist science and epistemology?

I still think a historical account is an important component of the feminist standpoint epistemologies: it can identify the shifts in social life that make possible new modes of understanding. A standpoint epistemology without this recognition of the "role of history in science" (Kuhn's phrase) leaves mysterious the preconditions for its own production. However, I now think that the kind of account indicated above retains far too much of its Marxist legacy, and thereby also of Marxism's Enlightenment inheritance. It fails to grasp the historical changes that make possible the feminist postmodernist challenges to the Enlightenment vision as well as to Marxism.

---

simultaneously and continually occurring in each person and in society. How this change is directed is the result of the confrontation between advocates and protagonists.

In this selection, Harding identifies the economic, political, and social specifics that constituted the milieu that eventually created the epistemological shift in the way women and men understand themselves and their relationships. The factors identified by Harding are affordable and efficient birth control; the growth in service occupations available to women; the civil rights movement; an increase in divorce; poverty, which brought more women into the workforce; and a less restricted lifestyle.

Finally, Harding validates the historical importance of the postmodern approach to knowledge, which is grounded in the messy experience of living rather than in the refined duality of the Enlightenment. She also recognizes the emergence of the *new woman,* who is capable of continuing her traditional feminine role while also assuming roles traditionally ascribed to men.

Many people consider the specifics identified by Harding as leading to societal change as negative and even immoral forces. Today, women are more liberated and self-actualized than they were in the past; men also are more liberated. It is appropriate to view these forces as inevitable, given the historical preconditions that led to their development. These forces did not spontaneously happen; they developed over a long period of time, reaching back to ancient epochs of human evolution. The feminist movement ushered in the most recent epoch in the human search for liberation and mandated the need to experiment with how freedom should function in society.

Educational administrators who are not in agreement with the successes of the feminist movement are fighting a battle that they cannot win. There is no turning back to the ways of the past. To attack the means and forces that led to this revolution is a futile endeavor. There are fewer and fewer male principals and superintendents who are hoping for a return to the past. The challenge for educational leaders is to promote the liberation of both women and men in policy and procedure development. To do so, employment policies and procedures that give equal opportunity to women are needed.

This same theme is carried forward in the writings of Susan Bordo. In the excerpt from "The Cartesian Masculinization of Thought" found in Selected Reading 6.4, Bordo explores the mind-set of philosophers who have perpetuated a male thought pattern that has had a significant negative impact on women.

Bordo considers the feminist movement significant enough to be compared to the Renaissance. The Renaissance explored the natural capability of humanity, in contrast to the Middle Ages, when humanity was under the controlling influence of the Church and a debasing concept of human nature; the feminist movement has sought liberation for women in a male-dominated culture. However, according to Bordo, no movement of liberation can be contained within artificial borders, but will spread to other conditions of domination. Bordo specifically mentions the domination of people of color and ethnic groups by a white male culture.

To appreciate the significance of Bordo's argumentation, it is important to have an understanding of the philosophy of René Descartes (1596–1650), whose method of argumentation has been termed *Cartesian* by subsequent philosophers. Descartes's main concern as a philosopher was the exploration of human knowledge, to which end he developed a method of argumentation known as *methodic doubt.* Descartes was convinced that truth and error are so intertwined

Selected Reading 6.4

The Cartesian Masculinization of Thought

Susan Bordo

. . . There is a certain similarity here with the Renaissance, in the cultural reawakening to the multiplicity of possible human perspectives, and to the role of culture in shaping those perspectives. But in our era, the reawakening has occurred in the context of a recognition not merely of the undiscovered "other," but of the *suppressed* other. Women, people of color, and various ethnic and national groups have forced the culture into a critical reexamination not only of diversity (as occurred for Renaissance culture), but of the forces that *mask* diversity. That which appears as "dominant," by virtue of that very fact, comes to be suspect: It has a secret story to tell, in the alternative perspectives to which it has denied legitimacy, and in the historical and political circumstances of its own dominance.

Fueled by the historicist tradition in epistemology, psychoanalytic thought, *and* the political movement for women's rights, representation, and participation in cultural life, feminist ethics and epistemology now appears as one of the most vital forces in the development of post-Cartesian focus and paradigm. The feminist exposure of the gender biases in our dominant Western conceptions of science and ethics—the revelation that the history of their development, the lenses through which they see the world, their methods and priorities have been decisively shaped by the fact that it has been men who have determined their course—has come as a startling recognition to many contemporary male philosophers. Inspired by the work of Gilligan, Chodorow, Harding, and Keller, feminist theory has been systematically questioning the historical identification of rationality, intelligence, "good thinking," and so forth, with the masculine modes of detachment and clarity, offering alternative models of fresher, more humane, and more hopeful approaches to science and ethics.

It is not only in explicitly feminist writing that these phenomena are occurring. Many of the "new paradigms" being proposed in the recent spate of literature on modernity and modern science are grounded in sympathetic, participatory alternatives to Cartesianism. (See Berman and Capra, in particular.) In philosophy, a whole slew of reconsiderations of traditional epistemological "problems" such as relativism, perspectivism, the role of emotions and body in knowledge, the possibility of ultimate foundations, and so on, has brought the feminine perspective in through the back door, as it were. Without explicit commitment to feminism or "the feminine," philosophers are nonetheless participating in a (long overdue) philosophical acknowledgment of the limitations of the masculine Cartesian model, and are recognizing how tightly it has held most modern philosophy in its grip.

This is not to say that detachment, clarity, and precision will cease to have enormous value in the process of understanding. Rather, our culture needs to reconceive the status of what Descartes assigned to the shadows. Such reevaluation has been a constant, although "recessive" strain in the history of philosophy since Descartes. Leibniz's declaration that each monad is its *own* "mirror" of the universe, Hume's insistence that "reason is and ought to be the slave of the passions," and perhaps most importantly, Kant's revelation that objectivity itself is the result of human structuring, opened various doors that in retrospect now appear as critical openings.

Hume, for example, may now be seen as having a rightful place—along with Nietzsche, Scheler, Peirce, Dewey, James, Whitehead, and more recently, Robert Neville—in the critical protest against the Cartesian notion that reason can and should be a "pure" realm free from contamination by emotion, instinct, will, sentiment, and value. Within this protest, we see the development both of a "nationalist" *anthropology* of the Cartesian ideals of precision, certainty, and neutrality (Nietzsche, Scheler, Dewey, and James), and a complementary *metaphysics* (Peirce, Whitehead, and Neville) in which "vagueness" as well as specificity, tentativeness, and valuation are honored as essential to thought.

In emphasizing the active, constructive nature of cognition, Kant undermined the Cartesian notion that the mind reflects and the scientist "reads off" what is simply *there* in the world. The Kantian "knower" is transcendental, of course, and Kant's "constructionism" begins and ends, like most Enlightenment thought, with a vision of universal law—in this case, the basic, ahistorical requirements of "knowability," represented by the categories. But the "Copernican Revolution in Thought," in asserting the activity of the subject, opened the door, paradoxically, to a more historical and contextual understanding of knowing. The knower, not the known, now comes under

that it is nearly impossible to disentangle them. Thus he postulated that there must be a fresh approach to proving the tenets of human knowledge. He hoped to demonstrate three things with this new approach: that the soul is immaterial, that God exists, and that there is an extended reality. He began by doubting everything, but finally was convinced that there was one thing that he could not doubt, his own existence. More specifically, the fact that Descartes could think scrutiny—and not as Descartes scrutinized the knower, for those contaminating elements which must be purged from cognition, but for those "active and interpreting forces," as Nietzsche says, "through which alone seeing becomes seeing *something.*" The postulation of an inner "eye" in which these forces "are supposed to be lacking . . . [is] an absurdity and a nonsense" (1996, 119).

The articulation of the historical, social and cultural determinants of what Nietzsche called "perspective" can be seen as one paradigm of modern thought. The main theoretical categories of that paradigm have been worked out by various disciplines: the "philosophical anthropology" of Max Scheler, Karl Mannheim's work on ideology, and, historically frontal, the dialectical materialism of Karl Marx. Marx, of course, was not primarily interested in epistemological questions. But he is nonetheless the single most important philosophical figure in the development of modern historicism, with his emphasis on the historical nature of all human activity and thought and our frequent "false consciousness" of this. It was Marx who turned the tables on the Enlightenment, encouraging suspicion of all ideas that claim to represent universal, fundamental, "inherent," or "natural" features of reality.

The Cartesian ideal of the detached, purely neutral observer is here viewed as a type of mystification, and the ideals of absolute objectivity and ultimate foundations seen as requiring historical examination. In the modern era, "universal" after "universal" has fallen, under the scrutiny of Marxists, anthropologists, critical theorists, feminists, philosophers of science, and deconstructionists. The various claims regarding human nature and human sexuality (the "naturalness" of competition, the "necessity" of sexual repression, the "biological" nature of gender differences) have been challenged. Rorty and Foucault, respectively, have argued that the "mind" and "sexuality" are historical "inventions." And Patrick Heelan has shown that our most basic perceptions of space have a cultural history.

---

convinced him of his own existence. This notion is often quoted in the Latin, *Cogito, ergo sum,* and is translated as "I think, therefore I am."

The major opposition to Descartes's philosophy rests in his proposition that a person can know something without sense experience. The thought process as an exercise in reasoning is the ultimate source of the type of knowledge that Descartes sought; his methodic doubt leaves one isolated in the mental order.[8]

According to Bordo, the historical identification of rationality with the male mode of thinking, with its detachment and clear-cut reasoning, has been systematically questioned by feminist theorists. Further, Bordo rightly points out that many other authors, female and male, are investigating the limitations of the Cartesian model. She identifies prominent philosophers—Leibniz, Kant, Hume, Nietzsche, Scheler, Peirce, Dewey, James, Whitehead, and Neville—who were critical of the Cartesian notion that reason could be free from emotion, instinct, sentiment, value, and will.

Bordo postulates a concern that has tremendous implications for curriculum development, both in science and in how the humanities and fine arts are interwoven into academic programs. The emphasis of the scientific method in the absence of serious humanities and fine-arts courses will give a distorted understanding of human knowledge. What is needed is a balanced and well-integrated curriculum that fosters the education of the whole person. Although this notion may seem obvious, some principals, superintendents, and other administrators do not sufficiently value humanities and fine-arts courses. The demands from parents and business leaders for more education in the use of technology also has placed a strain on the budgets of schools and school districts. Sometimes an easier answer for administrators is to cut or weaken programs and courses in the humanities and fine arts in order to free up funds for courses in technology.

FEDERAL LEGISLATIVE PROTECTION OF WOMEN'S RIGHTS

There is no doubt but that the feminist movement has brought about significant change in U.S. society. Advocates realized from the beginning, however, that change, particularly changing the way men think about and treat women, would take considerable time. Even as signs indicated that society was moving in the direction of equality for women, many advocates, individuals formally recognized as leaders of the feminist movement as well as others without such a designation, saw the need to substantiate equal rights for women in the labor market through federal legislation. Perhaps the struggle for equality would eventually have revolutionized the treatment of women anyway, but leaders both inside and outside the feminist movement took steps to bring about the desired change more effectively and more rapidly. They recognized that the liberation of women in all areas hinged on their economic security. Thus, advocates became political activists, demanding federal legislation that would provide equal opportunity for women in business and industry.

They were successful. Equal employment opportunity for women emanated primarily from the following federal laws: Title VII of the Civil Rights Act of 1964 as amended in 1972; Title IX of the Education Amendments of 1972; Public Law 95-555, which amended Title VII of the Civil Rights Act and is commonly known as the Pregnancy Disability Amendment; and the Equal Pay Act of 1963. These laws mandate compliance of employers, including school districts, with provisions that ensure equality in the employment and promotion of women in all positions.

The federal agency charged with enforcing these laws is the Equal Employment Opportunity Commission (EEOC), which was established by the Civil Rights Act of 1964 and significantly strengthened by the Equal Employment Opportunity Act of 1972. The jurisdiction of EEOC extends to all private employers of fifteen or more persons, all educational institutions, all state and local governments, public and private employment agencies, labor unions with fifteen or more members, and joint labor-management committees for apprenticeships and training.

The Civil Rights Act not only prohibits discrimination on the basis of gender, but also prohibits discrimination based on religion, national origin, race, and color. Title IX prohibits gender discrimination in educational programs and activities, including employment, in school districts receiving federal financial assistance. As there are virtually no school districts in the United States that do not receive some federal financial assistance, this law provides universal protection for women.

Public Law 95-555 seeks to eliminate unequal treatment of pregnant women in all employment-related situations. The guidelines from EEOC indicate that it is discriminatory for an employer to dismiss, refuse to hire, train, assign, or promote a woman solely because she is pregnant. Further, the law requires maternity leave for a predetermined time period, requires school districts to reemploy woman who have been on maternity leave, and requires school districts to grant seniority credit to a woman who has been on maternity leave. Finally, the law prohibits school districts from denying disability or medical benefits to a woman for disability or illness unrelated to but occurring during pregnancy, childbirth, or recovery from childbirth.

The Equal Pay Act requires employers, including school districts, to pay women and men the same salary or wage for equal work. Through court litigation, the definition of equal work has been broadened to mean *substantially* equal work; therefore, strict equality of jobs is not required. The act requires equal pay for jobs that demand equal skill, effort, and responsibility and that are carried out under similar working conditions. The implication for educational administrators is that the female coach of the girls' volleyball team cannot be paid less than the male coach of the boys' soccer team.

In 1991, Congress passed a new Civil Rights Act, which has two very important provisions. First, the law allows compensatory and punitive damages. Prior to enactment of this law, women who were discriminated against by a school district could receive lost pay and benefits, reinstatement, and attorney's fees. Now women can receive compensatory damages for emotional pain, inconvenience, and mental anguish. For administrators and school-board members, the second new provision of this law has tremendous significance. Now administrators and board members can be named as codefendants with the school district in a lawsuit, which means that punitive damages can be levied against them.

The progress in clarifying and advancing the dignity, equality, and liberation of women in U.S. society can be assessed through a directive issued by the Equal Employment Opportunity Commission in 1980, which declared sexual harassment to be a violation of Title VII of the Civil Rights Act of 1964. At the time of issuance, the personal treatment of women by men in the workforce was problematic. Since that time thousands of complaints have been filed with EEOC, some of merit and others frivolous. The directive enlightened everyone's understanding about the effectiveness of legal remedies that do not attack the manifestations of male dominance in the ordinary work environment. Certainly the more obvious discrimination in hiring and promoting women in the workplace could be addressed more effectively than the less obvious and often embarrassing harassment of women by male colleagues. This type of discrimination is more sinister because it is difficult to prove and the investigation that EEOC must conduct creates an opportunity for further abuse through untruthful testimony and innuendo.

The directive identifies two types of sexual harassment: *quid pro quo* discrimination and *hostile-environment* discrimination. Quid pro quo discrimination occurs when an employment or personnel decision is based on an applicant's or employee's submission to or rejection of unwelcome sexual conduct. For example, when a promotion is promised to a woman if she submits to a supervisor's sexual advances, it is considered sexual harassment.

Hostile-environment discrimination occurs when unwelcome sexual conduct interferes with an employee's job performance. The criterion for determining whether the conduct is harassment hinges on the reasonable person standard; if a reasonable person would have his or her job performance substantially hindered by the harassment, then there is environmental discrimination. Other factors to consider in investigating hostile-environment discrimination include whether the conduct was physical, verbal, or both; how often the conduct occurred; the job position of the harasser; whether other employees were involved; and whether the conduct was directed toward more than one person.

A mitigating circumstance is whether the conduct was unwelcome; an employee must tell the harasser that he or she wants the person to stop the abusive behavior. Further, the timing of the allegation and whether a prior consensual relationship existed with the alleged harasser are significant factors considered by EEOC.

School districts may be liable for the harassment actions of administrators because administrators are the *agents* of the districts. The school district is always liable in the case of quid pro quo harassment. In the case of hostile-environment harassment, the school district is liable if other administrators knew or should have known about the harassment. In coworker harassment, for example, the school district is liable if a supervisor knew that an employee under his or her supervision was harassing or was being harassed. When harassment is detected, the appropriate administrator must take action to remedy the situation. It is also the responsibility of a school administrator to protect employees from sexual harassment by nonemployees on school premises.

To demonstrate that sexual harassment will not be tolerated in a school district, the board of education should create a policy prohibiting such conduct and the superintendent of schools should develop administrative procedures for investigating and remedying harassment. Both the policy and the procedures should contain provisions for confidentiality and for protecting the victim of harassment from retaliation by the alleged harasser.

All employees in a school district should be required to participate in a staff development program that includes an explanation of the board policy and administrative procedures along with examples of conduct that is considered sexual harassment.[9]

THE FUTURE

There has been much postulating about the decline of Western culture and morality, specifically in the United States. However, many feminists propose that the real decline is in male dominance. What is happening is a reevaluation of the relationships that have existed in the past between women and men, between women and children, between women and women, and between women and society in general. Along with this analysis and questioning is the gradual replacement of male dominance not with female domination, but with gender equality. The targets for a shift to gender equality are corporations, governments, and educational institutions. The feminist movement has not resorted to violence to accomplish the goal of equality; rather, the movement has relied on the experiences of women, the practices and traditions of women, and women's thought and experimentation.

The philosopher Virginia Held conceptualizes the feminist society of the future by outlining certain aspects of the present structure of society and then pointing out how these conceptualizations are inadequate. The first view holds that the rule of law is supreme. The government may use violence to uphold the law and thus has ultimate authority in society. Economic, cultural, and educational activities are regulated by the government, and the government functions only with and under the consent of the governed. From a feminist perspective this situation is inadequate because it provides the government with the right to bring about the rule of law by force and violence. Further, the government shapes society, rather than the reverse, which is more appropriate.

The second view recognizes the economic base as the determination of everything in society. In a capitalist economic system, the government represents the economic interests of the capitalists. All societal structures, such as the educational system, are used to strengthen the economic system. The concern with this view is the lack of other influences on society. The vision of what the benefits should be of a capitalist society is much too narrow.

The third view identifies segments of society as overlapping but relatively independent. The economic, educational, and political institutions are self-determining. Society is viewed as pluralistic and as having multiple sources of influence. Even though the interests of the various institutions sometimes come into conflict, none overpowers the others. This third view is more compatible with the feminist agenda, but its lack of a unifying perspective may obscure the concerns of women.

Held then suggests a feminist alternative to these three views. She believes that society must recognize the centrality of the gender issues that permeate all institutions. Even though society must have independent and distinct institutions, these same institutions could be networked through relationships that are characterized by social caring and trust.[10]

The ideal society should have a democratic political system, an independent judicial system, and a strong economic base. In Held's view, the institutions of society should be evaluated in terms of their success in liberating women, children, minorities, elderly people, people with disabilities, and others. It is not necessary to change the principles under which institutions operate, but it might be necessary to limit their influence. The activism of various groups has succeeded in pointing out needed change, but such activism must be continual if real progress is to be a hallmark of society. The success of the civil rights movement for African Americans is a good example of the progress that can be made. The feminist movement also has made considerable strides. The cause of women is intertwined with the causes of maternal health care, child care, and early-childhood education as well as the cause to eliminate sexual victimization. These are only a few of the many interrelated concerns of the feminist movement.

The activism that has taken place in the United States has produced a considerable number of federal and state laws protecting the rights and dignity of women. U.S. Supreme Court decisions have further refined these rights. What is hoped for in the future is a society that does not need to resort to laws to guarantee the rights of everyone in all aspects of that society.

OTHER PHILOSOPHICAL APPROACHES TO THE ISSUES IN THIS CHAPTER

The language of rights in relation to women was initially articulated by philosophers as diverse as John Stuart Mill, Harriet Taylor, and Mary Wollstonecraft. Of particular significance is the work of Wollstonecraft, who wrote *A Vindication of the Rights of Women* toward the end of the eighteenth century. In this book she launched an aggressive attack on social conventions that denied women a basic education and addressed other rights that women needed to attain equality.

Though some of her thoughts were set forth in this chapter, the work of Virginia Held is worthy of further investigation. In addition, although they do not deal directly with feminism, the works of Michel Foucault in relation to social practices and power relations have relevance to gender-equity issues. Of particular significance is Foucault's idea that the limits and nature of human thought continue to change more often and more radically in relatively short periods of time; the effect of such changes on human theory and practice is monumental.

CROSSWALK TO ISLLC STANDARD FIVE

The contents of this chapter support the following dimensions of ISLLC Standard Five:

Knowledge
The administrator has knowledge and understanding of:
◆ various ethical frameworks and perspectives on ethics
◆ the values of the diverse school community

Dispositions
The administrator believes in, values, and is committed to:
◆ the principles in the Bill of Rights

Performances
The administrator:
◆ treats people fairly, equitably, and with dignity and respect
◆ demonstrates appreciation for and sensitivity to the diversity in the school community
◆ examines and considers the prevailing values of the diverse school community
◆ applies laws and procedures fairly, wisely, and considerately

ETHICAL CONSIDERATIONS PRESENTED IN THIS CHAPTER

◆ The education of children concerning the equality of females and males is a primary consideration in educational leadership.
◆ A genuine understanding of gender differences can only take place through continuous meaningful interaction between females and males;

thus, principals and superintendents are charged with developing such opportunities not only for students, but also for teachers, other administrators, and staff members.

◆ Educational leaders must be ever vigilant in eliminating gender-biased curricula and school practices and in eliminating gender-biased employment practices and working conditions.

◆ The welfare of both genders is intricately tied together; thus, educational leaders should promote the welfare of both females and males equally.

◆ Economic security is a major factor in gender equality. Thus, educational leaders should encourage students to enter the fields of study that will provide them with the greatest number of career options, and educational leaders should be concerned with providing district employees with equal opportunity to advance in their careers.

◆ Gender-biased attitudes are detrimental to all attempts at equalization. The language in school and school-district policies should be free from gender bias, which can be of significant help in changing attitudes.

◆ Civil rights laws provide a basic foundation for gender equity; strict adherence to these laws will help ensure the fair treatment of girls and women as students and as employees.

SUMMARY

Edith Stein patterned her philosophical methodology after the phenomenology of Edmund Husserl. She began with sense perceptions and submitted them to critical analysis through the tenets of reason. Her goal was to arrive at an intuitional understanding of essences, which rested on her belief that *being* is intelligible to the mind.

In her analysis of *woman* Stein used three different aspects: the human species, the woman species, and the individual. Stein held that a species is differentiated through a never-changing form and that changes occur through types. As a female grows and develops from childhood through adolescence toward adulthood, what changes is the type and what does not change is the person's form, or nature.

Stein's notion of grades within a species meant that a given person could be more or less fully a woman or a man and more or less fully human. The education a person receives can enhance or block that person's development and thereby can have an effect on the degree to which the person shares in femininity or masculinity and humanity. Stein further held that differences between women and men as species account for the holistic expression of personality found in women and the tendency toward the perfection of individual abilities found in men.

Simone de Beauvoir's book *The Second Sex* was considered the manifesto of the feminist movement in the 1950s. Beauvoir's position was that women are humans first and females second. Beauvoir believed that women and men are subjects who are free and capable of transcendence; they can transform themselves through taking responsibility for their lives and projecting futures that will be of their own creation.

Human authenticity demands that people affirm not only their own autonomy, but also that of others. By taking control of their lives, women are capable of progressing toward greater freedom and heightened consciousness. The vehicle for reaching this goal is entry into the world of work, which will bring with it economic security. From Beauvoir's perspective, women are responsible to themselves for searching out ways in which they can foster and develop their own coexistence with men.

One of Sandra Harding's contributions to the feminist movement is her clear argument that the historical milieu within which people are born situates them and erects barriers that will hinder them in their advance toward different understandings. She has identified economic, political, and social factors in this milieu that eventually created the epistemological shift in the way women and men understand themselves in their relationships.

This same theme is carried forward in the writings of Susan Bordo. Further, Bordo's position is in direct conflict with the historical identification of rationality with the male mode of thinking, with its detachment and clear-cut reasoning. Bordo believes that the emphasis in education on the scientific method in the absence of serious consideration for the humanities and fine arts gives a distorted understanding of human knowledge. Such an understanding has been used by men to claim intellectual superiority over women.

Virginia Held believes that the future feminist agenda will be concerned with trying to get society in general to recognize the centrality of the gender issue. Progress toward reaching the goals of this agenda can be evaluated in terms of the success of institutions in liberating women, children, minorities, elderly people, people with disabilities, and others. Hers is a more inclusive understanding of what the feminist agenda is trying to accomplish.

Leaders of the feminist movement recognized that the liberation of women in all areas of life hinged on their economic security. Thus, they became political activists, demanding federal legislation that would provide equal opportunity for women in business and industry. Equality of employment opportunity for women emanated primarily from four federal laws. Further, in 1991, Congress passed a new Civil Rights Act, which has two very important provisions affecting the employment of women. First, the law allows compensatory and punitive damages; second, individuals can be named as codefendants with institutions and companies in a lawsuit.

The federal agency charged with enforcing these laws is the Equal Employment Opportunity Commission (EEOC). EEOC issued a directive in 1980 declaring that sexual harassment is a violation of Title VII of the Civil Rights Act of 1964. This action has had a tremendous effect on the manner in which some women are treated in the workforce.

⤳ DISCUSSION QUESTIONS AND STATEMENTS

1. Explain the philosophical methodology used by Edith Stein.
2. In relation to Stein's concept of species, what did she mean by *form* and *type*?
3. What did Edith Stein mean by grades within a species?
4. Explain the gender complementarity view of the relationship between men and women.
5. What did Simone de Beauvoir mean by *bad faith*?
6. What is the key to female equality with men, according to Beauvoir?
7. Explain the concept of human authenticity as developed by Beauvoir.
8. Explain the epistemological shift that Sandra Harding claims has taken place in the way women and men understand themselves in their relationships.
9. According to Harding, what are the barriers that hinder people from advancing toward different understandings of the role of women and men?
10. In relation to the position of Susan Bordo, how do the humanities and fine arts affect human understanding?
11. What danger does Bordo identify as a result of overemphasizing rationality?
12. Explain the three views of Virginia Held that capture how the present structure of society is inadequate for the future emancipation of women.

⤳ CASE STUDY 6.1

Sexual Harassment?

A fourth-grade teacher at an elementary school is in her second year of teaching. While she was practice teaching at this same elementary school, one of the two fourth-grade teachers was diagnosed with a malignant brain tumor and had to resign her teaching position. Both the faculty and the principal recognized in the practice teacher the qualities that make a teacher great, and she was offered a substitute teacher contract for the one month remaining in the school year. She did an excellent job and as a consequence of her performance was offered the position on a permanent basis. She considered herself very lucky, because many of her university classmates were having a difficult time finding teaching jobs.

She remembers distinctly the conference she had with the principal when he offered to recommend her for the permanent substitute position and also the conference when he told her that he would recommend her for the teaching position on a permanent basis. In retrospect, the practice teacher is struck by several of the principal's remarks and actions during those two conferences. He seemed to emphasize the confidence that the superintendent of schools had in his recommendations, particularly in regard to the hiring and firing of teachers. She also thinks it was rather odd that he hugged her when he told her that she had the teaching position on a permanent basis. He even kissed her on the cheek. However, at the time she thought his intentions were honorable.

When she graduated from the university, which was during the time she was a substitute teacher, the principal sent flowers to her apartment with a card congratulating her and saying how happy he was to have hired her for the permanent position. The day before her birthday, the principal invited her to dinner as a way of celebrating. She declined because she felt uneasy about going to dinner with her boss. He seemed to take the rejection in good spirits, so she didn't give the incident much thought afterwards. However, she began to worry about his intentions when he dropped by her apartment on a Saturday afternoon. She let him in for a few minutes, but said that she was about to leave for an appointment. He hugged her and kissed her on the cheek.

The teacher did not know what to do. She discussed her concerns with a friend, who told her to confront the principal and clearly state that she was not interested in developing a personal relationship with him. This she did, and once again, he did not appear to be upset with the rejection. For a while he seemed to ignore her. When the teacher received her first-year evaluation, she felt that although it was not a bad evaluation, it was not reflective of her performance. The principal seemed rather hostile when she questioned the accuracy of his evaluation. He had stated that she was deficient in three areas: human relations skills, lesson-plan development, and the adaptation of instructional techniques to the needs of students. However, she decided not to make an issue of the evaluation.

In late September of her second year of teaching, the principal made an unscheduled visit to her class to evaluate her performance. The teacher was very upset because it was unusual for the principal to conduct teacher evaluations that early in the school year. Once again, the principal seemed rather hostile when she questioned why she was being evaluated at that time. He stated that he was doing her a favor because if she did not improve her performance, he would have no choice but to recommend nonrenewal of her probationary teacher contract. He further stated that she had time to rectify her performance and suggested that she begin by improving her human-relations skills.

Discussion Questions and Statements

1. Could this be a case of sexual harassment?
2. Explain what the teacher should do at this juncture.
3. What, if anything, should the teacher have done with regard to this situation during her first year of teaching?
4. Could the teacher have handled the principal's interest in her in a better manner?
5. Describe how the philosophers presented in this chapter would have handled this situation.
6. Has the principal violated any federal laws?

⤳ CASE STUDY 6.2

The Hiring Process

A school district has a vacancy for a high school principal. There are eight schools in the school district: five elementary schools, two middle schools, and one high school. Each elementary school has one principal; the two middle schools each have a principal and an assistant principal; the high school has a principal and three assistants. All the principals are men; one assistant principal is a woman.

The school district has a selection process that calls for a committee of parents, teachers, staff members, and other administrators to review applications, interview candidates, and make a recommendation of three candidates to the superintendent of schools. The superintendent then presents one candidate to the board of education.

Although women have applied for three building-level administrative positions in the past five years, none have been hired. The board of education has an affirmative action policy, but no implementation procedures.

Discussion Questions and Statements

1. Outline the procedures the superintendent should follow to implement the affirmative action policy.
2. What is the basic ethical principle concerning equality that may be lacking in this school district?
3. Describe how equality of employment opportunity affects the instructional program and the education of students.

4. What federal legislation affects the promotion and employment of women?

5. What attitudes about women might contribute to their underrepresentation in positions of educational leadership?

SELECTED BIBLIOGRAPHY

Arendt, Hannah. *The Human Condition.* Chicago: University of Chicago Press, 1958.

Aries, Philippe. *Centuries of Childhood: A Social History of Family Life.* New York: Vintage, 1962.

Baier, Annette. "Whom Can Women Trust." In *Feminist Ethics,* ed. Claudia Card. Lawrence: University Press of Kansas, 1991.

Beauvoir, Simone de. *The Second Sex,* trans. H. M. Parshley. New York: Alfred A Knopf, Inc., 1952.

————. *Memoirs of a Dutiful Daughter,* trans. James Kirkup. New York: Harper Collins Publishers, 1958.

Benhabib, Seyla, and Drucilla Cornell, eds. *Feminism as Critique: On the Politics of Gender.* Minneapolis: University of Minnesota Press, 1987.

Bordo, Susan. *The Flight to Objectivity: Essays on Cartesianism and Culture.* Albany: State University of New York Press, 1987.

Card, Claudia, ed. *Feminist Ethics.* Lawrence: University Press of Kansas, 1991.

Chodorow, Nancy. *The Reproduction of Mothering.* Berkeley: University of California Press, 1978.

Chow, Esther Ngan-Ling. "The Feminist Movement: Where Are All the Asian American Women?" In *From Different Shores: Perspectives on Race and Ethnicity in America,* 2d ed., ed. Takaki. New York: Oxford University Press, 1994.

Davis, Angela Y. *Women, Culture, and Politics.* New York: Vintage, 1990.

Friedman, Marilyn. "Beyond Caring: The De-Moralization of Gender." In *Science, Morality and Feminist Theory,* eds. Marsha Hanen and Kai Nielsen. Calgary, Canada: University of Calgary Press, 1987.

Gilligan, Carol. *In a Different Voice.* Cambridge: Harvard University Press, 1982.

Harding, Sandra. *The Science Question in Feminism.* Ithaca, New York: Cornell University Press, 1986.

Harding, Sandra, and Merrill B. Hintikka, eds. *Discovering Reality: Feminist Perspectives on Epistemology, Metaphysics, Methodology and Philosophy of Science.* Dordrecht, Holland: Reidel, 1983.

Held, Virginia. *Feminist Morality: Transforming Culture, Society, and Politics.* Chicago: The University of Chicago Press, 1993.

————."Terrorism, Rights, and Political Goals." In *Violence, Terrorism, and Justice,* eds. R. G. Frey and Christopher W. Morris. Cambridge: Cambridge University Press, 1991.

Keller, Evelyn Fox. *Reflections on Gender and Science.* New York: Yale University Press, 1985.

Stein, Edith. *The Collected Works of Edith Stein.* Washington, D.C.: ICS Publications, 1987.

Tong, Rosemary. *Women, Sex and the Law.* Totowa, N.J.: Rowman and Allenheld, 1984.

Wollstonecraft, Mary. *A Vindication of the Rights of Women, with Strictures on Moral and Political Subjects.* 1792. Ed. C. H. Poston. Reprint, New York: Norton, 1988.

Pluralism, Justice, Discourse Ethics, and Educational Leadership

Approximately 1.2 million immigrants arrive yearly in the United States; 36 percent are from Asia and nearly 40 percent are from the Americas. This phenomenon is changing both the ethnic composition and the religious orientation of the United States. The U.S. population is not only Christian and Jewish, but also Islamic, Hindu, and Confucian. The United States is now the most religiously diverse country on earth.

The fastest growing religious faith is Islam; there are more Muslims than Episcopalians, more Muslims than Presbyterians, and perhaps more Muslims than Jews. Chicago alone has over one million Muslims. The Council of Islamic Schools in North America counts approximately 180 full-time, private Islamic schools operating in the United States.[1]

Coupled with this religious diversity is the ethnic pluralism of the population. There is great diversity not only within each religious faith, but also within each ethnic group that embraces these various religions. Diversity and pluralism naturally initiate a concern for social justice. The rights and responsibilities of people as individuals and as members of various groups bring into play certain tensions that are often manifested through intolerance and discrimination. As a consequence of pluralism, racism in the United States is a problem that affects the lives of African, Chinese, Filipino, Hispanic, Korean, Indian, and other immigrants and members of these groups who are also U.S. citizens.

Religious and ethnic pluralism is further complicated by human rights issues revolving around discrimination based on age, disability, gender, illness, and lifestyle and by society's treatment of children and of people who are eccentric, elderly, innovative, marginalized, deviant, and dangerous.

Within the profession of educational leadership, the greatest current issue is how principals, superintendents, and other administrators will be able to exercise effective leadership within a milieu of tremendous diversity. These professionals are responsible for providing educational leadership not only to diverse groups of students and parents but also to diverse groups of teachers and staff members. The recruiting of members of diverse religious and ethnic groups into positions of educational leadership is a related issue.

Diversity of religious beliefs precludes recourse to religious norms as standards for human conduct. However, recourse to philosophical notions of humanity can serve as guides in striving for justice in schools and school districts and in preparing students to live in a diverse society. There is a need, therefore, to develop ideas and notions of social justice that can serve as a basis from which public-school administrators can exercise their leadership.

As in the past, immigrants today tend to congregate in neighborhoods where others share their customs, language, and traditions. But there is a significant difference between the immigrants of past generations and those of contemporary times. In the past most immigrants were motivated to assimilate into the general population as quickly as possible so that they and their children would be able to participate more fully in the American dream.

Today, immigrants are reluctant to seek complete assimilation and often take deliberate steps to preserve their heritage both for themselves and for the sake of their children. Assimilation is viewed as a continuum, with nonassimilation on the one end and complete assimilation on the other. Nonassimilation implies a conscious abrogation of other heritages in developing norms for living; total assimilation implies a conscious abrogation of personal heritage as a norm for living. However, it is impossible for a person or a group of people to be totally unaffected by the heritages surrounding them or to totally dismiss a heritage shared by the majority of people.

This situation constitutes an additional reason to develop ideas and notions that can become touchstones from which issues of social justice can be addressed. However, a first step must be engaging people in dialogue about how to proceed and about issues and problems endemic to such an endeavor. The following questions reflect possible issues or problems to be considered.

> Given the diversity and pluralism of society in general, what ideas and notions about social justice are possible?
>
> How do administrators, faculty, and staff members become aware of issues of social justice?
>
> How can the faculty and staff be engaged in meaningful discourse about diversity and pluralism in relation to social justice?
>
> How can issues of social justice be integrated into school programs and curricula?
>
> What are schools and school districts doing about the issues of diversity and pluralism in relation to social justice?
>
> Given the diversity and pluralism of faculties and staffs, what ideas and notions about social justice are even possible?

Given the educational mandate to search for truth, what is the relationship between social justice and differing concepts of human nature, politics, and the ethics of human conduct?

To address the issue of social justice effectively, it is necessary to acquire a better understanding of the pluralistic nature of U.S. society. This discussion will lead into a treatment of justice in relation to pluralism. Finally, discourse ethics is proposed as a method for arriving at a more just society. The unifying element throughout is educational leadership.

PLURALISM

A correct attitude about pluralism is extremely important to the effective practice of educational leadership. Three dimensions of pluralism form the bases on which this attitude may be developed. The first dimension centers on the conditional nature of values. The question of values has captured the attention of philosophers in every age; although viewpoints vary, most people believe that there are a number of genuine values that differ from culture to culture and from generation to generation. These values are worthy of consideration and must be contemplated from a perspective that appreciates diversity. A further distinction should be made between values that produce a benefit and values that result in harm to people.

Values in this context can be considered as either occurring naturally or caused by humans. Health and disease occur naturally; kindness and cruelty are caused by humans. Values caused by humans are desirable or not depending on the benefit or harm they produce. Receiving love and respect are certainly desirable and produce a benefit; humiliation and exploitation are undesirable and produce harm. Such values are generally considered universal and thus applicable to all cultures, generations, and societies. As such, they are considered primary values. The Universal Declaration of Human Rights promulgated by the United Nations in 1948 is a statement of primary values pertaining to human rights and is an excellent set of conduct norms specifically fashioned to safeguard the rights of all people, regardless of national affiliation. It is a pluralistic code of ethics.

Principals, superintendents, and other administrators exhibit a human-caused, desirable primary value when they treat with respect the teachers and other staff members whom they supervise. Administrators exhibit a human-caused, undesirable primary value when they supervise through coercion, for example, by threatening dismissal if a teacher or staff member does not meet their standards.

A principal who has cancer is experiencing a naturally occurring, undesirable primary value; a principal in good health is experiencing a naturally occurring, desirable primary value. These distinctions become important when a person is in the process of sorting out the various aspects of his or her personal response to daily occurrences; they bring clarity to ethical thinking and analysis.

There are also secondary values, which vary with historical periods, cultures, persons, and societies. Secondary values vary because of the diversity of opinions as to what constitutes a good life. Such variables as social roles (colleague, lover, parent, spouse, etc.), profession or occupation (carpenter, computer technician, teacher, etc.), personal aspirations (being ambitious, influential, liked, knowledgeable, etc.), and personal preference (aesthetic enjoyment, foods, hobbies, vacations, etc.) contribute to secondary personal values. The historical period of the 1960s ushered in significant cultural changes in the societies of Southeast Asia and the United States. The increase in drug usage, the change in sexual mores, and the challenge to traditional modes of authority were popularized through the art, clothing, music, and personal habits of that period. Because of the interdependence of the developed nations of the world, these dramatic changes influenced millions of people.

Primary values are subject to secondary values in the sense that there is significant variation in the forms and ways in which the benefits of primary values are sought and the harms of primary values are avoided. Even though nutrition is a primary value, the manner in which food is prepared, served, and eaten is subject to individual and cultural interpretation.

The manner in which a principal administers his or her school will be driven to a significant degree by that person's primary and secondary values. Because primary values are universal, there is usually minimal conflict between an administrator and staff members over the necessity to exhibit primary values in relationships with one another, with pupils, and with parents. Conflicts usually arise over how primary and secondary values are implemented. When a school experiences an influx of students from a different culture, the principal, teachers, and staff members will most likely need to reevaluate the school's procedures and policies. The student rights and responsibilities policy should be the first priority.

Even casual physical contact between students will differ significantly from culture to culture. For example, observing African, Asian, and European American students will quickly reveal differences in how members of these groups interact with one another. It is easy for an administrator to misinterpret this behavior if it is viewed only from his or her own cultural base. It can be disastrous for a principal to impose his or her culturally biased concepts of appropriate interpersonal behavior on the student body when the students come from a different culture. Obviously, because students return to culturally laden homes and neighborhoods after school hours, the imposition of an artificial school culture is doomed to failure, in addition to its being unethical. This is a human-caused, undesirable secondary value.

The conditionality of values implies that values are open to interpretation. The value of education for every child is conditioned by the rights of children with disabilities in the context of the rights of nondisabled children. These rights are acutely debated when there is a scarcity of human and material resources because the education of children with disabilities usually requires a larger expenditure of resources than is required to educate children without disabilities.[2]

The second dimension of pluralism centers on the observation that conflict is unavoidable because the perspective of what constitutes a good life and the values that facilitate it are diverse and varied. Further, these perspectives and values are such that the realization of one often prohibits the realization of others. Thus, conflicts over reasonable perspectives and values are unavoidable. Leading a good life includes coping with conflicts that arise because others have perspectives and values that they consider essential but that are incommensurable or incompatible with a given understanding of the good life. The idea of incommensurability refers to things that are so unlike that they cannot be compared, such as euthanasia and giving birth. Similarly, an individual may want to enjoy something that has a value that is incompatible with his or her other values. For example, a person may have a hobby that requires so much time and energy that he or she cannot spend quality time with his or her family.

From these concepts arises the notion that conflict always results from incommensurable or incompatible values. It is possible in some situations to rank values in order to arrive at a reasoned decision, but assigning rank depends on the participants' conceptions of the good life. According to people who advocate this approach, a reasoned decision does not require acceptance of a highest value or a mediating value or an authoritative value, but requires acceptance of any one of a plurality of equally reasoned values.

It is important to understand that a person cannot realize all the possibilities that he or she values; in fact, the good life unavoidably includes losing something valuable. A person may value justice and friendship. Justice requires impartiality, whereas friendship requires partiality. Therefore, to treat a friend justly creates a tension.[3]

One of the most common disappointments of neophyte administrators is the rather uncomfortable realization that colleagues modify the manner in which they relate to one of their own who accepts an administrative position. This situation is especially difficult if the administrator becomes the supervisor of former teaching colleagues. It is thus good administrative practice to place a newly appointed principal in a school in which he or she has not been a teacher.

That same principal will also quickly learn that some values of teachers, staff members, and parents may be significantly different from his or her values. Conflict is inevitable. The parent who believes that he or she has the right to choose who will instruct his or her child will create a conflict for the principal. The assignment of students to teachers is a rather complex administrative responsibility. The number of children who have disabilities, developmental delays, inadequate reading abilities, and problems at home must be taken into consideration by the principal in making student assignments. Gender and ethnic balancing are also considerations. Even though it is appropriate for a parent to express his or her wishes, the decision must remain with the principal.

The third dimension of pluralism involves the necessity of developing an approach to resolving conflicts. The very conditionality of values significantly influences the manner in which conflict resolution is carried out. Of course, the most important variable is the desire of the participants to arrive at a reasonable settlement. In addition, conflicts arise in concrete situations, which require a practical and reasoned resolution. Should a school district pay higher salaries to teachers, thereby increasing the pupil-teacher ratio because funds will then not be available to hire additional teachers? In such a situation should the board of education place before the voters a referendum asking for an increase in the property tax to fund both the salary increase and the hiring of additional teachers? Paying higher salaries would help retain good teachers who could be lured away from the school district by districts that pay more. Hiring more teachers would improve the situation of the children who are in classes so large that they are not getting the individual attention they deserve. Asking the taxpayers for an increase in local property taxes would put a financial strain on the young families who are at the lower end of the income curve in their professions and occupations, although these may be precisely the families who have contributed to the higher enrollments. In contemporary U.S. society, resolution usually occurs through a compromise, which dictates that one side must abandon certain values, or through the majority-rule approach, which dictates that the side with the most people wins. These compromise techniques are usually facilitated through strong emotions or political intimidation.

A more desirable approach to the resolution of conflict is based on a mode of thinking that views conflicts as unavoidable, given that values are conditional, incommensurable, and incompatible. This approach negates the perspective that conflict is a crisis produced by the stupidity or perversity of the adversary. Further, this approach can help the different parties see that a particular conflict over a given value can result in a more significant conflict or a series of conflicts because the value at hand is truly part of an entire system of values.

Conflicts usually occur within particular traditions or with particular persons. It is prudent to suspect that an entire system of values is hidden behind a given situation and therefore the disputants have a deep-seated and vested interest in the present conflict. When the conflict over values involves a single person, it usually centers on the person's concept of the good life.

The resolution of conflicts requires a sense of objectivity that allows a person to retreat from the conflict in order to evaluate how its resolution will ultimately affect the entire value system of the disputants or of the tradition. It can be helpful to focus on the values that are shared by the disputants. Thus, the conflict may shift from values to the means that will be used to reach the desired resolution. Unfortunately, school districts may not have enough time or resources to resolve a dispute successfully.

Shared values always connect at the level of primary values, but identification of shared secondary values can and often does promote conflict resolution. A prerequisite to conflict resolution is reasonableness. If one of the disputants sees a political reason for being unreasonable, he or she may deliberately sabotage the resolution process.

A certain value may be the linchpin of the system of values of a person or of an entire tradition. In such a situation, there will be no resolution unless the focus of the conflict can be shifted to the ways and means of implementing shared values. The best system for resolving disputes will incorporate a sense of flexibility and hospitableness into the process. In this manner, hostilities can be quelled and real issues are more likely to emerge.[4]

The parent who does not want his or her child in a particular teacher's class could be approached by the principal with a compromise, such as offering to review the situation at the end of the first quarter of the school year. A reasonable person may be made to appreciate that the placement of a child based solely on the wishes of a parent would set a precedent that could be disruptive to the entire school community.

Values are recognized as the constituents of a good life, which is made good through personal satisfaction and the moral merit that values embody. The good life is also predicated on the fruition of the possibilities that a person values. A large number of the many valued possibilities are incommensurable and incompatible. Therefore, the good life involves the selection of some possibilities and the abrogation of others. This process prompts a person to find some way of balancing, comparing, or ranking the possibilities that he or she values. For a person to accomplish this process of selection, certain conditions must be met.

The first condition is that the tradition within which the person lives must be a rich one; each person must have choices in order to realize his or her most valued possibilities. A second condition is the development of an active imagination. The person must have the ability to imagine how each possibility would lead to or enrich what he or she believes is the good life. The third condition is the freedom to make choices, which will be enhanced if there are a large number of possibilities.

As a person lives out what he or she considers the good life, the possibilities for others are expanded and enriched, even if not all people are living the good life. Pluralism must not be misunderstood as providing a common end for each person living in the same tradition, however. People striving to live the good life are not striving for the same goal.

Because values are incommensurable and incompatible, because there are many different valued possibilities, because people can exercise their active imaginations, and because people have freedom, conflicts are unavoidable. This plurality is something to be celebrated because it makes life enjoyable and it can be the basis for tolerating differences in other people. People who live varied lives are capable of coping with varied conditions.

A teacher who begins a master's degree program in educational administration has certainly been faced with this process. There are choices to be made and consequences to be weighed. Graduate education is expensive and will put a strain on the home budget, especially if the teacher has a family dependent on his or her salary. The time commitment is extensive and will cut into the time a person has to spend with family. On the other hand, leading a career in an area of interest can give a person great satisfaction, which might enhance the manner in which he or she interacts with family members. The monetary gains from an administrator's salary could compensate for the initial cost and ultimately could provide opportunities for other family members, which they would not have on a teacher's salary.

People who promote pluralism recognize that certain values are extremely important, but do not believe that any one value always overrides all other values that conflict with it. A distinction can be made between deep and variable conventions. Deep conventions are the safeguards of all good lives regardless of how they are conceived. Variable conventions indeed vary with traditions and conceptions of the good life.

Deep conventions must not be identified only with primary values. There are secondary values about which a person can have such a deep conviction that they are considered requirements of a good life. The following characteristics allow a secondary value to have the status of a deep convention: a particular traditions holds this value to be a requirement for the good life; reasonable people outside a given tradition recognize the value as a requirement for the good life within that tradition; and the value varies among traditions.

Primary values are universal to all humans; thus, the satisfaction of basic physiological, psychological, and sociological needs is recognized as necessary to the good life in every context. How these primary values are understood and maintained varies from context to context, however. It is helpful to view primary values as content laden and secondary values as context laden, that is, dependent on the form in which they are expressed. An extension of this concept is that some secondary values are independent of the context in which they are expressed; they represent ways in which primary values are implemented. However, these secondary values need not be accepted by all reasonable people in every situation.

Acknowledging pluralism means that a person accepts the position that there are some deeply held conventions that protect the requirements of the good life. This protection is expressed in primary and secondary values, which set limits that are recognized by all reasonable people in every tradition. Thus, for example, every reasonable person will agree that child abuse, slavery, torture, and vendettas are unethical.

In recent years the news media have revealed that there are teachers and principals who have had intimate relationships with students, which eventually led to sexual encounters. All reasonable people recognize that this is unethical behavior. There is a definite line of demarcation between a professional relationship and an abusive relationship, which is clear to reasonable people. First and foremost, a relationship between an educator and a student should be initiated by the educator for the purpose of helping the student be successful in the learning process. Students tend to reveal intimate details of their private lives to teachers and principals; thus, educators should encourage students to reveal only those aspects of their private lives that are relevant to the difficulties they are experiencing as members of the school community. A principal or teacher should never disclose to students the intimate details of his or her private life.

Physical contact between educator and student should be judiciously undertaken only to convey concern and acceptance. A professional relationship between principal and student and between teacher and student is a relationship with boundaries. All other relationships are abusive.

Finally, there must be some ideal that acts as a framework that maintains the tradition within which people pursue the good life. Such a framework would foster the realization of plural, conditional, incompatible, and incommensurable values without advocating some specific value. The need for an ideal that serves as a framework also applies to individual lives.

The freedom to make defining decisions is the arena within which all positive human interaction is played out. People should be allowed to experiment within this arena as long as it does not compromise the integrity of other people. Thus, the teacher who wants to experiment with different and sometimes unorthodox instructional methods should be allotted the freedom to do so by the principal; at the same time, both teacher and principal must be aware of the right of each student to an effective education.[5]

The real challenge lies with the supervising administrator—usually the principal at the school level and the superintendent of schools at the district level. These two leadership positions control the milieu within which freedom is exercised. In schools that have assistant principals, the principal supervises the assistant principals, who, in turn, supervise the teachers and staff members. In school districts large enough to have assistant superintendents, the superintendent supervises the assistant superintendents, and they, in turn, supervise the principals and other administrators. Thus, both the principal and the superintendent still control the milieu through the supervision of other educational leaders.

It is also important to realize that boards of education can affect the milieu within which freedom is exercised. The board in the aggregate supervises the superintendent of schools, and if the board does not understand or accept this notion of freedom, it will hinder not only the exercise of freedom of the superintendent, but also, ultimately, the exercise of freedom by all other administrators, teachers, and staff members.

JUSTICE

As pluralism produces conflict over values, which can lead to unjust treatment of people, there is a need to know and understand some basic notions about justice. *Justice* is the guide that regulates how people live out their lives as members of a given community. Everyone is a member of some society, even if he or she tries to live his or her life as a hermit. In Western society, computer technology and space satellites make it possible to locate where each person lives. There is no place where a person can hide and neglect his or her obligations to society.

The choice to retreat from society by living a completely solitary life no longer exists; rather, the very act of *being* brings with it social obligations.

Justice is the most important issue in contemporary society because the actions of people can have an effect on others with an immediacy unknown in previous societies. This immediacy leaves little time to ponder the far-reaching consequences of actions. In addition, actions today affect many more people than did actions in the past. The sophistication of communications has significantly altered the way people receive information, and the information they receive usually arrives having been fashioned by many interpretations and replete with political flair. Teacher strikes, student violence, and abuse of students by educators are reported on television and in newspapers filtered through commentary and editing, which foster a point of view interwoven with the facts of the events. For example, the killing of students by students using handguns brought commentary from those favoring and those opposing gun control.

The notion of justice implies that an individual or a group of people can be treated justly or unjustly, with justice or injustice, fairly or unfairly. The content of justice is an entitlement. In this context, individuals and groups of people have claims that are properly due them. The most obvious claims are services, goods, or money, but the content also can be an entitlement to fidelity or respect or a person's good reputation. The entitlements that affect a person permeate almost every dimension of human interaction. In education, and particularly in educational leadership, personal entitlements are essential to the practice of leadership. How can a principal effectively lead faculty members without possessing their respect? However, questions related to this issue might be: Has the principal earned the respect of the faculty? Has respect been unjustly withheld by the faculty?

By way of example, there are two aspects of respect as an entitlement. First, all people have an entitlement to a basic type of respect because they are human beings. All people, governments, and institutions must afford others this type of respect, which entails personal integrity, liberty, and equality of opportunity. The second aspect of respect is an entitlement due a person because of his or her leadership position. This latter dimension also entails trusting that the principal will perform his or her responsibilities, which are the entitlements due the faculty. In educational leadership, responsibilities and obligations can be considered entitlements.

The responsibilities and obligations of a society to its members usually entail social services. In contemporary society these services include education, medical care, police and fire protection, water, and sewage processing. Unfortunately, the economic principle of scarcity correctly states that there will be more needs than resources; thus, determining the scope of services and the processes for prioritizing and distributing services are of the utmost importance. Experience indicates that differences in opinion will continually emerge, giving rise to the need for more effective and efficient means of arriving at decisions.

In education, these responsibilities rest with the board of education, the superintendent of schools, principals, and other administrators. When disputes arise that cannot be resolved by these parties, the judicial system takes over. Turning to the judicial system to make decisions is extremely undesirable, because doing so places in the hands of judges and juries the responsibilities that are first and foremost those of the educational community.

When a person becomes a member of a society or a subsociety, such as the education community, that person assumes certain responsibilities to the society as a whole. Because education has a significant effect on the entire society, it is the responsibility of every person, whether or not he or she has children attending public or private schools. Education is a given in a democratic society, and the quality of that education ultimately affects the kinds and quality of services provided to the entire society. The most obvious responsibility of each citizen is to pay taxes, which are the resources necessary for a quality education. Public schools are financed primarily through local property taxes; state taxes constitute the second most significant source of funding, and federal taxes supply a much smaller amount.

The responsibilities of society to the individual are usually referred to as *distributive justice;* the responsibilities of individuals to society are referred to as *legal justice;* and the responsibilities and obligations that exist between people are commonly referred to as *commutative justice*. In educational leadership these responsibilities in a sense define the relationships that exist between administrators and all other individuals in the school community.

Figure 7.1 lists U.S. federal court decisions that represent distributive justice in relation to securing educational opportunity through racial desegregation.

Legal justice is exemplified through the obligation of people to pay taxes for the support of public schools. Commutative justice is played out in civil lawsuits when a dispute arises between individuals.

Identification of responsibilities may appear to be clear-cut, but this is not always the case. Consider children who have disabilities. Certainly the local school district is responsible for implementing the federal laws setting forth the rights of children with disabilities. However, the cost of such services is generally greater than the cost of educating children without disabilities. If the services to children without disabilities would be curtailed in order to provide services to children with disabilities, an obligation rests on the taxpayers of the community to provide additional money. Providing for the entitlement of people always places a corresponding responsibility on others. Considering entitlements apart from corresponding responsibilities is futile and precipitates many difficulties in the realm of educational leadership.[6]

Another consideration in the popular notion of justice is *restitution*. It is commonly recognized that the appropriate response to unjustly depriving someone of an entitlement requires not only the implementation of the entitlement, but also restoring what was withheld. Although easily accomplished in terms of services and goods, restitution is more difficult to implement in relation to personal qualities. A student who needs remedial reading services but has not received them should, of course, be provided such help. The student might need additional help, however, to regain what was lost during the time the service was withheld.

A. The Supreme Court ruled that racial segregation violated the Equal Protection Clause of the Fourteenth Amendment.

Brown v. *Board of Education*, 1954

B. Challenges to desegregation as set forth by the *Brown* decision.

Cooper v. *Aaron*, 1958

United States v. *Louisiana*, 1960

Griffin v. *County School Board*, 1964

Alexander v. *Holmes County Board of Education*, 1969

Carter v. *West Feliciana School Board*, 1970

Northcross v. *Board of Education*, 1970

Dandridge v. *Jefferson Parish School Board*, 1971

Guey Heung Lee v. *Johnson*, 1971

Gomperts v. *Chase*, 1971

Columbus Board of Education v. *Penick*, 1978

C. Challenges to busing students for integration.

North Carolina State Board of Education v. *Swann*, 1971

Drummond v. *Acree*, 1972

Bustop Inc. v. *Board of Education*, 1978

Board of Education of City of Los Angeles v. *Superior Court*, 1980

Washington v. *Seattle School District Number 1*, 1982

D. Challenges to integrating faculties for desegregation purposes.

Rogers v. *Paul*, 1965

Bradley v. *School Board I*, 1965

U.S. v. *Montgomery Board of Education*, 1968

Davis v. *Board of School Commissioners*, 1971

Bradley v. *School Board II*, 1974

FIGURE 7.1
Selected Landmark U.S. Federal Court Cases Concerning Racial Segregation

Contractarianism

To better understand the implications of justice in the practice of educational leadership, it is most beneficial to consider the major school of thought in political philosophy that constitutes the basis for the practice of justice. It is commonly referred to as contractarianism and holds that political society should be designed by the very people who will live in it and that the specifications for this design should be the needs of these individuals. Therefore, governments come into being and retain their existence through a contract or agreement among the people to be governed. The agreement seeks to remedy the problems that are inevitable when large numbers of people live together in order to provide opportunities for a better life, which are only possible through this assembly of people.

Thus, government is neither something natural to humanity nor transcendental, imposed from above by a deity. Rather, it is legitimized through the agreement. Many variations on this theme have been analyzed and developed by many philosophers. Here, the philosophy of John Rawls, who is considered a contemporary contractarian, will be presented.[7]

John Rawls's Theory of Justice

John Rawls is an influential American political philosopher who has written extensively about justice and has formulated a theory of *justice as fairness*. Rawls is considered a major defender of the social-contract theory found in the writings of Immanuel Kant, John Locke, and Jean-Jacques Rousseau. The basic premise of Rawls's theory is that the best principles of justice for the basic structure of any society are those that would be the object of an original agreement in the establishment of a society. These principles would be derived by free, rational persons as an initial position of equality. Further, these principles would form the basis for all future agreements and would specify social cooperation and forms of government.

This theoretical construct is a guide for evaluating the fairness of contemporary life. In all Western societies the original agreements are long past and constitute a faint glimmer in the society's collective consciousness. Only in the most primitive societies might there come an opportunity to simulate original agreements. In subsocieties, however, there is the possibility of simulating, albeit in an imperfect way, original agreements on justice.

Consider, for example, the process that occurs when a new school district is formed. The newly elected board of education is charged with the development of policies that will govern the school district. These policies will constitute the original agreements of equality. Although the board must operate within the parameters established by local ordinances, state and federal laws, and governmental agency regulations, there is still a sense of urgency and freedom in actualizing the governance structure. Policies will be needed on affirmative action and equal employment opportunity along with policies that address the rights and responsibilities of students.

In an even more micro manner, the establishment of a new school will require the development of policies to regulate the conduct of its members. Justice or fairness is a consideration in all deliberations that are regulatory. The importance of this perspective lies in the reality that it does simulate by analogy the concept of an original agreement on equality. By its very nature, the democracy that functions in the United States rests on the assumption that decisions are made by free, rational persons. Thus, the conditions set forth by Rawls are met to a degree that allows his notion of fairness to be played out in contemporary life.

From time to time all institutions go through periods of reevaluation and reform. Public education is no exception. The process of reevaluation gives rise to the opportunity to examine the policies of a school district or individual school through the lens of equality, using the concept of the reasonable person as a benchmark.

Rawls elucidated two principles that he believes people would choose as a means of implementing the notion of fairness. The first principle assigns basic rights and duties. The second principle holds that inequalities can exist only if they result in compensating benefits for everyone, and particularly for the least-advantaged people in society.

The first principle asserts that each person is to have an equal right to a system of liberties that is compatible with a similar system of liberties available to all people. The concept of a total system is extremely important because it establishes that the exercise of one liberty is most likely dependent on other liberties. Furthermore, according to Rawls, the principles of justice are to be ranked; for example, liberty can be restricted only for the sake of liberty. Thus, the personal right of students to express their self-identity through dress must not compromise the physical safety of other students. The wearing of gang symbols and colors could easily erupt into violent confrontations between rival gangs. Certainly the gang with fewer and less-experienced members would accept such a restriction on the liberty of its members.

The second principle asserts that any social and economic inequalities must benefit the least-advantaged individuals and that equal opportunity to secure offices and positions must be open to all. Once again, the principles of justice must be ranked. The principle of efficiency does not occupy the position of first priority. Legislation and court decisions pertaining to affirmative action and equal opportunity in employment have helped secure the second part of this principle together with legislation and case law that ensure equal opportunity to run for public office. Figure 7.2 provides an overview of four major federal laws that were passed by Congress to secure justice.

In explaining how present inequities may benefit people who are least advantaged, the principle of just savings must be considered. Thus, in a school district that has substandard school facilities, the superintendent of schools and the board of education may agree that capital-project financing is the only prudent way to make extensive capital improvements. Most school districts, particularly districts with low assessed values, do not have enough financial resources to use operating funds for such capital improvements.

To enable school districts to procure such funding most state legislatures have granted school districts the right to sell bonds to raise necessary money. Wealthy districts could use operating funds, which might be more effective because taxpayers, who would be responsible for redeeming the bonds through taxation, may vote against selling bonds. The notion embedded in the bond approach, though, is that facilities are long-term necessities, which will benefit many generations, not merely the current student body. Selling bonds that will be amortized over a twenty-year period rightfully spreads the burden over more than the present generation, but not over extended generations.

The Civil Rights Act of 1964 as Amended

Title VII of this act provides that people cannot be denied a job or unfairly treated during employment because of race, color, religion, sex, or national origin. This act also established the Equal Employment Opportunity Commission (EEOC), which monitors and prosecutes violations of this Law.

Age Discrimination in Employment Act of 1967

As amended, this act promotes the employment of older workers based on ability rather than age by prohibiting arbitrary discrimination. The law protects individuals who are at least forty years of age; it applies not only to employers but also to employment agencies and labor organizations. It is against this law for an employer to refuse to hire or otherwise to discriminate against older workers in terms of compensation and working conditions.

Title V of the Rehabilitation Act of 1973

This law prohibits recipients of federal financial assistance from discriminating against people with disabilities in relation to the following employment practices: recruitment, selection, compensation, job assignment/classification. Employers are also required to provide reasonable accommodations for employees with disabilities.

The Americans with Disabilities Act of 1990

This very comprehensive law is meant to protect the rights of individuals with disabilities. This law is set forth under five titles. Title I regulates employment practices; Title II regulates services, programs, and activities of state and local governmental agencies; Title III applies to public accommodations provided by the private sector; Title IV requires telecommunication companies to provide telecommunication relay services for people with hearing or speech disabilities; Title V contains a number of provisions including prohibiting taking retaliation against persons seeking redress under this act.

FIGURE 7.2
Selected Landmark U.S. Federal Legislation Concerning Human Rights

Further, the use of operating funds for capital improvements in most school districts could significantly decrease the money available to support the curricular program. The supplies and materials budget might be reduced, or teacher salary increases might be cut from the budget, resulting in the departure of excellent teachers to other districts that offer more substantial salaries.

The application of the second principle through this example demonstrates that a few generations of taxpayers will bear the burden of improving facilities in order to enhance the opportunities of extended generations. If facilities are not improved, they will continue to deteriorate and ultimately cost more to renovate, in turn costing future taxpayers even more money. Consequently, extended future generations are saved from becoming least advantaged through the present and immediate-future generation of taxpayers.

Selected Reading 7.1 contains excerpts from the writings of John Rawls in which he set forth the basis for his theory of justice and elucidates the rationale underpinning his principles of justice.

Justice in the United States as it pertains to the rights of citizens is embodied in certain documents, which were the cornerstones on which the United States was founded. The Bill of Rights, found in Appendix 7.1, and the Declaration of Independence, a selection from which is found in Appendix 7.2, as well as the Constitution of the United States, contain the principles concerning justice that are set forth in this chapter. Figure 7.3 summarizes certain constitutional amendments concerning human rights that are endemic to the American way of life.

Amendment XIII, section 1

Neither slavery nor involuntary servitude, except as a punishment for crime whereof the party shall have been duly convicted, shall exist within the United States, or any place subject to their jurisdiction.

Passed by Congress January 31, 1865. Ratified December 6, 1865

Amendment XIV, section 1

All persons born or naturalized in the United States, and subject to the jurisdiction thereof, are citizens of the United States and of the State wherein they reside. No State shall make or enforce any law which shall abridge the privileges or immunities of citizens of the United States, nor shall any State deprive any person of life, liberty, or property, without due process of law; nor deny to any person within its jurisdiction the equal protection of the laws.

Passed by Congress June 13, 1866. Ratified July 9, 1868.

Amendment XV, section 1

The right of citizens of the United States to vote shall not be denied or abridged by the United States or by any State on account of race, color, or previous condition of servitude.

Passed by Congress February 26, 1869. Ratified February 3, 1870.

Amendment XIX

The right of citizens of the United States to vote shall not be denied or abridged by the United States or by any State on account of sex.

Passed by Congress June 4, 1919. Ratified August 18, 1920.

FIGURE 7.3
U.S. Constitutional Amendments Concerning Human Rights
Source: http://www.nara.gov/exhall/charters/constitution/amendments.html

Selected Reading 7.1

A Theory of Justice
John Rawls

My aim is to present a conception of justice which generalizes and carries to a higher level of abstraction the familiar theory of the social contract as found, say, in Locke, Rousseau, and Kant. In order to do this we are not to think of the original contract as one to enter a particular society or to set up a particular form of government. Rather, the guiding idea is that the principles of justice for the basic structure of society are the object of the original agreement. They are the principles that free and rational persons concerned to further their own interest would accept in an initial position of equality as defining the fundamental terms of their association. These principles are to regulate all further agreements; they specify the kinds of social cooperation that can be entered into and the forms of government that can be established. This way of regarding the principles of justice I shall call justice as fairness.

Thus we are to imagine that those who engage in social cooperation choose together, in one joint act, the principles which are to assign basic rights and duties and to determine the division of social benefits. Men are to decide in advance how they are to regulate their claims against one another and what is to be the foundation charter of their society. Just as each person must decide by rational reflection what constitutes his good, that is, the system of ends which it is rational for him to pursue, so a group of persons must decide once and for all what is to count among them as just and unjust. The choice which rational men would make in this hypothetical situation of equal liberty, assuming for the present that this choice problem has a solution, determines the principles of justice. . . .

Justice as fairness begins, as I have said, with one of the most general of all choices which persons might make together, namely, with the choice of the first principles of a conception of justice which is to regulate all subsequent criticism and reform of institutions. . . .

One feature of justice as fairness is to think of the parties in the initial situation as rational and mutually disinterested. This does not mean that the parties are egoists, that is, individuals with only certain kinds of interests, say in wealth, prestige, and domination. But they are conceived as not taking an interest in one another's interests. . . .

I shall maintain instead that the persons in the initial situation would choose two rather different principles: the first requires equality in the assignment of basic rights and duties, while the second holds that social and economic inequalities, for example inequalities of wealth and authority, are just only if they result in compensating benefits for everyone, and in particular for the least advantaged members of society. These principles rule out justifying institutions on the grounds that the hardships of some are offset by a greater good in the aggregate. It may be expedient but it is not just that some should have less in order that others may prosper. But there is no injustice in the greater benefits earned by a few provided that the situation of persons not so fortunate is thereby improved. The intuitive idea is that since everyone's well-being depends upon a scheme of cooperation without which no one could have a satisfactory life, the division of advantages should be such as to draw forth the willing cooperation of everyone taking part in it, including those less well situated. Yet this can be expected only if reasonable terms are proposed. The two principles mentioned seem to be a fair agreement on the basis of which those better endowed, or more fortunate in their social position, neither of which we can be said to deserve, could expect the willing cooperation of others when some workable scheme is a necessary condition of the welfare of all. Once we decide to look for a conception of justice that nullifies the accidents of natural endowment and the contingencies of social circumstances as counters in quest for political and economic advantage, we are led to these principles. They express the result of leaving aside those aspects of the social world that seem arbitrary from a moral point of view. . . .

. . . I now wish to give the final statement of the two principles of justice for institutions. For the sake of completeness, I shall give a full statement including earlier formulations.

First Principle

Each person is to have an equal right to the most extensive total system of equal basic liberties compatible with a similar system of liberty for all.

Second Principle

Social and economic inequalities are to be arranged so that they are both:

a. to the greatest benefit of the least advantaged, consistent with the just savings principle, and

b. attached to offices and positions open to all under conditions of fair equality of opportunity.

First Priority Rule (The Priority of Liberty)

The principles of justice are to be ranked in lexical order and therefore liberty can be restricted only for the sake of liberty. There are two cases:

a. a less extensive liberty must strengthen the total system of liberty shared by all;

b. a less than equal liberty must be acceptable to those with the lesser liberty.

Second Priority Rule (The Priority of Justice over Efficiency and Welfare)

The second principle of justice is lexically prior to the principle of efficiency and to that of maximizing the sum of advantages; and fair opportunity is prior to the difference principle. There are two cases:

a. an inequality of opportunity must enhance the opportunities of those with the lesser opportunity;

b. an excessive rate of saving must on balance mitigate the burden of those bearing this hardship.

General Conception

All social primary goods—liberty and opportunity, income and wealth, and the bases of self-respect—are to be distributed equally unless an unequal distribution of any or all of these goods is to the advantage of the least favored.

By way of comment, these principles and priority rules are no doubt incomplete. Other modifications will surely have to be made, but I shall not further complicate the statement of the principles. It suffices to observe that when we come to nonideal theory, we do not fall back straightway upon the general conception of justice. The lexical ordering of the two principles, and the valuations that this ordering implies, suggest priority rules which seem to be reasonable enough in many cases. By various examples I have tried to illustrate how these rules can be used and to indicate their plausibility. Thus the ranking of the principles of justice in ideal theory reflects back and guides the application of these principles to nonideal situations. It identifies which limitations need to be dealt with first. The drawback of the general conception of justice is that it lacks the definite structure of the two principles in serial order. In more extreme and tangled instances of nonideal theory there may be no alternative to it. At some point the priority of rules for nonideal cases will fail; and indeed, we may be able to find no satisfactory answer at all. But we must try to postpone the day of reckoning as long as possible, and try to arrange society so that it never comes. . . .

By way of general comment, these principles primarily apply, as I have said, to the basic structure of society. They are to govern the assignment of rights and duties and to regulate the distribution of social and economic advantages. . . . As their formulation suggests, these principles presuppose that the social structure can be divided into two more or less distinct parts, the first principle applying to the one, and the second to the other. They distinguish between those aspects of the social system that define and secure the equal liberties of citizenship and those that specify and establish social and economic inequalities. The basic liberties of citizens are, roughly speaking, political liberty (the right to vote and to be eligible for public office) together with freedom of speech and assembly; liberty of conscience and freedom of thought; freedom of the person along with the right to hold (personal) property; and freedom from arbitrary arrest and seizure as defined by the concept of the rule of law. These liberties are all required to be equal by the first principle, since citizens of a just society are to have the same basic rights.

The second principle applies, in the first approximation, to the distribution of income and wealth and to the design of organizations that make use of differences in authority and responsibility, or chains of command. While the distribution of wealth and income need not be equal, it must be to everyone's advantage, and at the same time, positions of authority and offices of command must be accessible to all. One applies the second principle by holding positions open, and then, subject to this constraint, arranges social and economic inequalities so that everyone benefits.

These principles are to be arranged in a serial order with the first principle prior to the second. This ordering means that a departure from the institutions of equal liberty required by the first principle cannot be justified by, or compensated for, by greater social and economic advantages. The distribution of wealth and income, and the hierarchies of authority, must be consistent with both the liberties of equal citizenship and equality of opportunity.

Source: Reprinted by permission of the publisher from *A Theory of Justice* by John Rawls, Cambridge, Mass.: The Belknap Press of Harvard University Press, Copyright © 1971 by the President and Fellows of Harvard College. Excerpts from pages 11–13, 14–15, 302–303, 61.

DISCOURSE ETHICS

Implementation of the pluralistic point of view in educational leadership is a political issue because all school districts are governed at the local level either by elected officials or by people appointed by elected officials, commonly referred to as the board of education. Further, federal and state revenue supporting public education is appropriated by elected officials. At the local level, property taxes provide the bulk of funds utilized in developing and sustaining public education. This tax revenue is appropriated by direct vote of the citizens; bond revenue used to construct school buildings is also authorized by direct vote of the people. The decision to ask voters for an increase in property taxes or to place before voters a bond referendum is made by the board of education. Thus, educational leaders are called upon to expend public monies according to the dictates of Congress and state legislatures; in like manner, they are called upon to expend property-tax and bond-issue monies in accord with the wishes of the taxpayers in their school district.

An equally important responsibility of the superintendent of schools is to advise local boards of education when educational expenses require an increase in property-tax revenue and when capital improvements are necessary and beyond the scope of the annual budget. The entire bonding process is placed in motion through the leadership of the superintendent of schools, with the approval of the board of education.

It is common and appropriate educational administrative practice for superintendents and principals to engage the constituents of the school district and individual schools in public discourse before recommendations are made to the board of education. Further, it is common and appropriate practice for boards of education to engage the public in discourse before creating policies that affect the citizens in general, and the parents and students of the school district in particular, in terms of bond issues, curriculum development, educational programming, tax increases, human-resource policies, and student personnel policies.

The underlying basis for this type of engagement rests on the concept that legislators and school-board members are public officials responsible to the people who elected them. These voting citizens form a pluralistic constituency that demands for its representatives to know and act on its ideas and opinions. It is political suicide for elected officials to ignore advocacy groups and the parents of children when they enact legislation or policies affecting education.

Superintendents of schools and principals are equally vulnerable to this political reality if they ignore these people when they formulate educational recommendations, create administrative procedures, and initiate educational practices. People will be concerned if they feel that the extensive powers of the government are cut free from taxpayer influence such that legislators and boards of education can create unwanted legislation and policies affecting education.

Jürgen Habermas is a contemporary philosopher who views ethics as the pursuit of how conflicting interests can result in moral judgments. In his understanding, the pluralism of life makes it impossible to come to final answers about ethical norms. Individual and group mores are rooted in particular traditions to such an extent that general prescriptions cannot be formulated. Because what is considered the good life is so specific to particular "lifeworlds," immediate conflicts are sure to arise in any discourse. Thus, answers to such questions as How should I live my life? elude general prescription.[8]

However, pluralism does not preclude the establishment of a much narrower norm about justice because the purpose of such a norm is to fairly adjudicate conflicting ethical norms. Such a norm has universal appeal because of the many conflicts that arise about what is fair and equal in society in general and in specific societies. Justice thus becomes a willed norm binding on everyone. Embodied within Habermas's theoretical design is a procedure for moral argumentation, reasoned agreement by those who will be affected by the norm. The central principle of *discourse ethics* is that the validity of the norm rests on the acceptability of the consequences of the norm by all participants in the practical discourse. Thus, there is a shift away from the solitary moral reflection of individuals to the community of moral subjects in dialogue.[9]

Determining the fairness of a norm cannot take place only in the minds of moral agents, but must be played out in actual discourse with other moral agents. In Habermas's model each person must be willing and able to appreciate the perspective of other moral agents; thus there is a sense of empathy built into the process.[10]

In his book *Moral Consciousness and Communicative Action*, Habermas attempts to demonstrate the relationship between conceptual issues and empirical research. Specifically, he discusses the relationship of discourse ethics to social action through an examination of research in social psychology as it pertains to moral and interpersonal development.

Selected Reading 7.2 sets the stage for an explanation of discourse ethics by addressing the role and function of philosophy in this respect and by addressing the principle of universalization.

Obviously, the ordinary communication that takes place in everyday life touches on the most significant issues and problems facing contemporary humanity. Yet there is a lack of insight as to how this communication can effectively address and find a way to deal with the complexities of life. Habermas perceives the overarching problem to be isolation; an isolation of the tenets set forth by science, technology, the arts, and morality. Further, the philosophizing of those who have the status to demand attention tends to infuse culture with the hope of *arbitrating* a consensus, whereas Habermas believes that philosophers should assume the role of mediator rather than arbitrator. Arbitration seeks to give an answer, whereas mediation seeks understanding in order to facilitate. This is a profound distinction because it provides a framework within which people can communicate in a nondefensive manner.

∽ Selected Reading 7.2

Moral Consciousness and Communicative Action
Jürgen Habermas

In everyday communication, cognitive interpretations, moral expectations, expressions, and evaluations cannot help overlapping and interpenetrating. Reaching understanding in the lifeworld requires a cultural tradition that ranges across *the whole spectrum,* not just the fruits of science and technology. As far as philosophy is concerned, it might do well to refurbish its link with the totality by taking on the role of interpreter on behalf of the lifeworld. It might then be able to help set in motion the interplay between the cognitive-instrumental, moral-practical, and aesthetic-expressive dimensions that has come to a standstill today like a tangled mobile. This simile at least helps identify the issue philosophy will face when it stops playing the part of the arbiter that inspects culture and instead starts playing the part of a mediating interpreter. That issue is how to overcome the isolation of science, morals, and art and their respective expert cultures. How can they be joined to the impoverished traditions of the lifeworld, and how can this be done without detriment to their regional rationality? How can a new balance between the separated moments of reason be established in communicative everyday life?

. . . Everyday communication makes possible a kind of understanding that is based on claims to validity and thus furnishes the only real alternative to exerting influence on one another in more or less coercive ways. The validity claims that we raise in conversation—transcend this specific conversational context, pointing to something beyond the spatiotemporal ambit of the occasion. Every agreement, whether produced for the first time or reaffirmed, is based on (controvertible) grounds or reasons. Grounds have a special property: they force us into yes or no positions. Thus, built into the structure of action oriented toward reaching understanding is an element of unconditionality. And it is this unconditional element that makes the validity (*Gültigkeit*) that we claim for our views different from the mere de facto acceptance (*Geltung*) of habitual practices. From the perspective of the first persons, what we consider justified is not a function of custom but a question of justification or grounding. That is why philosophy is "rooted in the urge to see social practices of justification as more than just such practices."

The same urge is at work when people like me stubbornly cling to the notion that philosophy is the guardian of rationality. . . .

Discourse ethics, then, stands or falls with two assumptions: (a) that normative claims to validity have cognitive meaning and can be treated *like* claims to truth and (b) that the justification of norms and commands requires that a real discourse be carried out and thus cannot occur in a strictly monological form, i.e., in the form of a hypothetical process of argumentation, occurring in the individual mind.

Source: From Jürgen Habermas, *Moral Consciousness and Communicative Action* (Cambridge: The MIT Press), pp. 18–20, 68. Fourth printing, 1995. This translation © 1990 Massachusetts Institute of Technology. Reprinted by permission.

Thus, everyday communication can lead to influencing based on reason rather than on coercion. Further, the claims of validity that individuals set forth in their communication also transcends the present context and allows for future discourse.

A group of parents complaining to a superintendent of schools that the school district is neglecting the average learner in deference to children who are gifted can present their position on a number of occasions with rational argumentation, compelling the superintendent to take a stand for or against their position. The superintendent in turn exercises the status of philosopher when he or she advocates from a reasoned position with the board of education to secure a policy decision.

In this situation the superintendent is positioning the board of education to make a conscious choice, rather than permitting the current practice to continue without justification. Thus, the principle of universalization is operationalized because the discourse that took place between the parents and the superintendent and between the superintendent and the board of education had a basis in reason. More important, however, this reasoned position was derived through discourse rather than in a monological form that took place only in the mind of each parent and in the mind of the superintendent.

In Selected Reading 7.3, Habermas systematically addresses how discourse ethics is actualized. He makes the defining statement by asserting that the participants to any discourse must agree with his principle of universalization, and he asserts that this principle acts as a rule of argumentation to which he refers as the transcendental-pragmatic argument. Habermas then describes three levels of presuppositions for argumentation within the Aristotelian tradition. First is the logical-semantic level, which in itself has no ethical content and thus is not the best point of departure for the transcendental-pragmatic argument. Second is the dialectical level of procedures, which allows participants to test validity claims that have become problematic. At this level participants are in unrestrained competition for better argumentation. Third is the rhetorical level of processes, which presupposes an unrestricted communication community as an ideal condition. Participants are free from external and internal coercion other than the force of the best argument, which at that point supports the cooperative search for truth. Habermas analyzes R. Alexy's rules for discourse in order to capture the nuances of this level.

According to Habermas the discourse rules of Alexy are not meant to be rules in the strict sense of the term, but are meant to be the form within which an argument should take place. Discourse rules are implicit and intuitive. They are the pragmatic presuppositions of this special type of speech; thus, it is necessary to realize them only to a degree that will allow for argumentation. It is also necessary to institutionalize discourse because of the social context of life, which is limited by time and space. The topics to be discussed and the contributions of participants must be organized in terms of opening, adjournment, and resumption of discussions. Habermas makes an important point by asserting that this institutionalization must not predetermine the content of the discourse or the freedom of the participants. In fact, the participants must give at least implicit assent to the discourse rules. These conditions will ultimately lead to the realization of the principle of universalization, which, in turn, operationalizes the principle of discourse ethics. This principle stipulates that the only norms that can be valid are those that meet the approval of the participants in the practical discourse.

Selected Reading 7.3

Moral Consciousness and Communicative Action
Jürgen Habermas

We must return to the justification of the principle of universalization. We are now in a position to specify the role that the transcendental-pragmatic argument can play in this process. Its function is to help to show that the principle of universalization, which acts as a rule of argumentation, is implied by the presuppositions of argumentation in general. This requirement is met if the following can be shown:

Every person who accepts the universal and necessary communicative presuppositions of argumentative speech and who knows what it means to justify a norm of action implicitly presupposes as valid the principle of universalization, whether in the form I gave it above or in an equivalent form.

It makes sense to distinguish three levels of presuppositions of argumentation along the lines suggested by Aristotle: Those at the logical level of products, those at the dialectical level of procedures, and those at the rhetorical level of processes. First, reasoning or argumentation is designed to produce intrinsically cogent arguments with which we can redeem or repudiate claims to validity. This is the level at which I would situate the rules of a minimal logic currently being discussed by Popperians, for example, and the consistency requirements proposed by Hare and others. For simplicity I will follow the catalog of presuppositions of argumentation drawn up by R. Alexy. For the logical-semantic level, the following rules can serve as *examples:*

1.1   No speaker may contradict himself.

1.2   Every speaker who applies predicate F to object A must be prepared to apply F to all other objects resembling A in all relevant aspects.

1.3   Different speakers may not use the same expression with different meanings.

The presuppositions of argumentation at this level are logical and semantic rules that have no ethical content. They are not a suitable point of departure for a transcendental-pragmatic argument.

In *procedural* terms, arguments are processes of reaching understanding that are ordered in such a way that proponents and opponents, having assumed a hypothetical attitude and being relieved of the pressures of action and experience, can test validity claims that have become problematic. At this level are located the pragmatic presuppositions of a special form of interaction, namely everything necessary for a search for truth organized in the form of a competition. Examples include recognition of the accountability and truthfulness of all participants in the search. At this level I also situate general rules of jurisdiction and relevance that regulate themes for discussion, contributions to the argument, etc. Again I cite a few examples from Alexy's catalog of rules:

2.1   Every speaker may assert only what he really believes.

2.2   A person who disputes a proposition or norm not under discussion must provide a reason for wanting to do so.

Some of these rules obviously have an ethical import. At this level what comes to the fore are presuppositions common both to discourses and to action oriented to reaching understanding as such, e.g., presuppositions about relations of mutual recognition.

But to fall back here directly on the basis of argumentation in action theory would be to put the cart before the horse. Yet the presuppositions of an unrestrained competition for better arguments are relevant to our purpose in that they are irreconcilable with traditional ethical philosophies that have to protect a dogmatic core of fundamental convictions from all criticism.

Finally, in *process* terms, argumentative speech is a process of communication that in light of its goal of reaching a rationally motivated agreement, must satisfy improbable conditions. In argumentative speech we see the structures of a speech situation immune to repression and inequality in a particular way: it presents itself as a form of communication that adequately approximates ideal conditions. This is why I tried at one time to describe the presuppositions of argumentation as the defining characteristics of an ideal speech situation. I cannot here undertake the elaboration, revision, and clarification that my earlier analysis requires, and accordingly, the present essay is rightly characterized as a sketch or a proposal. The intention of my earlier analysis still seems correct to me, namely the reconstruction of the general symmetry conditions that every competent speaker who believes he is engaging in an argumentation must presuppose as adequately fulfilled. The presupposition of something like an "unrestricted communication community," an idea that Apel developed following Peirce and Mead, can be demonstrated through systematic analysis of performative contradictions. Participants in argumentation cannot avoid the presupposition that, owing to certain characteristics that require formal description, the structure of their communication rules out all external or internal coercion other than the force of the better argument and thereby also neutralizes all motives other than that of the cooperative search for truth.

Following my analysis, R. Alexy has suggested the following rules of discourse for this level:

3.1   Every subject with the competence to speak and act is allowed to take part in a discourse.

3.2   a.   Everyone is allowed to question any assertion whatever.

       b.   Everyone is allowed to introduce any assertion whatever into the discourse.

       c.   Everyone is allowed to express his attitudes, desires, and needs.

3.3   No speaker may be prevented, by internal or external coercion, from exercising his rights as laid down in (3.1) and (3.2).

A few explanations are in order here. Rule (3.1) defines the set of potential participants. It includes all subjects without exception who have the capacity to take part in argumentation. Rule (3.2) guarantees all participants equal opportunity to contribute to the argumentation and to put forth their own arguments. Rule (3.3) sets down conditions under which the rights to universal access and to equal participation can be enjoyed equally by all, that is, without the possibility of repression, be it ever so subtle or covert.

If these considerations are to amount to more than a definition favoring an ideal form of communication and thus prejudging everything else, we must show that these rules of discourse are not mere *conventions*; rather, they are inescapable presuppositions.

The presuppositions themselves are identified by convincing a person who contests the hypothetical reconstructions offered that he is caught up in performative contradictions. In this process I must appeal to the intuitive preunderstanding that every subject competent in speech and action brings to a process of argumentation. Here I will content myself with discussing a few examples, indicating what such an analysis might actually look like.

The statement

(1) Using good reasons, I finally convinced H that p

can be read as someone's report on the outcome of a discourse. In this discourse the speaker, by using reasons, motivated the hearer to accept the truth claim connected with the assertion that p, that is, to consider p true. Central to the meaning of the word "convince" is the idea that a subject other than the speaker adopts a view on the basis of good reasons. This is why the statement

    (2) *Using lies, I finally convinced H that p

is nonsensical, It can be revised to

    (3) Using lies, I finally talked H into believing that p.

I can refer someone to a dictionary to look up the meaning of the verb "to convince." But that will not explain *why* statement (2) is a semantic paradox that can be resolved by statement (3). To explain that, I can start with the internal connection between the expressions "to convince someone of something" and "to come to a reasoned agreement about something." In the *final* analysis, convictions rest on a consensus that has been attained discursively. Now statement (2) implies that H has formed his conviction under conditions that simply do not permit the formation of convictions. Such conditions contradict the pragmatic presuppositions of argumentation as such (in this case rule (2.1)). This presupposition holds not only for particular instances but inevitably for every process of argumentation. I can prove this by making a proponent who defends the truth of statement (2) aware that he thereby gets himself into a performative contradiction. For as soon as he cites a reason for the truth of (2), he enters a process of argumentation and has thereby accepted the presupposition, among others, that he can never *convince* an opponent of something by resorting to lies; at most, he can talk him into believing something to be true. But then the content of the assertion to be justified contradicts one of the presuppositions the proponent must operate with if his statement is to be regarded as a justification.

Similarly, performative contradictions can be demonstrated in the statements of a proponent who tries to justify the following sentence:

    (4) *Having excluded persons A, B, C, . . . from the discussion by silencing them or by foisting our interpretation on them, we were able to convince ourselves that N is justified.

Here A, B, C, . . . are assumed to be among the persons who would be affected by putting norm N into effect and to be indistinguishable in their capacity as *participants in argumentation* in all relevant respects from the other participants. In any attempt to justify statement (4), a proponent necessarily contradicts the presuppositions set out in rules (3.1) to (3.3).

In giving these presuppositions the form of rules, Alexy may well be promoting the misconception that all actual discourses must conform to these rules. In many cases this is clearly not so, and in all cases we have to be content with approximations. This misconception may have something to do with the ambiguity of the word "rule." Rules of discourse in Alexy's sense are not *constitutive* of discourses in the sense in which chess rules are constitutive of real chess games. Whereas chess rules *determine* the playing of actual chess games, discourse rules are merely the *form* in which we present the implicitly adopted and intuitively known pragmatic presuppositions of a special type of speech, presuppositions that are adopted implicitly and known intuitively. If one wanted to make a serious comparison between argumentation and chess playing, one would find that the closest equivalents to the rules of chess are the rules for the construction and exchange of arguments. These rules must be followed in *actual fact* if error-free argumentation is to take place in real life. By contrast, discourse rules (3.1) to (3.3) state only that participants in argumentation must assume these conditions to be approximately realized, or realized in an approximation adequate enough for the purpose of argumentation, regardless of whether and to what extent these assumptions are counterfactual in a given case or not.

Discourses take place in particular social contexts and are subject to the limitations of time and space. Their participants are not Kant's intelligible characters but real human beings driven by other motives in addition to the one permitted motive of the search for truth. Topics and contributions have to be organized. The opening, adjournment, and resumption of discussions must be arranged. Because of all these factors, institutional measures are needed to sufficiently neutralize empirical limitations and avoidable internal and external interference so that the idealized conditions always already presupposed by participants in argumentation can at least be adequately approximated. The need to institutionalize discourses, trivial though it may be, does not contradict the partly counterfactual content of the presuppositions of discourse. On the contrary, attempts at institutionalization are subject in turn to normative conceptions and their goal, which spring *spontaneously* from our intuitive grasp of what argumentation is. This assertion can be verified empirically by studying the authorizations, exemptions, and procedural rules that have been used to institutionalize theoretical discourse in science or practical discourse in parliamentary activity. To avoid the fallacy of misplaced concreteness, one must carefully differentiate between rules of discourse and conventions serving the institutionalization of discourses, conventions that help to actualize the ideal content of the presuppositions of argumentation under empirical conditions.

If after these cursory remarks we accept the rules tentatively set down by Alexy (pending a more detailed analysis), we have at our disposal, in conjunction with a weak idea of normative justification (i.e., one that does not prejudge the matter), premises that are strong enough for the derivation of the universalization principle (U).

If every person entering a process of argumentation must, among other things, make presuppositions whose content can be expressed in rules (3.1) to (3.3) and if we understand what it means to discuss hypothetically whether norms of action ought to be adopted, then everyone who seriously tries to *discursively* redeem normative claims to validity intuitively accepts procedural conditions that amount to implicitly acknowledging (U). It follows from the aforementioned rules of discourse that a contested norm cannot meet with the consent of the participants in a practical discourse unless (U) holds, that is,

> Unless all affected can *freely* accept the consequences and the side effects that the *general* observance of a controversial norm can be expected to have for the satisfaction of the interests of *each individual*.

But once it has been shown that (U) can be grounded upon the presuppositions of argumentation through a transcendental-pragmatic derivation, discourse ethics itself can be formulated in terms of the principle of discourse ethics (D), which stipulates,

> Only those norms can claim to be valid that meet (or could meet) with the approval of all affected in their capacity as participants in a practical discourse.

The justification of discourse ethics outlined here avoids confusions in the use of the term "moral principle." The only moral principle here is the universalization principle (U), which is conceived as a rule of argumentation and is part of the logic of practical discourses. (U) must be carefully distinguished from the following:

- Substantive principles or basic norms, which can only be the *subject matter* of moral argumentation
- The normative content of the presuppositions of argumentation, which can be expressed in terms of rules, as in (3.1) to (3.3)
- The principle of discourse ethics (D), which stipulates the basic idea of a moral theory but does not form part of a logic of argumentation

Previous attempts to ground discourse ethics were flawed because they tended to collapse *rules, contents, presuppositions* of argumentation and in addition confused all of these with moral principles in the sense of principles of philosophical ethics. (D) is the assertion that the philosopher as moral theorist ultimately seeks to justify. The program of justification I have outlined in this essay describes what I regard as the most promising *road* to that goal. This road is the transcendental-pragmatic justification of a rule of argumentation with normative content. This rule is selective, to be sure, but it is also formal. It is not compatible with all substantive legal and moral principles, but it does not prejudge substantive regulations, as it is a rule of argumentation only. All contents, no matter how fundamental the action norm involved may be, must be made to depend on real discourses (or advocatory discourses conducted as substitutes for them). The moral theorist may take part in them as one of those concerned, perhaps even as an expert, but he cannot conduct such discourses by *himself alone*. To the extent to which a moral theory touches on substantive areas—as Rawls's theory of justice does, for example—it must be understood as a contribution to a discourse among citizens.

Source: From Jürgen Habermas, *Moral Consciousness and Communicative Action* (Cambridge: The MIT Press), pp. 86–94. Fourth printing, 1995. This translation © 1990 Massachusetts Institute of Technology. Reprinted by permission.

Selected Reading 7.4 further explains Habermas's theory, yet it does so in an interview format, which helps pinpoint specific issues. Only four of Habermas's written responses to Nielsen's questions are presented here; these four contain concepts especially relevant to the study of educational leadership.

The first question inquires, among other issues, why Habermas focuses on justice in his theory. Habermas responds by first reinforcing his position that unforced conviction of a rationally motivated agreement is the objective of his theory. Thus, discourse ethics can be effective only if it is applied to questions that can be dealt with through impartial judgment; it is hoped that the process will lead to an answer that is equally beneficial to all stakeholders. Endemic to this process, therefore, is the issue of justice. Habermas is making a distinction between moral judgment, which must meet with the agreement of all stakeholders, and ethical judgment, which is concerned with questions that deal with an individual's or a limited group's understanding of the good life.

In the second question, Nielsen signals an ambiguity in Habermas's theory; specifically, whether the participants in a discourse can eventually agree to disagree. Habermas's answer emphasizes the procedure of discourse, which is meant to generate convictions rather than collective decisions. Habermas further asserts that various kinds of discourse can be beneficial to the participants, such as those dealing with the self-understanding of an individual or a group. However, this type of discourse does not constitute moral discourse, which is the objective of Habermas's theory. This second question also points out the confu-

Selected Reading 7.4

Justification and Application: Remarks on Discourse Ethics
Jürgen Habermas

Torben Hviid Nielsen: Discourse ethics offers a view of ethics that is narrow or minimal in two respects: its approach is deontological, cognitivistic, formalistic, and universalistic, and it focuses on issues of justice as its primary subject matter. Thus, the traditional concern with the good or happiness (or a combination of both) is excluded. Why this exclusive focus on justice? Do you regard this as a necessary feature of all modern ethical theories?

Jürgen Habermas: Under modern conditions of life none of the various rival traditions can claim prima facie general validity any longer. Even in answering questions of direct practical relevance, convincing reasons can no longer appeal to the authority of unquestioned traditions. If we do not want to settle questions concerning the normative regulation of our everyday coexistence by open or covert force—by coercion, influence, or the power of the stronger interest—but by the unforced conviction of a rationally motivated agreement, then we must concentrate on those questions that are amenable to impartial judgment. We can't expect to find a generally binding answer when we ask what is good for me or for us or for them; instead, we must ask what is *equally good for all*. This "moral point of view" throws a sharp, but narrow, spotlight that picks out from the mass of evaluative questions practical conflicts that can be *resolved* by appeal to a generalizable interest; in other words, questions of justice.

In saying this, I do not mean that questions of justice are the only relevant questions. Usually ethical-existential questions are of far more pressing concern for us—problems, that is, that force the individual or group to clarify who they are and who they would like to be. Such problems of self-clarification may well be of greater concern to us than questions of justice. But only the latter are so structured that they can be resolved equitably in the equal interest of all. Moral judgments must meet with agreement from the perspective of all those possibly affected and not, as with ethical questions, merely from the perspective of some individual's or group's self-understanding or worldview. Hence moral theories, if they adopt a cognitivist approach, are essentially theories of justice. . . .

Torben Hviid Nielsen: Your moral theory takes the form of an examination of moral argumentation. The only moral principle you lay down is a principle of universalization, which is supposed to play a role in moral argumentation similar to that played by the principle of induction in deciding empirical-theoretical questions. It specifies that a norm is valid only if it could be accepted by all potentially affected in a real process of argumentation, meaning that the norm must be capable of satisfying the interest of each participant. But why should the participants agree to the consequences of the general observance of the norm? Often they merely arrive at a consensual determination of their disagreement. That would be similar to the procedure of political will formation resulting in a consensus that certain issues and controversies must be left to *other* forms of discussion.

Jürgen Habermas: Argumentation is not a decision procedure resulting in *collective decisions* but a problem-solving procedure that generates *convictions*. Of course, argumentative disputes concerning the truth claims of assertoric statements or the rightness claim of normative statements may remain undecided and no agreement be reached; then the questions are left open for the time being, though on the assumption that only one side can be right. In practical discourses, however, it may transpire that the conflict at issue is not a moral one at all. It may be an ethical-existential question affecting the self-understanding of a given individual or group, in which case any answer, however rational, will be valid only relative to the goal of my or our good, or not unsuccessful, life and cannot claim to be universally binding. Or perhaps it is a pragmatic question of balancing opposed but nongeneralizable interests, in which case the participants can at best reach a fair or good compromise. Thus, the breakdown of attempts at argumentation in the sphere of practice may also reflect the realization that self-interpretive discourses or negotiations are called for rather than moral discourses.

Parliamentary processes of will formation also have a rational core, for political questions admit of discursive treatment either from empirical and pragmatic or a moral and ethical points of view. There is a definite time frame within which decisions must be reached in legally institutionalized processes of belief formation such as these. The standard procedures combine elements of belief formation orientated to truth with majoritarian will formation. From the perspective of a theory of discourse that seeks to sound out the normative potential of such procedures, majority rule must retain an internal relation to the cooperative search for truth. Ideally, then, a majority decision must be reached under discursive conditions that lend their results the presumption of rationality: the content of a decision reached in accordance with due procedure must be such as can count as the rationally motivated but fallible result of a discussion provisionally brought to a close under the pressure of time. Hence, one should not confuse discourse as a procedure for making moral or ethical *judgments* with the legally institutionalized procedures of political *will* formation (however much the latter are mediated by discourse).

Torben Hviid Nielsen: You defend cognitivism in moral theory by maintaining an analogy between truth claims and normative validity claims. However, this analogy can be upheld only by identifying the norms that underlie the principle of universalization with normative validity as such. How can, and why must, moral theory neglect norms that have de facto social currency but are not valid in the strict sense? And is this exclusion possible without severing the dialectical connection between abstract morality and social ethics?

Jürgen Habermas: Viewed from the performative perspective of their addressees, norms claim to be valid in a manner analogous to truth. The term "analogous" indicates, of course, that the mode of validity of norms should not be assimilated to the truth of propositions. The differences can be seen even prior to divergences at the level of rules of argumentation and in the specific nature of the arguments admissible in either case; they already begin with the fact that normative validity claims are embodied in norms, that is, in structures that are on a higher level than individual moral actions and regulative speech acts, whereas truth values are ascribed only to individual assertoric statements and not to theories. In the latter case, the higher-level structures—the theories—owe their validity to the set of true propositions derivable from them, whereas particular commands and prohibitions obtain their validity from the norms underlying them.

One interesting difference is that taking propositions to be true has no impact on what is essential to the truth of sentences, the existence of states of affairs. By contrast, the fact that norms are taken to be right has immediate consequences for the regulation of action essential to norms. As soon as a norm governing action gains sufficient recognition among, and is adhered to by, its addressees, a corresponding practice is generated, regardless of whether the norm can be justified and *deserves* recognition or whether it is merely *de facto* recognized for the wrong reasons, for example, or is adhered to out of sheer habit. For this reason, it is important to distinguish between the validity of a norm and its social currency, the fact that it is generally held to be valid. I can agree with you thus far.

However, I am not sure that I understand the meaning of your question. The *moral theorist* adopts a normative point of view; he shares the attitude of an addressee of the norm who participates in discourses of justification and application. From this perspective, we must begin by abstracting from existing traditions, customary practices, and present motives, in short, from the established ethical life of a society. On the other hand, it is primarily this ethical life that must interest the *sociologist*. But the latter adopts the objectifying attitude of a participant-observer. We cannot simultaneously adopt the second-person attitude of an addressee of a norm and the third-person attitude of a sociological observer. What you have in mind is presumably the complicated case where knowledge acquired in the one attitude is interpreted in the other. That is the situation of the sociologist who assesses a descriptively formulated belief in the legitimacy of an observed, socially valid order in terms of the reasons that could be adduced in support of its legitimacy from the perspective of *potential* addressees. The participant in argumentation (or the moral theorist, as his philosophical alter ego) switches his role accordingly the moment he views the empirical aspects of matters in need of regulation through the spectacles of a legislator and takes account in his reflections of the reasonableness or acceptability of regulations. These different ways of viewing things and their different objects must be clearly distinguished from one another, but such differences yield no arguments in support of a fallacious sociologization of moral theory.

You spoke of empirically valid norms that do not have (normative) validity. Strictly speaking, this formulation applies only to conventions such as table manners, that is, to customary rules that are followed for the most part without needing, or being amenable to, rational justification. . . .

Torben Hviid Nielsen: In a series of articles that have appeared since the original publication of *Moral Consciousness and Communicative Action*, you have discussed the Hegelian concept of "ethical life" *(Sittlichkeit)* or, alternatively,

sion found in the terms used by Habermas. In this publication, one of his most recent, Habermas uses the term *moral discourse* to explain his theory. However, *discourse ethics* is the most common designation.

Habermas also makes a distinction in his answer between political will formation and discourse ethics. Political will formation is played out within a given period of time. Legislatures have time constraints; individual legislators try to understand the will of the people and contrive compromises with other legislators in order to complete their task within a given time frame. However, the procedure for political will formation must include elements of belief formation oriented to truth; thus, a majority-rule decision should be reached through discourse conditions.

of a "pragmatic ethics," in an effort to mediate between discourse ethics and social reality. You gauge the rationality of a form of life by the degree to which it enables and encourages its members to develop a moral consciousness guided by principles and to convert it into practice. But can rationality be identified with morality? . . .

Jürgen Habermas: The concept of communicative rationality comprises a number of different aspects of validity, not just the moral aspects of the normative validity of commands or actions. Hence the rationality of a form of life is not measured solely by the normative contexts or the potential sources of motivation that facilitate the translation of postconventional moral judgments into practice. Nevertheless, what seems to me to be essential to the degree of liberality of a society is the extent to which its patterns of socialization and its institutions, its political culture, and in general its identity-guaranteeing traditions and everyday practices, express a non coercive, non authoritarian form of ethical life in which an autonomous morality can be embodied and take on concrete shape. Intuitively we recognize fairly quickly—like ethnologists who have been integrated into a foreign society—how emancipated, responsive, and egalitarian our surroundings really are, how minorities, marginal social groups, the handicapped, children, and the elderly are treated, the social significance of illness, loneliness, and death, how much tolerance there is toward eccentricity and deviant behavior, the innovative and the dangerous, and so on.

Source: From Jürgen Habermas, *Justification and Application: Remarks on Discourse Ethics* (Cambridge: The MIT Press), pp. 150–151, 158–161, 171. This edition © 1993 Massachusetts Institute of Technology. Reprinted by permission.

In the third question, Nielsen asks whether questions of moral theory must neglect norms that have de facto social acceptance. Habermas replies that people adhere to norms in the same way in which they acknowledge truth. People hold their theories as valid because of the truth of the propositions from which those theories are derived. Further, people hold valid certain commands or prohibitions because of the norms underlying them. As soon as norms are recognized and adhered to, it is inconsequential whether they were derived norms or merely de facto norms, even if they are recognized for the wrong reason.

The final issue raised by Nielsen is the ever-present concern about the relationship of reason to morality. Habermas's answer is significant because it brings into focus the issues that must be addressed in a rational society cognizant of its ethical responsibilities. He sees the degree to which a society, its institutions, its political culture, its traditions, and its everyday practices permit a noncoercive and nonauthoritarian form of ethical living as the hallmark of rational ethics; an ethics that is based on discourse. The manifestation of a rational society can be seen in the way certain groups are treated: minorities, marginal social groups, people with disabilities, children, elderly people. Further manifestations of a rational society are revealed in its attitude toward illness, loneliness, and death, and in its level of tolerance for eccentricity and deviant behavior.

OTHER PHILOSOPHICAL APPROACHES
TO THE ISSUES IN THIS CHAPTER

The position set forth in this chapter on justice was derived primarily from a contractarian rather than a utilitarian philosophical perspective. Other contractarian philosophers who have had a significant impact on political philosophy are Jean-Jacques Rousseau, John Locke, and Thomas Hobbes; utilitarian philosophers equally important are John Stuart Mill and Jeremy Bentham. The two best-known political philosophers from the classical period are Aristotle and Plato. Although not recognized as a political philosopher, David Hume wrote extensively about justice, the structure of society, and issues that impinge on political theory.

Some of the views presented on pluralism are in contradiction with those held by Ronald Dworkin, Thomas Nagel, and Isaiah Berlin. Also, some of the ideas in the section on discourse ethics have been challenged and in some cases enhanced by such philosophers as Theodor W. Adorno, Michel Foucault, Max Horkheimer, Jean-François Lyotard, and Herbert Marcuse.

CROSSWALK TO ISLLC STANDARD FIVE

The contents of this chapter support the following dimensions of ISLLC Standard Five:

Knowledge

The administrator has knowledge and understanding of:

- various ethical frameworks and perspectives on ethics
- the values of the diverse school community

Dispositions

The administrator believes in, values, and is committed to:

- the ideal of the common good
- the principles in the Bill of Rights

Performances

The administrator:

- treats people fairly, equitably, and with dignity and respect
- demonstrates appreciation for and sensitivity to the diversity in the school community
- examines and considers the prevailing values of the diverse school community
- opens the school to public scrutiny
- applies laws and procedures fairly, wisely, and considerately

ETHICAL CONSIDERATIONS PRESENTED IN THIS CHAPTER

- Given the fact that the children, parents, teachers, staff members, and other administrators with whom educational leaders work may hold values emanating from Buddhism, Christianity, Confucianism, Hinduism, Islamism, Judaism, some other religion, or no religion, it is important to recognize that such diversity enriches the educational and professional experience of everyone.
- Educational leaders will be better prepared to meet the opportunities of diversity if they realize that some conflict is unavoidable because of such diversity in values.
- A crucial disposition for educational leaders is that conflict can be resolved through a practical, reasoned approach that respects the opinions of everyone in the search for solutions.
- To promote the importance of diversity, educational leaders need to recognize that although certain values are extremely important, there is no one value that always overrides all other values that conflict with it.
- The fundamental rights of students, parents, teachers, staff members, and administrators are enumerated in the Declaration of Independence and the Bill of Rights.

- ◆ Educational leaders must learn to utilize the executive, judicial, and legislative branches of government at the local, state, and national levels in the United States in order to guarantee the fundamental rights of students, parents, teachers, staff members, and other administrators.

- ◆ The degree to which the least-advantaged members of society are guaranteed their fundamental rights is the ongoing criterion for assessing the effectiveness of schools and school districts as institutions responsible for transmitting the heritage of the United States.

- ◆ Developing norms of conduct in schools should take place through dialogue and discourse with all those who will be affected by the norms.

- ◆ Freedom from coercion other than the force of the best argument should be the approach educational leaders utilize in dialogue and discourse.

- ◆ The unconventional student, parent, teacher, staff member, or administrator should be guaranteed his or her right to be different as long as it does not impinge on the rights of others.

SUMMARY

There are three dimensions of pluralism. The first centers on the conditionality of values. There is a multiplicity of genuine values, which differ from culture to culture and from generation to generation. These values must be considered from a perspective that appreciates diversity. It is helpful to make a distinction between primary and secondary values. A further useful distinction can be made between values that produce a benefit and values that produce a harm in people. Values are either naturally occurring or caused by humans. Health and disease are naturally occurring; kindness and cruelty are caused by humans.

Values caused by humans are generally universal and thus are considered primary values. Secondary values vary with historical periods, cultures, persons, and societies. Secondary values vary because of the diversity in opinion as to what constitutes the good life. Such variables as social roles, profession or occupation, personal aspirations, and personal preference contribute to secondary personal values. It is important to recognize that even primary values are subject to secondary values in the sense that there is significant variation in the forms and ways in which the benefits of primary values are sought and the harm of primary values is avoided. This situation implies that primary values are subject to interpretation, which in turn means that they are conditional.

The second dimension of pluralism centers on the observation that conflict is unavoidable because perspectives of what constitutes the good life and the values that facilitate it are diverse and varied. The realization of one value often prohibits the realization of others. Further, the idea of incommensurability refers to things that are so different that they cannot be compared, such as euthanasia and giving birth; also, a person may want to enjoy something that has a value that is incompatible with his or her other values. Conflict always results from incommensurable or incompatible values. In reconciling these conflicts, a reasoned decision does not require acceptance of a highest value or a mediating value or an authoritative value; it requires accepting any one of a plurality of equally reasoned values. Finally, a person cannot realize all the possibilities he or she values, and the good life unavoidably includes losing something valuable.

The third dimension of pluralism relates to resolution of conflicts. The conditionality of values significantly influences the manner in which conflicts are resolved; the most important variable is the desire of the participants to arrive at a reasonable settlement. As conflict arises in concrete situations, a practical and reasoned resolution is required. An effective approach to conflict resolution centers on the perspective that conflict is not a crisis produced by the stupidity or perversity of the adversary, but is unavoidable given that values are conditional, incommensurable, and incompatible. To resolve a conflict, a person needs a sense of objectivity that allows him or her to evaluate how potential resolutions will ultimately affect the entire value system of the disputants. It can be helpful to focus on the values that are shared by the disputants.

The good life involves the selection of some possibilities and the abrogation of others, which requires a person to find some way of balancing, comparing, or ranking his or her valued possibilities. This selection process is facilitated if the person comes from a tradition that offers a large number of choices and if the person has an active imagination. As people live out their ideas of the good life, the possibilities for others to live what they consider the good life are expanded because of the profound effect individuals have on others.

The importance given to certain values can be defended on context-independent grounds. Although certain values are extremely important, no one value always overrides all other values that conflict with it. This is better understood from the perspective of deep and variable conventions. Deep conventions are the safeguards of all good lives regardless of how they are conceived; variable conventions vary with traditions and conceptions of the good life. Deep conventions are secondary values about which a person can have such a conviction that they are requirements for the good life. Although primary values are universal to all human beings, how they are understood and maintained varies from context to context. Thus, primary values are content laden. Secondary values are context laden; however, some secondary values are context independent in the sense that they represent ways in which primary values are implemented regardless of the context.

There must be an ideal that acts as a framework that fosters plural, conditional, incompatible, and incommensurable values without advocating some specific value. The arena within which is played out all positive human interaction is freedom, the freedom to make defining decisions.

Justice regulates how people live out their lives as members of a given community. The substance of justice is entitlement, the rights to which individuals and groups of people have a claim. Distributive justice refers to the responsibilities of society to the individual; legal justice refers to the responsibilities of each person to society; and commutative justice refers to the responsibilities that exist between individuals. Justice also involves restitution, the right of a person to have restored an entitlement that was withheld.

One school of thought in political philosophy that provides a basis for the practice of justice is contractarianism. Contractarianism involves the notion that society should be designed by the very people who will live in it. Government comes into existence through a contract or agreement among the people to be governed.

John Rawls is a contemporary contractarian who describes his theory of justice in terms of fairness. His basic premise is that the best principles of justice for the basic structure of any society are those that would be the object of an original agreement in the establishment of a society. These principles would be derived by free, rational people as an initial position of equality, would form the basis for all future agreements, and would specify social cooperation and forms of government. People would choose two initial principles to implement the notion of fairness. The first principle asserts that each person is to have an equal right to a system of liberties that is compatible with a similar system of liberties available to all people. The second principle asserts that social and economic inequalities must benefit the least-advantaged members of society and that equal opportunity to secure offices and position must be open to all. The principle of just savings explains how present inequities may benefit those who are least advantaged.

Jürgen Habermas is a contemporary philosopher who views ethics as the pursuit of how conflicting interests can result in moral judgments. His theoretical design includes a procedure for moral argumentation known as discourse ethics, which is reasoned agreement by those who will be affected by a norm. The validity of the norm rests on the acceptability of the consequences of the norm by all participants in a practical discourse. Moral reflection thus shifts away from solitary individuals to the community of moral subjects in dialogue. Making a decision about the fairness of a norm must be played out in actual discourse with other moral agents, and each person must be willing and able to appreciate the perspective of other moral agents.

Habermas believes that the role of the philosopher in contemporary society is to mediate and facilitate a framework within which people can communicate in a nondefensive manner. Further, the reasoned validity that people elucidate in discourse tends to transcend the present context and sets the stage for future discourse.

Habermas's principle of universalization is operationalized within the context of a discourse that eventuates in a reasoned position. Reasoning is the basis of all discourse, and participants must agree to this rationality if it is to be effective. Participants should be free from external and internal coercion other than the force of the best argument. Because of the limitations of time and space, it is necessary to institutionalize discourse; the topics to be discussed and the contributions of participants must be organized in terms of opening, adjournment, and resumption of discussion.

Discourse ethics can be effective only if it is applied to questions that can be addressed through impartial judgment so that the process will lead to an answer that is equally beneficial to all stakeholders. Discourse does not seek to reach consensus; rather, its aim is to generate convictions in the participants. The degree to which a society, its institutions, its political culture, its traditions, and its everyday practices permit a noncoercive and nonauthoritarian form of ethical living is the hallmark of rational morality, which is derived from discourse. Developing a working knowledge and understanding of pluralism, justice, and discourse ethics will lead to more effective resolution of value-laden conflicts.

✍ DISCUSSION QUESTIONS AND STATEMENTS

1. How do diversity and pluralism affect the practice of educational leadership?

2. Explain the difference between primary and secondary values.

3. Why is conflict of values unavoidable?

4. Explain how conflicts can be resolved.

5. What is the difference between content- and context-laden values?

6. Why are some values incommensurable and incompatible?

7. Define justice.

8. Explain the differences between distributive, legal, and commutative justice.

9. What does John Rawls mean when he asserts that justice is fairness?

10. Elucidate Rawls's principles of justice.

11. What is the central principle of discourse ethics?

12. Explain Jürgen Habermas's principle of universalization.

13. According to Habermas, what is the hallmark of rationality in a society?

14. What deters some educational leaders from initiating discourse and dialogue?

⌐ CASE STUDY 7.1

The Desegregation Program

The court-ordered desegregation program has been in effect for three years. It was intended to correct the de facto segregation of African American students in three of the county's school districts; the other six school districts are composed primarily of European American students. After two years of meetings and testimony, the nine school districts reached an agreement through the court calling for the voluntary transfer of African American students and European American students across district lines. The state was required to provide incentive money to be used for increased staffing in districts that received additional students and to counteract any loss in state aid resulting from decreased enrollments in districts that lost students. The state was also required to pay for cross-district busing and to fund magnet schools in five of the districts in order to attract students into the voluntary-transfer program.

The superintendent of schools for one of the six primarily European American school districts has been the superintendent for four years. He came to the district the year before the lawsuit was filed with the federal district court concerning segregation. He participated willingly in the two years of meetings with the other superintendents and their attorneys; he was even called to give testimony about the settlement agreement, which he wholeheartedly endorsed. He believed that the court order would eventually solve the problem of segregation by changing the attitudes of the children who attended school together. Although a few parents opposed the agreement, the administrators, teachers, staff members, and board of education were satisfied with the settlement. The vast majority of people seemed to be optimistic about the opportunity to be part of the solution to the problem of segregation in the county.

Implementation of the program went better than the superintendent had expected. There were some problems with transportation, and the schedule of disbursement of the additional state aid created a minor cash-flow problem, but the mechanics of the program were in full operation from the start. At the end of the first semester, however, there were some problems within the individual schools of the district. Principals raised questions about the conduct of some African American students, and the parents of some African American students expressed concern that their children's first-semester grades were lower than the grades they had earned in their home schools.

Toward the end of the second semester, the president of the teachers' union met with the superintendent of schools to discuss several issues. Some European American teachers were having a difficult time coping with the culture of the transfer students. Further, African American students had raised questions about the content of textbooks and lesson plans that neglected the role of African Americans in the history of the United States and in the development of the various academic disciplines.

The situation deteriorated further during the first semester of the next academic year. The parents of European American students claimed that the administration had established a dual system of discipline and was more lenient with African American students. The parents of African American students claimed that the grading system used by teachers was slanted in favor of European American students.

The superintendent feared that the voluntary-desegregation program in the school district was in jeopardy of being cited for contempt of the federal court order. Consequently, he asked the board of education to allocate an additional $50,000 to implement a research-and-development program to save the district from being found out of compliance with the court order. The superintendent, together with a committee of teachers and principals, proposed that the board hire a consulting firm to conduct focus groups and to survey the parents of both African American and European American students to learn what issues they felt should be addressed to create a successful voluntary-transfer program. These same techniques were to be used also with principals, teachers, staff members, and students.

The information obtained from the focus groups and the surveys was to be used in developing programs to address the identified issues. Further, nationally recognized experts in the areas of race relations, multicultural-curriculum construction, and diversity appreciation were to be identified and invited to conduct seminars for all stakeholders to help them understand cultural differences. It would be just as important for African Americans to understand the European American culture as it would be for European Americans to understand the culture of African Americans. Finally, ongoing committees composed of representatives from all the stakeholder groups were to be formed so that the superintendent and the board of education would continually receive information about the progress of the voluntary-desegregation program.

While these plans were being implemented, some African American leaders were beginning to raise the consciousness of the federal court judge and public officials about their concern over the transfer of significant numbers of students out of their neighborhood schools and the possible effect this would have on the stability of the neighborhoods, especially because of the importance of the school as a focal point of interest and activity in the communities.

Discussion Questions and Statements

1. How does the superintendent's plan address the secondary values of the *conditionality of values* thesis?

2. Describe how the superintendent's plan is a reasonable attempt to resolve the conflicts arising from the voluntary-transfer program.

3. Does the voluntary-transfer program reflect the notion that the good life involves the balancing, comparing, or ranking of values?

4. Can the concerns of the leaders in the African American community be reconciled on context-independent grounds?

5. Does the voluntary-transfer program truly represent progress toward a closer approximation of valued possibilities for humanity as a whole?

6. Explain how the superintendent's plan supports Jürgen Habermas's central principle of discourse ethics.

7. Does the plan meet the institutionalizing requirement for discourse?

8. Does the superintendent's plan allow for reaching consensus or the generation of conviction in the participants?

SELECTED BIBLIOGRAPHY

Baier, Annette. *Postures of the Mind*. Minneapolis: University of Minnesota Press, 1985.

Berlin, Isaiah. "Two Concepts of Liberty." In *Four Essays on Liberty*. Oxford, England: Oxford University Press, 1969.

Habermas, Jürgen. *Legitimation Crisis*. Boston: Beacon Press, 1975.

———. *The Structural Transformation of the Public Sphere: An Inquiry into a Category of Bourgeois Society*. Cambridge: The MIT Press, 1989.

———. *Moral Consciousness and Communicative Action*. Cambridge: The MIT Press, 1990.

———. *Justification and Application: Remarks on Discourse Ethics*. Cambridge: The MIT Press, 1990.

Harvey, David. *The Condition of Postmodernity*. Cambridge, Mass.: Blackwell, 1995.

Kekes, John. *The Morality of Pluralism*. Princeton, N.J.: Princeton University Press, 1993.

McCarthy, Thomas. *The Critical Theory of Jürgen Habermas*. Cambridge: The MIT Press, 1978.

Moon, Donald J. *Constructing Community: Moral Pluralism and Tragic Conflicts*. Princeton, N.J.: Princeton University Press, 1993.

Nagel, Thomas. *Mortal Questions*. Cambridge, Mass.: Cambridge University Press, 1979.

Nussbaum, Martha C. *The Fragility of Goodness*. Cambridge, Mass.: Cambridge University Press, 1986.

Rawls, John. *A Theory of Justice*. Cambridge: The Belknap Press of Harvard University Press, 1971.

Raz, Joseph. *The Morality of Freedom*. Oxford, England: Clarendon Press, 1986.

Rehg, William. *Insight and Solidarity: A Study in the Discourse Ethics of Jürgen Habermas*. Berkeley: University of California Press, 1994.

Sen, Amartya. *On Ethics and Economics*. Cambridge, Mass.: Blackwell Publishers, 1994.

Williams, Bernard. *Moral Luck*. Cambridge, Mass.: Cambridge University Press, 1981.

Bill of Rights

Preamble

> Congress of the United States
>
> begun and held at the City of New York, on
>
> Wednesday the fourth of March, one thousand seven hundred and eighty-nine

The Conventions of a number of the States, having at the time of their adopting the Constitution expressed a desire in order to prevent misconstruction or abuse of its powers, that further declaratory and restrictive clauses should be added: And as extending the ground of public confidence in the Government will best ensure the beneficent ends of its institution.

Resolved by the Senate and House of Representatives of the United States of America in Congress assembled, two thirds of both Houses concurring that the following Articles be proposed to the Legislatures of the several states as Amendments to the Constitution of the United States, all or any of which articles, when ratified by three fourths of the said Legislatures to be valid to all intents and purposes as part of the said Constitution. Vis.:

Articles in addition to, and Amendment of the Constitution of the United States of America, proposed by Congress and Ratified by the Legislatures of the several States, pursuant to the fifth Article of the original Constitution.

Amendment I

Congress shall make no law respecting an establishment of religion, or prohibiting the free exercise thereof; or abridging the freedom of speech, or of the press; or the right of the people peaceably to assemble, and to petition the Government for a redress of grievances.

Amendment II

A well regulated Militia, being necessary to the security of a free State, the right of the people to keep and bear Arms, shall not be infringed.

Amendment III

No Soldier shall, in time of peace be quartered in any house, without the consent of the Owner, nor in time of war, but in a manner to be prescribed by law.

Amendment IV

The right of the people to be secure in their persons, houses, papers, and effects, against unreasonable searches and seizures, shall not be violated, and no Warrants shall issue, but upon probable cause, supported by Oath or affirmation, and particularly describing the place to be searched, and the persons or things to be seized.

Amendment V

No person shall be held to answer for a capital, or otherwise infamous crime, unless on a presentment or indictment of a Grand Jury, except in cases arising in the land or naval forces, or in the Militia, when in actual service in time of War or public danger; nor shall any person be subject for the same offence to be twice put in jeopardy of life or limb; nor shall be compelled in any criminal case to be a witness against himself, nor be deprived of life, liberty, or property, without due process of law; nor shall private property be taken for public use, without just compensation.

Amendment VI

In all criminal prosecutions, the accused shall enjoy the right to a speedy and public trial, by an impartial jury of the State and district wherein the crime shall have been committed, which district shall have been previously ascertained by law, and to be informed of the nature and cause of the accusation; to be confronted with the witnesses against him; to have compulsory process for obtaining witnesses in his favor, and to have the Assistance of Counsel for his defense.

Amendment VII

In Suits at common law, where the value in controversy shall exceed twenty dollars, the right of trial by jury shall be preserved, and no fact tried by a jury, shall be otherwise reexamined in any Court of the United States, than according to the rules of the common law.

Amendment VIII

Excessive bail shall not be required, nor excessive fines imposed, nor cruel and unusual punishments inflicted.

Amendment IX

The enumeration in the Constitution, of certain rights, shall not be construed to deny or disparage others retained by the people.

Amendment X

The powers not delegated to the United States by the Constitution, nor prohibited by it to the States, are reserved to the States respectively, or to the people.

Ratified December 15, 1791

Source: National Archives and Records Administration, *The Preamble to The Bill of Rights* and *The First 10 Amendments to the Constitution as Ratified by the States,* available from http:/www.nara.gov/exhall/ charters/billrights/preamble.html, 1999 and http:/www.nara.gov/exhall/charters/billrights/billrights. html, 1999.

The Declaration of Independence

In Congress, July 4, 1776
The Unanimous Declaration of the
Thirteen United States of America

When in the Course of human events, it becomes necessary for one people to dissolve the political bands which have connected them with another, and to assume among the Powers of the earth, the separate and equal station to which the Laws of Nature and of Nature's God entitle them, a decent respect to the opinions of mankind requires that they should declare the causes which impel them to the separation.

We hold these truths to be self-evident, that all men are created equal, that they are endowed by their Creator with certain unalienable Rights, that among these are Life, Liberty and the pursuit of Happiness.—That to secure these rights, Governments are instituted among Men, deriving their just powers from the consent of the governed,—That whenever any Form of Government becomes destructive of these ends, it is the Right of the People to alter or to abolish it, and to institute new Government, laying its foundation on such principles and organizing its powers in such form, as to them shall seem most likely to effect their Safety and Happiness. Prudence, indeed, will dictate that Governments long established should not be changed for light and transient causes; and accordingly all experience hath shewn, that mankind are more disposed to suffer, while evils are sufferable, than to right themselves by abolishing the forms to which they are accustomed. But when a long train of abuses and usurpations, pursuing invariably the same Object evinces a design to reduce them under absolute Despotism, it is their right, it is their duty, to throw off such Government, and to provide new Guards for their future security.—Such has been the patient sufferance of these Colonies; and such is now the necessity which constrains them to alter their former Systems of Government. . . .

Source: From National Archives and Records Administration, *The Declaration of Independence,* available from http://www.nara.gov/exhall/charters/declaration/declaration.html, 1999.

Epilogue

The contemporary milieu is very difficult to describe because the people making the analyses are part of the milieu. Distanced objectivity is lacking. Nonetheless, attempts at description are necessary in order to chart a course of action for the future. Educational leaders are particularly vulnerable when they set forth analyses because the material under investigation is the ever-changing human condition, as viewed within schools and school districts.

With this in mind, a brief analysis will be set forth here in the hope of identifying the challenges that are facing educational leaders. Joseph J. Feeney made an interesting observation about one of his former students, which probably captures much of the attitudes prevalent among students in today's society. "This former student of mine, I suggest, embodies the wounded postmodernist. His emotions are exhausted, his expectations minimal, his hopes few. And he protects himself with humor."[1]

This may be a description not only of many students, but also of many adults who teach these students. The cause of this condition is probably rooted in the excessive materialism of contemporary life, which requires *more* of everything in order to reach fulfillment and happiness. On reflection, most people realize that more of everything does not by itself bring fulfillment and happiness. Further, the shocking voyeurism prevalent in the entertainment industry, on television, and in books and magazines leaves nothing to the imagination. People tend to believe that they have seen or read it all, yet they still want more. Finally, the continual abuse of power and position by political leaders and the pettiness of public officials does not help people believe that a better world is on the horizon.

Downsizing and buyouts in the private business sector, with the accompanying loss of job security, affect both students and educators. Fewer jobs mean less tax money, which ultimately affects the paychecks of administrators, teachers, and staff members. Teachers are less likely to remain in a given school district when other districts offer larger salaries and better fringe benefits. Longevity in a school or school district is circumstantial. Some educators begin to question their loyalty, yet quickly realize that financial obligations sometimes require them to seek employment in other districts or even outside education.

Violence, sexual abuse and harassment, and drug and alcohol abuse by students and colleagues, both in and out of the school environment, have produced in administrators, teachers, and staff members a sense of disillusionment and discouragement. As a result, educators become cynical and emotionally exhausted, with minimal expectations and hopes.

The level of stress increases and the profession becomes nothing more than a job. Despite this rather discouraging picture of the conditions under which educational leadership is practiced, many administrators remain optimistic. This is the challenge, to remain optimistic in the face of such adversity.

PRINCIPLES OF ETHICAL LEADERSHIP

Optimism is a quality that must be nurtured or it will quickly diminish. This nurturing must be primarily internal to each person because external nurturing is usually not available. It is almost impossible for an educational administrator to remain in a state of optimism without a set of principles that will sustain him or her as he or she is faced with the decision-making process.

The following five principles are not exhaustive and are presented as a starting point for administrators as they develop or refine their own set of principles.[2]

The human dignity of each person is the foundation of all decision making. Human dignity establishes the right of every person to be a member of the academic community. Administrators sometimes are forced to work in a frenzied atmosphere that requires decisions to be made instantaneously. It is easy to lapse into a mode of decision making that is set on making those people happy who have the most influence or the loudest voices. Consideration of the rights and responsibilities of individuals is the cornerstone on which all decisions are correctly based.

However, these rights and responsibilities are exercised in a social context. Schools and school districts are communities wherein each member's actions affect the rights or responsibilities of others. The effective accomplishment of both a school's and a school district's mission is directly dependent on the quality of the instructional and learning processes and the employer-employee relationship. The engagement between people will be effective to the degree that each participant is valued as a person and is allowed to become a fully participating member of the community. Such participation not only promotes the growth and development of individuals, but also protects their dignity and, further, promotes the common good.

Administrators, teachers, and staff members have a right to the empowerment that is necessary in order to exercise their responsibilities. Employment within a school district constitutes more than merely a job that is necessary to make a living. Because of the human phenomenon, work is the vehicle that either promotes or devalues human dignity. In a sense, it is a continuation of the creating evolutionary process. As such, the basic rights of workers take on a transcendental importance, to the person, to the school district, and to the other communities to which people belong. Employees have a right to productive work and to receive fair wages and fringe benefits. To this end, administrators are compelled to recognize the rights of other administrators, teachers, and staff members to organize into associations and unions.

Under these preconditions, school-district administrators can empower other administrators, teachers, and staff members to fulfill their responsibilities without undo interference. Such professionals have firsthand knowledge of the issues and problems facing colleagues, students, and parents. The proper assumption is that because of this proximity to the situation, they can find answers and solutions in a more effective and efficient manner. Thus, bureaucracy is a hindrance rather than a help; and no higher level of organization within a school district should perform any function that can be performed at a lower level by people individually or in groups.

By the very nature of their profession, educators are called to solidarity with students who are at risk. This principle is rather difficult to put into practice because administrators, teachers, and staff members also have a clear duty to students who are not at risk. At times, the rights of both groups of students will clash. *At-risk* students in this context means students who come from dysfunctional families, who are poor, who use drugs or alcohol, who are ill, who have a physical or learning disability, who are underachievers, who have been in trouble with law enforcement, who are violent, and so on. In some schools and school districts, at-risk students might be those with average intelligence and abilities because they are the forgotten minority. Taken to an extreme, this designation can refer to all students, because they are in their formative years and thus are particularly vulnerable.

Administrators, teachers, and staff members certainly know and understand who are the at-risk students in their schools. What makes this principle so important is the human tendency to neglect or divert attention from those who are troublesome or require extraordinary effort and to focus on those who are responsive, respectful, and easy to work with. In some schools there is a tendency to get tough with at-risk students and to relegate them to second-class status. However, the efforts expended with at-risk students are a service not only to those students, but also to the communities in which these students will live in the future. They cannot be productive members of society if educators give up on them, and some could eventually cause great harm to themselves and others. Success in school is sometimes the only possible way for these students to become productive members of society.

Equality of opportunity for students and educators is embedded in the goals of schools and school districts. It is a contradiction for school or school-district administrators to promote human growth and development in students and not to include in the curriculum and in practice issues concerning equality of members of minorities. Defining who is a member of a minority group is sometimes difficult; usually being in a minority means being different from the general population in some respect. That difference can involve age, disability, ethnicity, gender, illness, intelligence, physical characteristics, race, religious beliefs, sexual preference, wealth, or other factors, depending on the specific school or school district.

The underlying issue is that of plurality and the need to educate and practice diversity. U.S. society is continually changing such that some who had previously been designated as belonging to a minority group might find themselves in the majority in a given school or school district. Neighborhoods once predominantly African or European American may become Hispanic or Asian neighborhoods. Neighborhood schools change in the same way.

These dynamics also change the affirmative action and recruitment thrusts of a school district. It is important to search out qualified applicants who represent the ethnic makeup of the community for all positions within a school district. The challenge for educators is to instill in students and colleagues a sense of appreciation and respect for members of other ethnic and racial groups in U.S. society.

Further, this challenge calls for actions by administrators that will clearly show students, other administrators, teachers, staff members, parents, and the community that everyone is respected and valued in the school community regardless of differences that distinguish them from the general population. The tragic occurrences of violence against gay people and members of certain religious groups is a condition in society that cries out for attention in the curriculum and practices of schools and school districts.

Stewardship of school and school-district assets is a public trust impinging on all members of the school, school district, and community. The idea of assets goes beyond the equipment, physical facilities, money, and supplies of a given school or school district. Assets also include employees, students, parents, and community. All the various components of a school or school district are valuable resources that can be engaged in carrying out the educational mission. It is appropriate to think of each school and school district as a single unit composed of human and material resources that must be considered when developing short- and long-range plans. The most important assets are the people who work for the school or school district, because without their commitment and support, the mission of education can never be achieved. A major threat to this commitment is lack of adequate compensation, which is prevalent in many school districts.

Inadequate compensation is more than a personal financial problem for employees; it affects the welfare of people not even associated with the school district. Only through economic security can people exercise their responsibility to promote the common good of others. Personal economic security is a necessary condition for people to help others achieve their own economic security, which is promoted through taxation for social services and through voluntary financial contributions to not-for-profit agencies that supplement governmental social services.

The fiscal resources of the district include the potential for raising taxes to pay higher wages and to provide better fringe benefits. These steps may also be needed to meet other operational needs and necessary capital projects. The strategic plan that prioritizes the goals of the various schools and the entire school district must have attached a fiscal plan that details the money that will be needed to implement the strategic plan. When financial resources must be increased to accomplish the strategic plan, stewardship of a school and school district requires every employee, student, parent, and community member to work for the passage of the tax referendum. Stewardship is a joint responsibility that impinges equally on all members of the school and community.

Thus, the ethical school administrator is a person who makes decisions with the dignity of each person in mind, who empowers others, who has a sense of solidarity with at-risk students, who promotes equality in all aspects of education, and who is a responsible steward of school-district assets.

Appendix: Ethical Orientation Self-Test

The purpose of this self-test is to provide the individual with an assessment of his or her understanding of ethical principles as they relate to his or her professional actions. The perspective presented in this exercise is based on the material in this book as it relates to Standard Five of the ISLLC Standards. On a scale of 1 to 3 (1 = never, 2 = sometimes, 3 = always) rate the degree to which your actions comply with the following statements:

Rating

____ When confronted with an ethical situation, I take into account what is best for the greatest number of students.

____ Based on their level of maturity, I try to find ways to empower students because I value their freedom of self-determination.

____ The quality of the academic program is of concern to me in making decisions because I believe that students have a *basic right* to such a program.

____ In making decision I utilize both administrative and ethical principles.

____ When confronted with a situation, I subordinate my personal career interest to what is best for the school community.

____ In developing plans for school program improvement, a major objective of mine is creating a learning community wherein everyone is concerned about the well-being of all other community members.

____ I try to incorporate ways to help parents understand that they are integral members of the school community.

_____ Because my position as an educational administrator carries with it tremendous influence, I seize the opportunity to help others develop a positive attitude toward the school community.

_____ I use the influence of my position as an educational leader to effect change in the school community that promotes high performance in providing services to parents and students.

_____ I utilize the influence of my position as an educational leader to promote quality compensation and services to all employees of the school community.

_____ When I make a decision, I accept the consequences without making excuses or placing the blame on circumstances or on other people.

_____ I know and utilize the principles embodied in the Bill of Rights when I make decisions in carrying out my responsibilities.

_____ Before making serious professional decisions, I try to consider a number of ethical frameworks and perspectives.

_____ When confronted with a situation, I consider the tenets of a professional code of ethics before I make a decision.

_____ When developing administrative policy, I consider the importance that diverse cultures bring to the entire school community.

_____ I try to consider the relationship between my personal and professional values when making educational decisions.

_____ I attempt to live my private life in unison with my professional responsibilities so that people consider me an ethical person.

_____ I want to be a role model for students and other professional educators.

_____ I try to carry out my duties at a high level of performance and in such a way that others will want to do the same.

_____ I know and want others to know that I accept responsibility for the quality of school operations.

_____ I know and want others to know that I understand the positive and negative affects that my administrative practices can have on all members of the school community.

_____ I treat all members of the school community with equal respect because they are human beings worthy of such treatment.

_____ I treat all members of the school community with fairness because as human beings they have equal dignity.

_____ When making professional decisions I avoid considerations of personal gain.

_____ In carrying out my professional responsibilities, I understand how crucial it is to comply with all legal mandates and to apply their provisions in a fair and equitable manner.

_____ I understand how important it is to the school community to fulfill my contractual obligations.

_____ I believe that the schools belong to the public because all school operations are financed by taxpayers and thus the public has a right to criticize how the schools operate.

_____ Even though I have considerable authority, I recognize and respect the fact that others also have authority over school operations.

_____ It is clear to other people with whom I work that I expect them to act in an ethical manner.

_____ When developing administrative policy, I consider the values of the various cultures that are represented by members of the school community.

_____ I demonstrate in my administrative practice the importance of student and employee confidentiality.

_____ **Total**

A maximum rating of 93 indicates that a person always understands ethical principles as they relate to professional actions. A rating of 47 can be used as a median score for purposes of analysis.

Endnotes

CHAPTER 1

1.   Council of Chief State School Officers, *Interstate School Leaders Licensure Consortium: Standards for School Leaders* (Washington, D.C.: The Council, 1996), pp. 18–19.

2.   Oliver A. Johnson, *Ethics: Selections from Classical and Contemporary Writers*, 8th ed. (New York: Harcourt Brace College Publishers, 1999), p. 1.

3.   Ibid., pp. 4–11.

4.   Aristotle, "Metaphysics," in *The Basic Works of Aristotle*, ed. Richard McKeon (New York: Random House, 1941), p. 980a.

5.   Richard E. Palmer, *Hermeneutics: Interpretation Theory in Schleiermacher, Dilthey, Heidegger, and Gadamer* (Evanston, Ill.: Northwestern University Press, 1985), p. 13.

6.   Florian Coulmas, *The Writing Systems of the World* (Cambridge, Mass.: Basil Blackwell Ltd., 1990), p. 3.

7.   Ibid., p. 4.

8.   Ibid., pp. 3, 9, 11, 12.

9.   Ibid., p. 13.

10.   Ibid., p. 14.

11.   Gayle L. Ormiston and Alan D. Schrift, eds., *The Hermeneutic Tradition: From Ast to Ricoeur* (Albany: State University of New York Press, 1990), p. 4.

12.   Ibid., p. 4.

13.   Ibid., p. 103.

CHAPTER 2

1.   Bruno de Solages, "Christianity and Evolution," trans. Harry Blair, in *Bulletin de Litterature Ecclesiastique* 4 (1948): 7–8.

2.   John Hitchcock, *The Web of the Universe: Jung, the "New Physics," and Human Spirituality* (New York: Paulist Press, 1991), p. 25.

3.   de Solages, "Christianity and Evolution," pp. 7–8.

4.   Ibid.

5.   Teilhard de Chardin, *The Phenomenon of Man* (New York: Harper & Row, Publishers, Inc., 1959), pp. 302–303.

6.   Richard M. Gula, *What Are They Saying about Moral Norms?* (New York: Paulist Press, 1982), p. 18.

7.   Ibid., pp. 18–21.

8.   Ibid., p. 34.

9.   Charles E. Bouchard, *Whatever Happened to Sin?* (Liguori, Mo.: Liguori Publications, 1995), p. 23.

10.   Ibid.

11.   Ibid., pp. 24–25.

12.   Gula, *Moral Norms*, pp. 35, 37, 39, 41–47.

13.   Mark O'Keefe, *What Are They Saying about Social Sin?* (New York: Paulist Press, 1990), pp. 2, 7, 13, 16, 46–47.

14.   Piet Schoonenberg, *Man and Sin: A Theological View*, trans. Joseph Donceel (Notre Dame, Ind.: Notre Dame Press, 1965), p. 104.

15.   O'Keefe, *Social Sin*, pp. 19, 20, 24, 35–39, 43.

16.   Schoonenberg, *Man and Sin*, pp. 63, 76, 80, 89, 90, 91, 111–113, 115.

17.   Ibid., p. 80.

18.   O'Keefe, *Social Sin*, pp. 8, 12.

19.   Bouchard, *Whatever Happened to Sin?*, pp. 35, 56–61.

20.   Ibid., pp. 35–38.

21.   Gula, *Moral Norms*, pp. 60–62.

22.   Viktor E. Frankl, *Man's Search for Meaning: An Introduction to Logotherapy* (New York: A Touchstone Book, Simon & Schuster, Inc., 1984), pp. 101–136.

23.   Lucien Richard, *What Are They Saying about the Theology of Suffering?* (New York: Paulist Press, 1992), pp. 1–2.

24.   Ibid., p. 110.

25.   Ibid., pp. 105–106.

26.   Ibid., p. 115.

CHAPTER 3

1.   Stephen P. Robbins, *Organizational Behavior: Concepts, Controversies, and Applications*, 6th ed. (Upper Saddle River, N.J.: Prentice Hall, 1993), pp. 408–412.

2.   Ibid., p. 418.

3.   Ibid., p. 427.

4.   David Ingram and Julia Simon-Ingram, eds., *Critical Theory: The Essential Readings* (New York: Paragon House, 1992), pp. 307, 313, 314, 317–318.

5.   Robbins, *Organizational Behavior*, p. 601.

6.   Ibid., p. 602.

7.   Carolyn Gratton, *The Art of Spiritual Guidance: A Contemporary Approach to Growing in the Spirit* (New York: The Crossroad Publishing Company, 1995), pp. 2–3.

8.   Diana L. Eck, "Challenged by a New Geo-religious Reality: U.S. as a Hindu, Muslim, Buddhist, Confucian Nation," *In Trust* 8 (New Year 1997): 10–12.

9.   John Hitchcock, *The Web of the Universe: Jung, the "New Physics," and Human Spirituality* (New York: Paulist Press, 1991), pp. 50, 64, 71, 74–76.

10.   Carl G. Jung, ed., *Man and His Symbols* (New York: Dell Publishing, 1968), pp. 5, 24.

11.   J. O. Urmson and Jonathan Rée, eds., *The Concise Encyclopedia of Western Philosophy and Philosophers* (Boston: Unwin Hyman, 1991), p. 156.

12.   Ibid., pp. 213–214.

13.   Immanuel Kant, *Grounding for the Metaphysics of Morals* with *On a Supposed Right to Lie because of Philanthropic Concerns*, 3d ed., trans. James W. Ellington (Indianapolis: Hackett Publishing Company, 1993), p. v.

14.   Ibid., pp. v–vi.

15.   Urmson and Rée, *The Concise Encyclopedia*, pp. 156–157.

16.   Frederick Copleston, *A History of Philosophy*, vol. 7, *Fichte to Nietzsche* (Westminster, England: The Newman Press, 1963), pp. 159–161.

17.   Georg Wilhelm Friedrich Hegel, *Philosophy of Right*, trans. T. M. Know (London: Oxford University Press, 1942), pp. 89–92, 107, 161, 194.

18.   Urmson and Rée, *The Concise Encyclopedia*, pp. 23–24.

19.   Copleston, *History of Philosophy*, vol. 7, p. 92.

20. Ibid., p. 95.

21. Marcus Aurelius Antoninus, *Meditations*, trans. Maxwell Staniforth (New York: Penguin Books, Inc., 1964), p. 1.

22. Ibid., pp. 9–10.

23. Urmson and Rée, *The Concise Encyclopedia*, p. 123.

24. Ibid.

25. Ibid.

CHAPTER 4

1. Jean-Jacques Rousseau, *On the Social Contract, or Principles of Political Right*, ed. and trans. Charles M. Sherover (New York: New American Library, 1974), p. vii.

2. J. O. Urmson and Jonathan Rée, eds., *The Concise Encyclopedia of Western Philosophy and Philosophers* (Boston: Unwin Hyman Inc., 1991), p. 279.

3. Rousseau, *On the Social Contract*, pp. vii–ix.

4. Ibid., p. ix.

5. Ibid., pp. x–xi.

6. Ibid., pp. xi–xii.

7. Jean-François Lyotard, *The Postmodern Condition: A Report on Knowledge*, trans. Geoff Bennington and Brian Masumi (Minneapolis: University of Minnesota Press, 1984), pp. 1–20.

8. Council of Chief State School Officers, *Interstate School Leaders Licensure Consortium: Standards for School Leaders* (Washington, D.C.: Council of Chief State School Officers, 1996), pp. 10, 12, 14, 16, 20.

9. John R. Hoyle, Fenwick W. English, and Betty E. Steffy, *Skills for Successful 21st Century School Leaders* (Arlington, Va.: American Association of School Administrators, 1998), pp. 4–5.

10. Susan Moore Johnson, *Leading to Change: The Challenge of the New Superintendency* (San Francisco: Jossey-Bass Publishers, 1996), pp. 91–93.

11. M. Scott Norton et al., *The School Superintendency: New Responsibilities, New Leadership* (Needham Heights, Mass.: Allyn & Bacon, 1996), pp. 31–34.

12. Urmson and Rée, *The Concise Encyclopedia*, pp. 318–321.

13. John Stuart Mill, *Utilitarianism*, ed. George Sher (Indianapolis: Hackett Publishing Company, 1979), pp. vii–xiii.

14. Hoyle, English, and Steffy, *Skills*, p. 12.

15. Amy Goldstein, "Stress in the Superintendency: School Leaders Confront the Daunting Issues of the Job," *School Administrator* 9, no. 49 (October 1992): 8–17.

CHAPTER 5

1. Thomas Hobbes, *Leviathan*, ed. Richard Tuck (Cambridge: Cambridge University Press, 1996), p. ix.

2. Ibid., pp. xii–xiv.

3. Frederick Copleston, *A History of Philosophy*, vol. 7, *Bentham to Russell* (Westminster, England: The Newman Press, 1966), pp. 45–46.

4. Ibid., pp. 46–47.

5. Petra E. Snowden and Richard A. Gordon, *School Leadership and Administration: Important Concepts, Case Studies and Simulations*, 5th ed. (Blacklick, Ohio: McGraw-Hill, 1998), pp. 107–108.

6. Ibid., p. 16.

7. Jeremy Bentham, *An Introduction to the Principles of Morals and Legislation* (New York: Hafner Publishing Company, 1948), pp. vii–xv.

8. Paul D. Travers and Ronald W. Rebore, *Foundations of Education: Becoming a Teacher*, 2d ed. (Upper Saddle River, N.J.: Prentice Hall, 1990), pp. 379–380.

9. Paul D. Travers and Ronald W. Rebore, *Foundations of Education: Becoming a Teacher*, 3d ed. (Upper Saddle River, N.J.: Prentice Hall, 1995), p. 64.

10. Paula M. Short and John T. Greer, *Leadership in Empowered Schools: Themes from Innovative Efforts* (Upper Saddle River, N.J.: Merrill/Prentice Hall, 1997), p. 160.

11. Ibid., pp. 160–163.

12. Joe Park, ed., *Selected Readings in the Philosophy of Education* (New York: The Macmillan Company, 1968), pp. 185–187.

CHAPTER 6

1.   Laurence Thomas, "Sexism and Racism: Some Conceptual Differences," in *Applied Ethics: A Multicultural Approach*, 2d ed., eds. Larry May, Shari Collins-Chobanian, and Kai Wong (Upper Saddle River, N.J.: Prentice Hall, 1998), p. 428.

2.   Prudence Allen, "The Human Person as Male and Female," in *Images of the Human: The Philosophy of the Human Person in a Religious Context*, eds. Hunter Brown, Dennis L. Hudecki, Leonard A. Kennedy, and John J. Snyder (Chicago: Loyola Press, 1995), pp. 399–430.

3.   Ibid., pp. 420–422.

4.   Ibid., pp. 422–428.

5.   Janine D. Langan, "The Human Person as Co-Existent," in *Images of the Human: The Philosophy of the Human Person in a Religious Context*, eds. Hunter Brown, Dennis L. Hudecki, Leonard A Kennedy, and John J. Snyder (Chicago: Loyola Press, 1995), pp. 537–544.

6.   Ibid., pp. 561–569.

7.   Virginia Held, *Feminist Morality: Transforming Culture, Society, and Politics* (Chicago: The University of Chicago Press, 1993), pp. 3–4.

8.   Reginald F. O'Heill, *Theories of Knowledge* (Upper Saddle River, N.J.: Prentice Hall, 1960), pp. 135–137.

9.   Ronald W. Rebore, Sr., *Personnel Administration in Education: A Management Approach* (Boston: Allyn & Bacon, 1998), pp. 40, 46–47, 63–69.

10.   Held, *Feminist Morality*, pp. 215–229.

CHAPTER 7

1.   Diana L. Eck, "Challenged by a New Geo-religious Reality," *In Trust* 8, no. 2 (New Year 1997): 10–12.

2.   John Kekes, *The Morality of Pluralism* (Princeton, N.J.: Princeton University Press, 1993), pp. 17–21.

3.   Ibid., pp. 21–23.

4.   Ibid., pp. 23–27.

5.   Ibid., pp. 27–37.

6.   Charles E. Bouchard, *Whatever Happened to Sin?* (Liguori, Mo.: Liguori Publications, 1996), p. 59.

7.   J. O. Urmson and Jonathan Rée, eds., *The Concise Encyclopedia of Western Philosophy and Philosophers* (Boston: Unwin Hyman Inc., 1991), pp. 250–251.

8.   Jürgen Habermas, *Moral Consciousness and Communicative Action* (Cambridge: The MIT Press, 1995), pp. vii–viii.

9.   Ibid., p. vii.

10.   Ibid., pp. vii–ix.

EPILOGUE

1.   Joseph J. Feeney, "Can a Worldview Be Healed? Students and Postmodernism," *America* 177, no. 15 (November 15, 1997): 12–13.

2.   William J. Byron, "Ten Building Blocks of Catholic Social Teaching," *America* 179, no. 13 (October 31, 1998), 10–11.

Index

Index